The Practice of
PUBLIC RELATIONS

Kathryn Lancioni

Kendall Hunt
publishing company

Chapters 3, 4, 5, and 6 are From *Public Relations Principles: Strategies for Professional Success*, by Shawn T. Wahl and Michelle M. Maresh Fuehrer. Copyright © 2016 Kendall Hunt Publishing Company. Reprinted by permission.

Cover image © Shutterstock.com

www.kendallhunt.com
Send all inquiries to:
4050 Westmark Drive
Dubuque, IA 52004-1840

Copyright © 2020, 2021 by Kendall Hunt Publishing Company

PAK ISBN: 978-1-7924-5322-9
Text ISBN: 978-1-7924-5321-2

All rights reserved. No part of this publication may be reproduced, stored in a retrieval system, or transmitted, in any form or by any means, electronic, mechanical, photocopying, recording, or otherwise, without the prior written permission of the copyright owner.

Published in the United States of America

TABLE OF CONTENTS

ABOUT THE AUTHOR IV
INTRODUCTION V

PART 1: INDUSTRY FUNDAMENTALS

CHAPTER 1: PUBLIC RELATIONS AND THE PPR MODEL 2
CHAPTER 2: HISTORY OF PUBLIC RELATIONS 18
CHAPTER 3: ETHICS AND PUBLIC RELATIONS 36
CHAPTER 4: PUBLIC RELATIONS THEORY 64
CHAPTER 5: PLANNING AND STRATEGIC COMMUNICATION 82
CHAPTER 6: PUBLIC RELATIONS WRITING AND SOCIAL MEDIA 110
CHAPTER 7: PR MEASUREMENT AND EVALUATION 148

PART 2: THE PRACTICE OF PUBLIC RELATIONS

CHAPTER 8: MEDIA RELATIONS 170
CHAPTER 9: INVESTOR RELATIONS 186
CHAPTER 10: COMMUNITY RELATIONS 206
CHAPTER 11: CORPORATE SOCIAL RESPONSIBILITY 224
CHAPTER 12: CRISIS MANAGEMENT 242
CHAPTER 13: PUBLIC AFFAIRS 266
CHAPTER 14: EMPLOYEE RELATIONS 284
CHAPTER 15: CUSTOMER RELATIONS 298

INDUSTRY CASES AND SPOTLIGHTS 309
REFERENCES 331

ABOUT THE AUTHOR

Kathryn Lancioni is an internationally recognized expert in the field of public relations. With more than 25 years of experience in the industry, Ms. Lancioni has a unique appreciation and understanding of its dynamic landscape working as a journalist, public relations executive, communications strategist and college professor.

Over the past several decades, Ms. Lancioni has helped dozens of domestic and multinational companies conquer their market research, branding, and public relations and investor relations challenges. She has worked with media at the highest levels, taken companies public on the New York Stock Exchange, directed global communications programs, counseled clients through monumental crises, and relaunched lagging brands.

Starting with her earliest days in the field, Ms. Lancioni has been continually challenged to help companies discover their competitive edge. She has empowered start-ups to realize unexpected target markets, developed insightful growth-minded strategies for beleaguered brands, and constructed out-of-the box communication programs for global powerhouses.

From the mid-1990s to early 2000s, Ms. Lancioni had the opportunity to work for some of the world's leading PR agencies, including Edelman, Ogilvy, and Weber-Shandwick. After nearly on the agency side, she moved into the corporate arena, advising both emerging and established organizations. From 2001 to 2006, she led the global communications and investor relations program of PanAmSat. In 2006, she launched Communication Insights, a communications consultancy providing strategic guidance and support to a variety of domestic and global organizations.

Alongside her industry work, Ms. Lancioni has been teaching the nuances of public relations to students in colleges and universities across the United States. She has served on the faculty of Farleigh Dickinson University, Montclair State University, Rutgers University, Seton Hall University, St. John Fisher College, and William Paterson University. She has guest lectured at Columbia Business School, Cornell University, and Rutgers University, and been the featured speaker at several national conferences. Her articles about the communications field have been published in several national and regional magazines. She serves on the Advisory Council of Entrepreneurship at Cornell University and on the Advisory Board of the Market Research Center in the Stillman School of Business of Seton Hall University.

Ms. Lancioni is the author of three books: *Communication Research, Public Relations: The Changing Global Landscape* and *The Practice of Public Relations,* all published by Kendall Hunt.

She earned a bachelor's of science in communications from Cornell University and a master's of science in journalism from the Graduate School of Journalism of Columbia University.

INTRODUCTION

The Practice of Public Relations provides an overview of the nuances and intricacies of the public relations industry from the perspective of a corporate public relations practitioner. The idea for the book, and the PPR Model discussed in Chapter 1, come from the simple fact there are very few, if any, textbooks that explore the relationship between an organization's public relations department and its other communication-based functions such as investor relations, community relations, and employee relations. Through careful study and discussion of the theories and concepts outlined in this book, aspiring public relations professionals should gain an appreciation for the industry's fundamentals, as well as the strategic role it plays in supporting other areas of an organization. The reality is public relations professionals do not work in a silo; they provide the framework for and support to the organization's communication infrastructure.

The book is divided into two sections: Industry Fundamentals and the Practice of Public Relations beginning with an overview of the PPR Model in Chapter 1. In the first section (Chapters 2–8), the pillars of the industry are explored: history, ethics, theory, planning, writing, and measurement. The one topic deliberately excluded is research because many colleges and universities offer separate courses in this area. In the second section (Chapters 9–15), each function in an organization supported by the public relations department is defined and explained. This includes media relations, investor relations, community relations, crisis management, public affairs, employee relations, and customer relations. A separate chapter on corporate social responsibility (CSR) is contained because of its increasing significance in the business world, as well as its connection to public relations. The last portion of the book, Spotlights & Cases, highlights CSR programs and community relations initiatives successfully implemented by global brands such as Coca-Cola, Starbucks, Warby-Parker, and water.org, each written by emerging public relations professionals.

The knowledge, insights, and observations shared in these chapters come from nearly three decades of experience working as an agency and corporate public relations executive. These ideas are not meant to be edict but instead to serve as the basis for conversation and discussion about the past, present, and future of the public relations industry.

PART 1: INDUSTRY FUNDAMENTALS

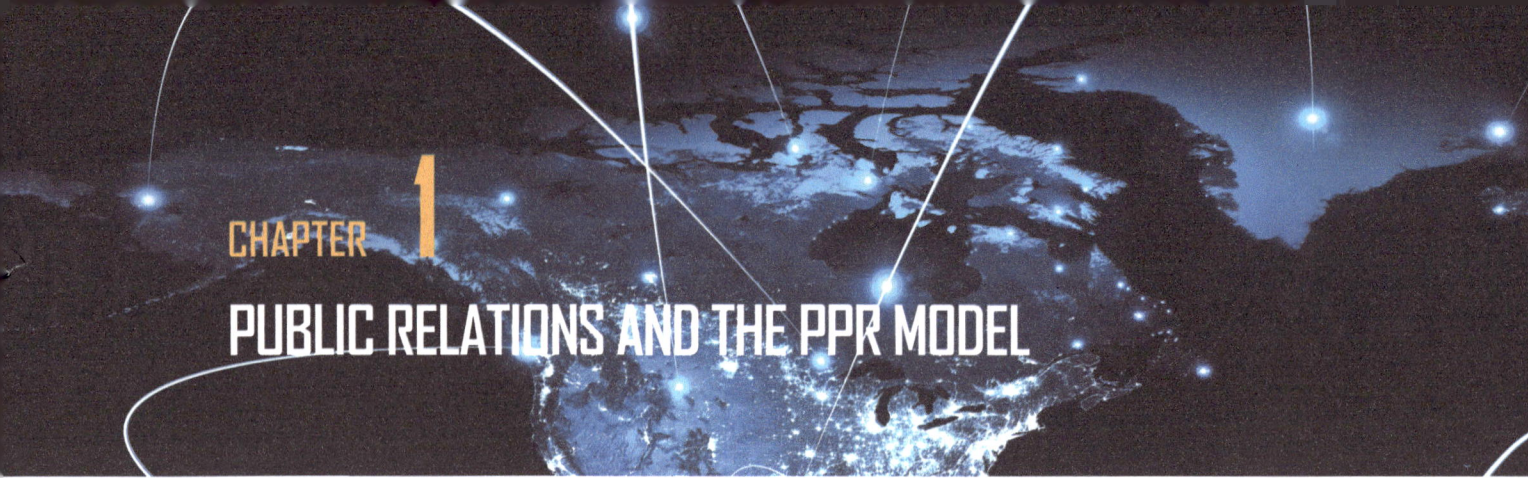

CHAPTER 1
PUBLIC RELATIONS AND THE PPR MODEL

Public relations is the essential piece in an executing an organization's communication strategy.

CHAPTER OUTLINE

The PPR Model: The Practice of Public Relations
Public Relations: The Communications Command Center
- Employee Relations
- Media Relations
- Investor Relations
- Community Relations
- Customer Relations
- Public Affairs
- Crisis Management
- The Crisis Communication Process

Summary and Application of the PPR Model
Strategies for Professional Success
Executive Summary
Key Terms
Discussion Questions

CHAPTER OBJECTIVES

After studying this chapter, you should be able to:

1. Define and explain the PPR Model.
2. Understand the role of the public relations team plays in supporting communication activities of other departments.
3. Denote the differences between the functional areas supported by the PR team.

THE PRACTICE OF PUBLIC RELATIONS

The idea of and concepts behind public relations are not new. The field of public relations dates back hundreds of years (as we will see in **Chapter 2**) and has evolved to what it is today. Industry forefathers such as Edward Bernays, Ivy Ledbetter Lee, and Arthur W. Page could never have imagined the strategic role public relations would play in the contemporary business arena. As you will learn in the coming chapters, an organization's public relations department plays a critical role in supporting all facets of its operations—ranging from the execution of its communication strategy to the achievement of its business objectives. The astounding reality is most people in an organization have no appreciation for the art or practice of public relations. Many cannot even define the term.

At the most basic level, the idea of public relations is quite simple. Essentially, the role of the public relations professional is to connect an organization to its external audiences, commonly referred to as publics. This work is done through the creation and execution of a comprehensive plan specifically designed to address the needs of a company's targeted publics. Most public relations agencies use the RPIE model as the basis for these plans. Every public relations program begins with the establishment of campaign specific goals and objectives, supported by the implementation of a select portfolio of strategies and tactics.

> RPIE: Refers to the research, planning, implementation and evaluation steps of PR campaigns.

The goals of most public relations programs include: creating, maintaining, and protecting the organization's reputation, enhancing the value of its brand, and presenting a positive image of the company to the outside world and its targeted publics.

As you will learn in **Chapter 8** (Media Relations), market research studies, including one specifically by Nielsen Research, show consumers make purchase decisions based on a company's reputation as reflected in the media, suggesting public relations efforts can have a strong influence on a company's sales and revenue.

Many programs also aspire to create and foster a sense of good will for the organization. This involves the public relations team interfacing with other areas of an organization including employee relations, investor relations, media relations, community relations, and public affairs. The public relations program may also strive to educate audiences about specific facets of the organization including its: business model, vision and objectives, CSR program and community policies, product line, crisis management programs, and public affairs initiatives. For example, a nonprofit organization may use its PR team to educate the public relative to its position on a certain cause or to work with trade associations to create educational programs relating to industries or policies they support. The public relations department is at the cross roads of an organization's communications activity. In the ideal world, this means it directs, manages or supports the communication campaigns of all other communication-based functions.

THE PPR MODEL: THE PRACTICE OF PUBLIC RELATIONS

Given its vast responsibility, the public relations department serves as the communications command center of an organization. Not only does it direct the organization's external communications efforts, it also determines and manages its overall communications strategy. This includes the establishment of communication objectives, the development of key messages and the translation of these messages to the company's target audiences, including: investors, customers, suppliers, employees, local and state governments, community members, and the media. This work is done partnership with other areas of the organization as explained in the model below. Members of a corporate PR team also act as spokespersons and play a significant role in the management of a crisis.

As illustrated in the diagram below-the Practice of Public Relations Model (PPR)—the public relations department influences the majority, if not all, of an organization's communication initiatives. It is a dynamic process whereby departments within an organization continually seek the insight or feedback of public relations professionals.

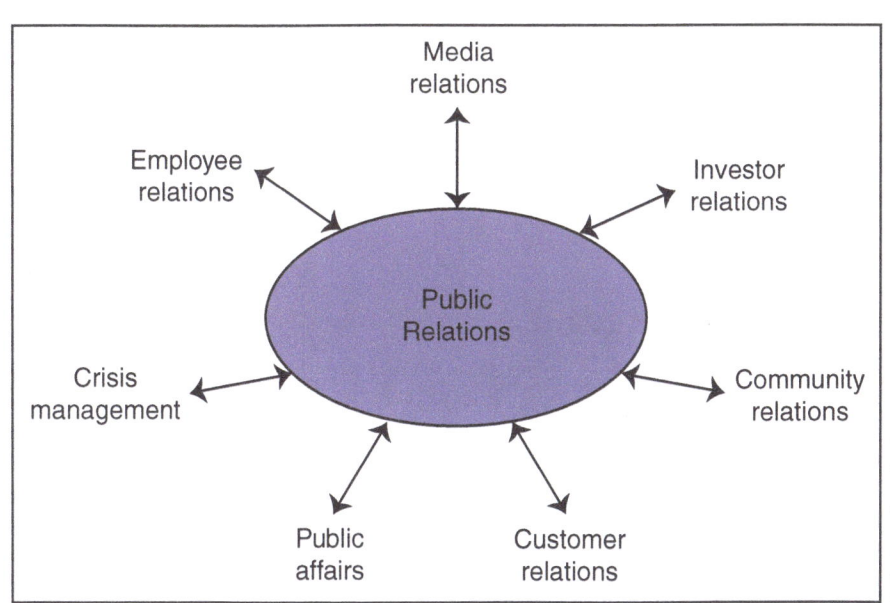

THE PPR—PRACTICE OF PUBLIC RELATIONS MODEL

Public relations practitioners support other departments in a variety of ways—ranging from writing materials and drafting presentations to designing plans and overseeing or implementing programs. This mandates "listening to the constituencies on which an organization depends, as well as analyzing and understanding the attitudes and behaviors of those audiences. Only then can an organization undertake an effective public relations campaign" (INC). As highlighted in the PPR model, the role of the public relations professional extends well beyond its defined responsibilities into many other areas of an organization.

PUBLIC RELATIONS: THE COMMUNICATIONS COMMAND CENTER

Within most organizations, there are at least seven different functional areas that look to the public relations department for direction, guidance, and support, including: employee relations, crisis management, media relations, public affairs, investor relations, community relations, and customer relations. Each group relies on the PR department in a different way, with their needs varying depending upon the situation at hand. In many circumstances, the PR department will work simultaneously with more than one area. For example, if a company has a product recall, the PR team is likely to work with the customer relations team, media relations, and IR team. If, however, it has a crisis associated with one of its executives, the PR team will work with the crisis team, media relations, investor relations, and employee relations. Since every situation is different, there is no way of categorically saying how involved the PR team will become. Let us now review each of the areas the PR department typically influences and supports.

Employee Relations

The concept of **employee relations (ER)** refers to the relationship between employers and employees. ER focuses on the individual and group relationships in the workplace between peers, managers and their team members. As explained in the article "All You Need to Know About Employee Relations," by Neelie Verlinden, "Employee relations covers the contractual, practical, as well as the physical and emotional dimensions of the employee-employer relationship. The term employee relations is also used to highlight the efforts a company—or the HR department—makes to manage that relationship. These efforts are usually formalized in an employee relations policy or program." In most organizations, employee relations is part of its human resources department.

For most companies, "happy employees" translates into "productive employees" and a "successful company." "Maintaining healthy employee relations in an organization is a prerequisite for organizational success," explains Prachi Juneja in the article titled "Employee Relations—Importance and Ways of Improving Employee Relations." Juneja notes, "Strong employee relations are required for high productivity and human satisfaction. [It] . . . depends upon healthy and safe work environment, cent per cent involvement and commitment of all employees, incentives for employee motivation, and effective communication system in the organization. Healthy employee relations lead to more efficient, motivated and productive employees which further lead to increase in sales level."

How does public relations support employee relations? In most organizations, the public relations team works with the employee relations team in several ways, including (Sarno 2016) the following:

- Developing key messages for significant news announcements.
- Providing updates of corporate news announcements.
- Showcasing media coverage of the company.
- Supporting crisis situations.
- Promoting company and employee success.
- Offering communications training in business communication, networking, and most importantly, crisis management, and media relations.

In **Chapter 15** of this book, we will further explore the connection between PR and employees relations.

> **Employee Relations (ER):** The relationship between employers and employees

Media Relations

The New York Times' slogan, "All the News That's Fit to Print" has been a staple of the media business since 1896. For most PR practitioners, the phrase has great meaning since many perceive their role as one thing and one thing only—to secure media coverage for their client. The reality, however, is media relations is just one part of the field of public relations. In **Chapter 8** of this book, we explore the practice of media relations and its connection to the field of public relations.

Media relations is simply the development of positive relationships between PR professionals and members of the media: journalists, editors, directors, producers, photographers, bloggers, influencers, and citizen journalists.

You might be wondering why media relations is included in The PPR Model. Isn't media relations part of the public relations function? Yes, it is but the media also serves as a targeted public for most organizations. As you will see in **Chapter 8**, media relations is not the only thing PR practitioners do. In some large public relations agencies, there are account teams that don't serve a specific client; instead, their job is focused on working directly with the media on behalf of the firm's clients. In many corporations, there is an internal public relations team that sets the strategy and an outside agency that handles the company's media relations function. Again, think of the PR team as the group that sets the communications strategy, messages, and programming for the organization. The media relations team—similar to the investor relations team—works

> **Media Relations:**
> It is simply the development of positive relationships between PR professionals and members of the media—journalists, editors, directors, producers, photographers, bloggers, influencers, and citizen journalists

to interpret and disseminate this program to the media, which is one of the company's outside audiences.

Investor Relations

Investor Relations is one of the most interesting yet least studied areas of communication. In **Chapter 9**, we examine the field of investor relations to shed some light and hopefully perk some interest in this area of communications. Media relations and investor relations share many common traits with the primary difference being their audience. In media relations, the audience is the media, while with investor relations the audiences are investors and financial analysts.

According to NIRI (National Investor Relations Institute), **Investor relations** is "a strategic management responsibility that integrates finance, communication, marketing and securities law compliance to enable the most effective two-way communication between a company, the financial community, and other constituencies, which ultimately contributes to a company's securities achieving fair valuation" (NIRI n.d.). IR practitioners must be comfortable with financial statements and understand accounting practices and corporate law. All public companies and many private companies have either an investor relations department or use an outside investor relations firm such as APCO, Edelman, ICR, The Prosek Partners, Vested, The Equity Group or Westwicke.

Investor Relations (IR): A strategic management responsibility that combines finance, communication, marketing, and securities law compliance to provide the most effective two-way communication between an organization, the financial community, and other audiences

THE PRACTICE OF PUBLIC RELATIONS

In most corporations, investor relations is a separate department that reports into the Chief Financial Officer (CFO).

Community Relations

Community Relations: The establishment and development of positive relationships between an organization and its community

Community relations focuses on establishing and developing positive relationships between an organization and its community. This community is segmented into several groups bridging both the real and virtual worlds. Most community relations programs go well beyond simple donations to local charities; they encompass a variety of activities, ranging from developing and coordinating volunteer opportunities for employees to offering internship and skill-development programs to high-school and college students. We will explore this rapidly growing field of communications in **Chapter 10**. We will also look at the relationship between Community Relations and Corporate Social Responsibility, which we will learn more in **Chapter 11**. In some organizations, community relations is a separate functional area, while in others it could be part of the public relations or human resources department.

Customer Relations

Customer Relations: The programs and initiatives a company takes to increase a consumer's confidence in its product and service offerings

Most people understand the concept of **customer relations** from the perspective of customer service. Almost every company in the world that sells or markets a product or service has a customer service hotline and email address—but customer relations is much more than that. According to the European Confederation of Public Relations (CERP), customer relations can be defined as the "actions taken for improving consumer confidence

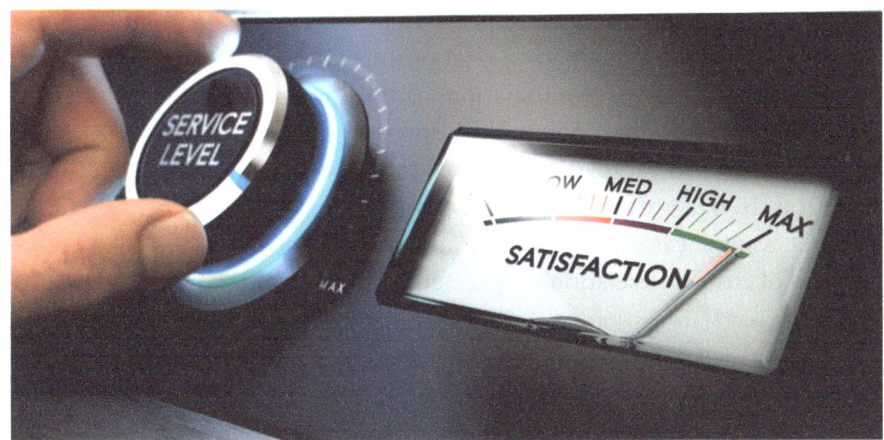

in the quality of products and services" (Faulkner 2017). Most customer relations departments offer a vast portfolio of programs designed to bolster the reputation of a company, as well as provide an organized, systematic methodology for supporting interactions with the consumer.

The importance of a comprehensive customer relations program cannot be underscored, and its role is becoming increasingly influential every day. A 2018 study by Microsoft suggests 59% of consumers have greater expectations for customer service than they did in 2017. In many ways, the idea of customer service has transformed into the customer experience to include all aspects of the consumer buying process. A 2014 research study by Nielsen, reveals a direct correlation between media relations and the consumer buying process. We will explore this relationship in **Chapter 8.**

Customer relations cuts across all parts of a company, but its actions are most evident in the customer service department. Most customer service departments focus on maintaining positive relationships between the organization and its customers. Typically, this is done through a combination of traditional and digital technologies, with web-based applications becoming increasingly popular.

Similar to public relations, most customer relations programs feature a combination of proactive and reactive communication outreach. Proactive efforts are targeted at developing the relationship with the customer, while reactive efforts are focused on solving issues or problems identified by the customer. Similar to the relationship between media relations and public relations, customer service and customer relations have both similarities and differences. Most customer service programs are reactive in nature—designed to address, and ideally solve, problems identified by customers. Customer relations entails both proactive and reactive actions. It encompasses both the company's ability to respond to problems (reactive) and support the development of company's relationship with customers (proactive). Most companies use a combination of traditional technologies such as 800-numbers and email communication and evolving technologies such as chatbots and social media platforms to support their customer relations programs. In most organizations, customer relations is a distinct functional area but is some cases it is housed in the sales department. We will explore the field of customer relations in greater detail in **Chapter 14.**

Public Affairs

Public Affairs (PA):
The issues resulting from the relationships of the public to a government body or financial institution

According to the PR Council, **public affairs (PA)** can be defined as a communication team that manages "issues arising from the relationships of the public to an organization such as a government body or financial institution" (PR Council n.d.). Simply put, it refers to matters that directly affect the public, such as legislation, policing, and public administration (Hawin 2016). Public affairs practitioners continually strive to influence public opinion and, in the process, influence government actions or decisions in ways that support their client's interests. In some circumstances, they act as advisers to global/multinational organizations attempting to shift the balance of power in favor of their client operating in a competitive industry. In the United States, most of this work occurs in Washington, D.C. at the federal level, as well as at the state level in the capital cities of each state. In many companies, public affairs is its own department,

especially if it focuses on influencing a significant amount of legislative policy. Due to the complexity of the practice, some organizations chose to outsource their public affairs programs to outside firms.

How do PR and PA differ? Each focus on different areas as it relates to the public. While public relations centers on developing, supporting, and nurturing the relationships between a company and its many publics, public affairs focuses on the policies that affect the public. Despite this fundamental difference, PA practitioners and PR practitioners still work together. In most organizations, the public affairs department views the public relations team as the eyes and ears of the organization and relies on it for:

- Corporate messaging
- Media coverage
- Financial and industry analyst reports
- Competitor updates and announcements
- Crisis planning

We will explore the field of public affairs in greater detail in **Chapter 13**.

Crisis Management

According to the Institute for Public Relations, a crisis is defined as "a significant threat to operations or reputations that can have negative consequences if not handled properly. In crisis management, the threat is the potential damage a crisis can inflict on an organization, its stakeholders, and an industry. A crisis can create three related threats: (1) public safety, (2) financial loss, and (3) reputation loss (Coombs 2014)." Some crises, such as industrial accidents and product malfunction, can cause death or serious injury. Crises can also cause extreme financial loss to an organization when it is forced to suspend operations, it experiences a drop in market share or has lawsuits filed against it in the aftermath of a crisis.

Crisis: A significant threat to an organization's operations or reputation that could have negative ramifications if not properly handled

Crisis Management:
A response process designed to mitigate the effects of the crisis on the organization and its stakeholders

Successful crisis management manages the response to a crisis sequentially focusing on three main areas: public safety, reputation, and financial loss. **Crisis management** isn't a reaction; it is a response process designed to mitigate the effects of the crisis on the organization and its stakeholders. Most crisis management plans can be divided into three phases (Coombs 2014):

1. Pre-crisis: Focus on prevention and preparation of a crisis
2. Crisis response: Response to an actual crisis
3. Post-crisis: Examination of ways to prepare more effectively for any potential, or unforeseen, future crises

Some organizations have an in-house crisis management function, while other choose to outsource it. The field of crisis management is explored in several areas of this book but we do a thorough examination of it in **Chapter 12**.

The Crisis Communication Process

In most organizations, a crisis response is carried out by the public relations team in partnership with senior management. Crisis communication involves proactively identifying and evaluating any potential risks an organization may face, creating a response strategy, enacting that strategy in the event the crisis occurs, and evaluating the response and adjusting the original strategy where appropriate to improve the organization's crisis communication policies.

SUMMARY AND APPLICATION OF THE PPR MODEL

The PPR Model illustrates the role of the public relations department as the communications hub of an organization. In coordination with the executive team, it is the central unit that develops and disseminates an organization's overarching communications strategy, crafts key messages and translates these messages to its various constituencies. In times of crisis or conflict, the PR team establishes the strategy and works with other parts of the organization to manage it in the marketplace. There is no other team in the organization that has greater influence of the communications program than the public relations department. In the subsequent chapters of this book, you will learn more about the public relations industry, the duties of the public relations professional and the critical role the public relations team plays in supporting other parts of the organization.

STRATEGIES FOR PROFESSIONAL SUCCESS

To be successful in public relations, it comes down to one thing—honesty. Regardless of whether you are pitching a reporter, texting an influencer, writing a thought-leadership piece, drafting messages or coaching an executive, the most important thing you can do as a public relations professional is to strive for honesty. Despite the fact public relations is an industry allegedly based on the idea of spin, the concept of honesty is fundamental to the successful practice of it. Without honesty, you have no credibility. The word spin should be thought of as positioning, which is an essential element of an public relations campaign. Even in the most dire of circumstances, it is important you focus on the truth. If positioned properly, even the worst of circumstances can be explained in a satisfactory manner. As a public relations professional, your focus should be ensuring honesty throughout your organization's communications campaigns, even in the most difficult of circumstances.

In the end, it will go a long way in solidifyig your relationship with the media and enhancing the image of your client.

EXECUTIVE SUMMARY

Now that you have finished this chapter you can:

- Define and explain the PPR Model.
- Explain the role of the public relations department as the communications hub of the organization.

- Explain the relationship between the public relations department and each of these functional areas:
  - Employee Relations
  - Media Relations
  - Investor Relations
  - Community Relations
  - Customer Relations
  - Public Affairs
  - Crisis Communication

KEY TERMS

Community Relations: The establishment and development of positive relationships between an organization and its community. *p. 10*

Customer Relations: The programs and initiatives a company takes to increase a consumer's confidence in its product and service offerings. *p. 10*

Crisis: A significant threat to an organization's operations or reputation that could have negative ramifications if not properly handled. *p. 13*

Crisis Management: A response process designed to mitigate the effects of the crisis on the organization and its stakeholders. *p. 14*

Employee Relations (ER): The relationship between employers and employees. *p. 7*

Investor Relations (IR): A strategic management responsibility that combines finance, communication, marketing, and securities law compliance to provide the most effective two-way communication between an organization, the financial community, and other audiences. *p. 9*

Media Relations: It is simply the development of positive relationships between PR professionals and members of the media—journalists, editors, directors, producers, photographers, bloggers, influencers, and citizen journalists. *p. 8*

Public Affairs (PA): The issues resulting from the relationships of the public to a government body or financial institution. *p. 12*

RPIE: Refers to the research, planning, implementation and evaluation steps of PR campaigns. *p. 4*

DISCUSSION QUESTIONS

1. What is the PPR Model?
2. Explain the basic theory of the PPR Model?
3. How is the PR department the communications hub of an organization?
4. What are the different practice areas of public relations?
5. Which practice area appears to be the most dependent on the organization?

CHAPTER 2
HISTORY OF PUBLIC RELATIONS

Republican Presidential nominee Warren Harding operating a newsreel camera. At right is a photojournalist at the Senator Harding's Washington home. Ca. June 1920.

CHAPTER OUTLINE

History of the Public Relations Industry
The Birth of PR
Evolution of Modern Public Relations: Edward Bernays
Bernays' Innovative Approaches: From Politics to Children
Ivy Ledbetter Lee and the World of Public Relations
Lee's Bold Public Relations Tactics
Beyond Bernays and Lee: Arthur Page
Continued Growth of PR in Europe
Public Relations: A Global Phenomenon
New Millennium, New Challenges
Strategies for Professional Success
Executive Summary
Key Terms
Discussion Questions

CHAPTER OBJECTIVES

After studying this chapter, you should be able to:

1. Explain the evolution of the public relations industry.
2. Realize the impact of early industry pioneers: Edward Bernays and Ivy Ledbetter Lee on the modern PR industry.
3. Appreciate the historical significance of modern PR tactics such as press releases, media pitches and media measurement.
4. Discuss the differences between the evolution of PR in the U.S. and Europe.

HISTORY OF THE PUBLIC RELATIONS INDUSTRY

In the 21st century, most organizations regardless of whether they are public or private, domestic or global, for-profit or not-for-profit have someone either internally or externally employed who has an understanding of public relations. Some professionals have a broad understanding of the industry, while others may have specialized knowledge relative to a specific industry such as technology or financial communication or an application of public relations such as crisis communication. Regardless of the knowledge or background of the public relations practitioner, each is working in a segment of a field from which the basic practices are commonly derived.

The origins of public relations date back to ancient Greece where philosophers such as Plato and Aristotle wrote on the art of rhetoric to assist speakers in their persuasion of the people. It was also present during the British abolitionist movement in the late 17th century, where books, leaflets, and lectures were presented to influence public opinion toward eliminating global slave trade.

Although this was public relations in its infancy, the concept of public relations as we know it today didn't start until the birth of mass communication in the beginning of the late nineteenth century. (https://www.curzonpr.com/theprinsider/from-the-beginning-the-history-of-pr/)

THE BIRTH OF PR

The ideas and practices of today's public relations industry began in Europe. In 1870, Krupp, a steel company in Germany, formed the world's first public relations department. It was tasked with writing articles, brochures, and other communications about the company. (Betteke and Dejan 2004, 161). In 1889, George Westinghouse created the United States' first public relations department at the Westinghouse Electric Corporation (Reddi 2010, 110). Westinghouse hired two men to promote the company's project on alternating current (AC) electricity (Lawrence and Weber 2014, 429). It is believed the first time the phrase "public relations" appeared in print was in the *1897 Year Book of Railway Literature* (*Source: 1897 American Journalism's Exceptional Year*).

The first public relations agency in the United States was a Boston-based agency named The Publicity Bureau. Founded in 1900 by three former newspapermen George V.S. Michaelis, Herbert Small and Thomas O. Marvin, there is very little information available about the early operations of the firm. The firm's first ad appeared in 1901 noting Michaelis as president, Marvin as treasurer and Small as secretary. It started with business clients and expanded into other areas. Its first major account was American Telephone & Telegraph which it secured in 1903. By 1906, the firm's major accounts were the country's railroads who were looking for guidance in battling regulations being proposed by President Theodore Roosevelt and his administration. The firm only lasted 12 years and ultimately it is unclear what caused its demise (*Journalism Quarterly*, Volume: 43 issue: 2, p. 269 Issue published: June 1, 1966).

In the United Kingdom, the Marconi company distributed its first news release in 1910. In 1924, Britain's first public relations agency, Editorial Services, opened its doors in London (Evans 2013, 126). Started by Sir Basil Clarke, considered the father of public relations in Great Britain, it was the leading public relations firm in the country during the 1920s. Some of firm's clients included the National Milk Publicity Council, the National Union of Teachers, and the greyhound racing industry (Clarke 1969, 8–13). It also worked with the Manufacturers' Union to promote the idea of motorcycling and with the Telephone Development Association to support the emerging telephone industry (Evans 2013, 129).

Krupp: Germany steel company that formed the world's first public relations department.

The Publicity Bureau: First public relations agency in the U.S.

Editorial Services: Britain's first public relations agency.

EVOLUTION OF MODERN PUBLIC RELATIONS: EDWARD BERNAYS

Despite these significant early achievements in the United States and Europe, the idea of public relations and corporate communications did not truly begin well into the 20th century.

In the United States, public relations started in earnest between World War I and World War II. There are two men credited with the birth of public relations in the United States—Edwards Bernays and Ivy Ledbetter Lee. Often referred to as "the father of public relations," Bernays was "one of the first people to expand what had been a narrow concept of press agentry, or working to influence government policy, into a far more ambitious—and controversial—realm of seeking to influence and change public opinion and behavior" (*New York Times*).

To Bernays, public relations was not a gimmick but a necessity, as he explains in his 1928 work *Propaganda* (Bernays 1947, 114):

> The conscious and intelligent manipulation of the organized habits and opinions of the masses is an important element in democratic society. Those who manipulate this unseen mechanism of society constitute an invisible government which is the true ruling power of our country. We are governed, our minds are molded, our tastes formed, and our ideas suggested, largely by men we have never heard of.... It is they who pull the wires that control the public mind.

To Bernays, public relations was an acceptable form of propaganda. His approach is rooted in the concept of "the engineering of consent" (Bernays 1928), as outlined in his 1947 article entitled "The Engineering of Consent." As Bernays explains, in the United States, "Every resident is constantly exposed to the impact of our vast network of communications which reach every corner of the country, no matter how remote or isolated. Words hammer continually at the eyes and ears of America. The United States has become a small room in which a single whisper is magnified thousands of times. Knowledge of how to use this enormous amplifying system becomes a matter of primary concern to those who are interested in socially constructive action" (Bernays 1947, 113).

Edward Bernays: Referred to as the father of PR, he developed many of the practices used in modern PR.

Engineering of Consent: Bernays famous article in which he outlines his beliefs about PR.

To Bernays, success in public relations comes from an individual's ability to control and influence the masses without them realizing it. Bernays' believed, "Only by mastering the techniques of communication can leadership be exercised fruitfully in the vast complex that is modern democracy in the United States" (Bernays 1947, 113).

BERNAYS' INNOVATIVE APPROACHES: FROM POLITICS TO CHILDREN

Over the course of several decades, Bernays was instrumental in the development of opinion-shaping techniques used to support businesses across a wide variety of industries, as well as welfare and civic groups, and governments at home and abroad. Bernays created the celebrity endorsement, a technique that capitalizes on support from opinion leaders, celebrities, doctors, and other recognized authorities to bolster an organization's position. He also pioneered the use of surveys, experiments, and polls to support the execution of PR campaigns (*New York Times*).

In addition to his innovative ideas, Bernays had an impressive list of clients, ranging from manufacturers such as General Electric, Procter & Gamble, and the American Tobacco Company, to media giants such as CBS and politicians such as Calvin Coolidge (Gunderman 2015). Coolidge enlisted Bernays' help prior to his run for President to negate his stuffy public image. Bernays once again proposed an unusual tactic by suggesting Coolidge meet in-person with members of the public. Bernays arranged a series of public events for Coolidge where potential voters would have the opportunity to meet him face-to-face. These events included pancake breakfasts and White House concerts with Al Jolson and other Broadway performers popular at the time. The approach worked and Coolidge won the 1924 presidential election (Gunderman 2015).

In many ways, Bernays was a legend before his time in his approach to public relations. An example is the campaign Bernays' designed to support American

Tobacco's Lucky Strike cigarettes. In the early to mid-1920s, it was unacceptable for women to smoke cigarettes in public. If a woman was seen smoking a cigarette in public, it would tarnish her reputation. To combat, and ultimately sway societal opinion, Bernays held a demonstration during the 1929 Easter parade in New York City featuring fashionable young women smoking cigarettes, which he deemed their "torches of freedom" (Gunderman 2015). This type of creativity was the hallmark of Bernays' public relations programs. His out-of-the-box approaches garnered attention from the media and in the public, ultimately resulting in the successful establishment of many brands.

In addition to influencing the public perception of smoking cigarettes, Bernays also promoted the sale of cigarettes. When surveys revealed women were opposed to purchasing Lucky Strikes because its green packaging and red bull's-eye clashed with the colors of their clothes, he launched a campaign to make green the must-have color. Once again, Bernays devised and implemented a multi-faceted approach unlike any other. For this campaign, his techniques included: a green fashion luncheon, green galas (at which green gowns were worn), and window displays outside of department stores in New York City adorned with green suits and dresses. The campaign was overwhelmingly successful and according to sales figures at the time, contributed greatly to the establishment of Lucky Strike as a brand and the overall growth in the popularity of cigarettes (*New York Times*). His promotion of the cigarette industry continued through the 1930s. Deviating from the concepts of fashion and freedom, he pivoted, ironically, to the health-conscious. Throughout the 1930s, Bernays positioned cigarettes as soothing and slimming (Gunderman 2015), despite the fact he knew of the negative effects it had on the body.

Bernays used the same ingenious techniques in marketing products to children. When working with Ivory soap, he held soap sculpture competitions and floating contests to promote the idea of taking a bath. His goal was to prove Ivory soap bars were more buoyant than competing products. When selling Dixie cups, he created a campaign to scare people into believing only disposable cups were sanitary. As part of this effort, he founded the Committee for the Study and Promotion of the Sanitary Dispensing of Food and Drink (Gunderman 2015).

As written in his *New York Times* obituary in 1995, Bernays "regarded himself as a professional opinion maker who, by following precise principles, could produce desired changes in attitudes." To Bernays, "Public relations, effectively used, helps validate an underlying principle of our society—competition in the market place of ideas and things."

IVY LEDBETTER LEE AND THE WORLD OF PUBLIC RELATIONS

In addition to Edward Bernays, the other significant pioneer in the field of public relations is Ivy Ledbetter Lee. Best known for his work with the Rockefeller family, his career in public relations began early in 1904 when he established the firm *Parker & Lee* in New York City. The firm operated on the basis of three principles: accuracy, authenticity, and interest. To Lee, each of these principles could be explained in the following way:

- **Accuracy:** The distribution of true and honest information.
- **Authenticity:** The use of real and genuine information.
- **Interest:** The commitment to keep the public engaged by the information distributed (Hill n.d.).

Ivy Ledbetter Lee: Considered another pioneer in the field of PR, best known for his work with the Rockefeller family.

Declaration of Principles: Lee's doctrine outlining how public relations should be conducted.

In 1906, *Parker & Lee* issued its Declaration of Principles, which was Lee's attempt to explain how public relations should be conducted. In this document, Lee outlines two of his main beliefs: the public's right to know and the importance of a thorough explanation of an organization's activities to the media. This declaration had a significant impact "on the evolution of press agentry into publicity and publicity into public relations" (Cutlip 2013, 48). In fact, many modern-day PR practitioners consider this document to be one of Lee's most significant contributions to the field (Hill n.d.).

© Everett Historical/Shutterstock.com

Parker & Lee's first client was the *Pennsylvania Railroad*. The railroad's reasons for hiring the firm and engaging Lee's services was explained in a letter from a vice-president at the Pennsylvania Railroad to a colleague at the Southern Pacific Railroad in January 1907:

> We came to the conclusion, last June, that the time had come when we must take "offensive" measures as it were. To place our "case" before the public and we engaged a publicity firm ... to perform the work for us under our supervision. The engagement was made, as an experiment, for six months and we afterwards renewed it for an additional six months. Their work has been very satisfactory, and if you are considering making any such arrangements and have not yet completed them, I am inclined to think than an interview with Mr. Lee might be of advantages you. (Cutlip 2013, 48)

LEE'S BOLD PUBLIC RELATIONS TACTICS

Lee's beliefs on the relationship between public relations practitioners, the media, and the public are exemplified in his handling of an incident with the Pennsylvania Railroad in 1906. Rather than agreeing with company executives to release no information about an accident involving one of its trains, Lee convinced them to take another approach. He issued a statement to the media containing details of the incident. This statement is considered to be the industry's the first press release (Hill n.d.).

In addition to issuing the statement, Lee went one step further and arranged a visit to the accident site for interested reporters. He also made Pennsylvania Railroad company executives available to answer questions and speak directly to the media. Lee's transparent approach in managing this situation was well received and led to other railroad companies adopting a similar perspective in the formulation and execution of their PR strategies. Ultimately, this viewpoint resulted in the creation of a better relationship between the railroad companies and the public (Hill n.d.).

PR TIP

Appreciate the significance of Lee's early innovations including the press release, open access of executives and the employee newsletter when thinking about modern day PR programs.

Lee worked with many other railroads including: the New York Central, the Baltimore and Ohio, and the Union Pacific. He also formed the Association of Railroad Executives, which provided specialized services support to the industry, including public relations. He advised several major industrial corporations across a wide variety of industries including steel, automotive, rubber, and meat packing. He counseled banks, public utilities, and several foreign governments. In addition to his doctrine of principles and the creation of the first press release, he pioneered the idea of an employee newsletter for corporations, as well as stockholder reports to shareholders (Heath 2005, 482–486).

Apart from his strong influence on the public relations industry, Lee is also famous for his revolutionary theory regarding employee productivity. The "Ivy Lee Method," a strategy designed to improve workplace productivity, dates back to 1918, when Lee was hired by Charles M. Schwab, the president of the Bethlehem Steel Corporation, to improve his company's efficiency (*Source*: Clear 2016). Lee's method is based on the following guidelines:

- At the end of each day, write down the six most important things you need to accomplish tomorrow—limit it six tasks.
- Prioritize those six items in order of importance.
- When you arrive the next morning, concentrate only on the first task. Work until you have complete the first task before moving on to the second task.
- Approach the rest of the list in the same way. At the end of the day, move any unfinished items to a new list of six tasks for the following day.
- Repeat this process every work day.

Despite the fact this approach is over 100 years old, it is still used by people around the world.

BEYOND BERNAYS AND LEE: ARTHUR PAGE

While Bernays and Lee are credited with laying the early foundation of the public relations industry, the application of public relations was developed on the ground as it was adopted by various industry segments including: oil and gas, utilities and manufacturing. One of the most significant PR practitioners of the time was Arthur W. Page. Often referred to as "the father of corporate public relations" (Litwin 2009, 9) for his work at AT&T, the telecommunications pioneer, Page's efforts were instrumental in helping it combat public scrutiny. At the time, the company was experiencing resistance from the public to its monopolization efforts. Page took a wholistic approach to public relations, believing it involved not just one facet of an organization but instead its entire infrastructure. In his mind, public relations was a set of beliefs and behaviors that applied to an entire organization. It was not the sole responsibility of the communications department; but instead the company as a whole (Brooks 1976).

Arthur W. Page: Referred to as the pioneer of corporate PR and most famous for his work with AT&T.

For AT&T, Page developed a series of five corporate public relations principles the entire company would follow:

- Make sure management thoughtfully analyzes its overall relationship with the public.
- Provide a communications infrastructure capable of informing all employees of the (company's) general policies and practices.
- Give contact employees (those having direct dealings with the public) the knowledge needed to be reasonable and polite to the public.
- Develop a feedback mechanism that incorporates employee and customer questions and criticism of the organization to management.
- Ensure honesty in communicating with the public about the company's actions (Seitel, 1997).

CONTINUED GROWTH OF PR IN EUROPE

Simultaneous to Page's work at AT&T there was an increasing emphasis on the use of public relations techniques, particularly through the formation of national associations in countries such as the United Kingdom and Finland. In addition, the creation of the International Public Relations Association (IPRA) in the early 1950s had a significant impact on the growth of the field across the continent.

IPRA: Founded in the early 1950s, it was the first international public relations association.

According to IPRA's website, the idea of creating an international public relations association began in London in November 1949 in a meeting between Dutch and British public relations practitioners. While discussing their respective projects, the idea of establishing an organization for public relations "with the objective of raising standards of public relations practice in the various countries and improving the quality and efficiency of practitioners" (IPRA n.d.) was born.

Despite low membership following its inception, the IPRA's influence on the growth of the public industry across Europe in the 1950s and 1960s was significant. In 1961 at a meeting in Venice, the group created its IPRA Code of Conduct focused on "establishing accepted standards of professional ethics and behavior in the field of public relations to be adhered to by all members of the Association worldwide" (IPRA n.d.). As the first official public relations code of conduct, it influenced the development of similar codes of conduct by other organizations around the globe.

In 1965, the IPRA expanded the scope of its original code during a meeting in Athens. Commonly referred to as the "Code of Athens" this doctrine "constitutes the Association's moral charter, its principles having been inspired by the United Nations Declaration of Human Rights" (IPRA n.d.). This expanded doctrine includes an array of amendments, including, most notably the first codes of professional practice and ethics which was widely adopted from 1965 onwards.

In the United States, the **Public Relations Society of America** (PRSA) was formed in 1948 to represent the interests of public relations professionals across the country. Today, PRSA remains the world's largest public relations membership association with more than 30,000 members, primarily in the United States (PRSA n.d.). PRSA offers members an array of services including professional development programs, networking opportunities and educational programs. It serves as the primary watchdog for enforcing, maintaining and promoting the use of fair and ethical practices across the industry. Through these efforts, the organization hopes to maintain a consistent voice "on public policy issues that strengthen the perceived value of the communications profession and position our members as industry thought leaders." PRSA also has a Code of Ethics which lays out principles and guidelines that uphold "the core values of the ethical practice of public relations, including advocacy, honesty, loyalty, professional development and objectivity." The organization has 110 chapters and 14 professional interest sections, as well as affiliated student chapters at over 370 U.S. colleges and universities. Each of these student run chapters operates under the name of PRSSA (Public Relations Student Society of America).

Public Relations Society of America (PRSA): Formed in 1948, it is the premier association for PR professionals in the U.S.

PUBLIC RELATIONS: A GLOBAL PHENOMENON

The global boom in the public relations started in the 1960s after the expansion of several major U.S. public relations firms—such as Hill & Knowlton, Burson-Marsteller, and Edelman—outside North America. As an example, Hill and Knowlton, founded in 1927 by John W. Hill, grew as a result of client expansion across Europe and areas of the Middle East. The industry's growth was also due to the enlargement of European transnational companies, ultimately leading to the establishment of corporate communication departments and the rise of consumer public relations, with its highly tactical publicity style (Greer and Singh n.d.).

By the late 1960s, public relations emerged as a full-blown professional industry with several hundred public relations agencies and more than 100,000 individual practitioners across the United States. Public relations professionals became an integral part of most organizations, often reporting directly to the president or CEO (Greer and Singh n.d.).

The tumultuous global political climate dominating the 1960s and 1970s was one of the catalysts for this growth. It was also the evolving consumer movement that "sought to protect the average person against unsafe products, unsanitary working conditions, unfair pricing and other breaches, real and alleged, of the expanding social contract that said, in effect, the 'Customer is King.' Corporations, in particular, found themselves crafting 'Bills of Rights' for their customers, recasting their credit agreements in 'plain English,' and instituting numerous other reforms to guarantee customer satisfaction" (Bates 2006, 15). Organizations of all types, including everything from global power houses to nonprofits, were forced to reexamine how they addressed the needs of their publics. For public relations professionals, this meant altering messages, adjusting strategies, and manipulating tactics to support the needs of clients.

During the 1980s and 1990s, the public's focus shifted to the environment and an individual's quality of life. Organizations were now the targets for initiatives "aimed at curbing air pollution, water pollution, deforestation, and the general threat of ecological disaster caused by global warming and the destruction of the world's natural habitats" (Bates 2006, 15). In response, public relations professionals counseled clients, redirected programs, and supported massive changes to communication outreach programs. During this time there was "growth and extension of consumer activism around issues such as unfair labor practices and unbridled corporate expansion and market control" (Bates 2006, 16).

An unexpected development in 1989 was the collapse of Berlin Wall and the former Eastern Bloc. As a result of these events, public relations began in

this part of the world. For some, this development is viewed as "new PR" coming out of the introduction of democratic governments. Others consider it a continuation of practices from the formerly socialist countries. Many of the governmental communications and propaganda professionals employed in these countries lost their jobs and became public relations practitioners, leveraging many of the same techniques and contacts (Vercic, Ruler, Btuschi, and Flodin, 2001, 380).

Throughout the 1990s, Europe led the public relations world in two ways. First, it was in 1988 with the formation of the International Communications Consultancy Organization (ICCO). The organization is the "voice of public relations consultancies around the world" (ICCO n.d.). Its membership includes associations representing over 3,000 PR firms from 66 countries across Europe, Africa, Asia, the Americas, the Middle East and Australasia. The organization's mission is to provide a forum for "senior management of the world's best PR consultancies to meet and address endues of mutual interest and concern" (ICCO n.d.). The second was the interpretation of the "Quality Assurance" movement into the public relations field (Vercic, Ruler, Btuschi, and Flodin, 2001, 381).

ICCO: Formed in 1988, it acts as the voice of PR agencies around the globe.

NEW MILLENNIUM, NEW CHALLENGES

With the dawn of the millennium, came new challenges for PR practitioners. The collapse of the stock market in the late 1990s post the dot.com era was quickly followed by the Enron and Worldcom scandals. The meltdown of

these two companies made it harder for PR professionals to "prove their value in assisting clients and employers to serve the public interest while pursuing private goals" (Bates 2006, 19). Just as the industry was recovering came the 9/11 terrorist attacks. Almost instantly, the focus of most corporate public relations shifted to corporate social responsibility.

Immediately following 9/11, public relations professionals were in uncharted waters. Not only had thousands of innocent people perished, but public relations counselors were scrambling to meet their client's needs. As experts in communications, "they played a major role in fashioning and disseminating advisories and announcements to these audiences amidst the chaos of the moment" (Bates 2006, 19). This was the case across most industries, especially those involving finance and transportation. At Merrill Lynch, for example, whose global headquarters where nearly decimated from the attacks, their communications goal was to guarantee the safety of employees, while simultaneously trying to calm the nerves of investors.

For the transportation industry, the communications challenges were very different. Not only did the attacks strand thousands of travelers across the country but it also terrified would-be travelers about the prospect of flying. At Delta Airlines, the communication challenges were immense—just as they were at all of the airlines. Public relations professionals had to focus on a massive number of issues, including: communicating with travelers' and employees' families, issuing statements to the media, and disseminating information about new safety policies. This was on-the-job training for many public relations

professionals as neither the PR industry nor the transportation industry ever faced a crisis of this kind (Bates 2006, 20).

As a result of 9/11, most organizations developed and implemented policies for handling terrorist attacks and other crises. The event underscored the importance of crisis planning for all organizations and helped to highlight the flaws existing in systems. As Don Bates wrote in *"Mini-Me" History: Public Relations from the Dawn of Civilization,* "If nothing else, 9/11 dramatically reinforced the need for and efficacy of sound public relations in helping institutions and the people and communities they serve to cope during time of life threatening crisis, then move forward with strength and determination to reconstitute their lives and reaffirm the moral and political values that are at the core of a society's very survival" (Bates 2006, 22).

With the end of the second decade of the 21st century, public relations has become a major communication practice in the United States, Europe, and around the globe. With its humble beginnings in a small room at The Publicity Bureau in the early 1900s to the global force it has become today, there are few who would argue that public relations is not an incredibly powerful force in the world of global communication.

As Ivy Ledbetter Lee once said,

> "Tell the truth because sooner or later, the public is going to find out anyway. And if the public doesn't like what you are doing, change your policies and bring them into line with what people want."

STRATEGIES FOR PROFESSIONAL SUCCESS

After tracking its evolution, it is important to revisit the fundamentals of the modern public relations industry in order to appreciate the significant influence of the past on the present:

What is public relations? A profession dedicated to establishing and maintaining mutually beneficial relationships between an organization and the audiences or "publics" on which the success of these entities depend. Such publics may include: investors, employees, customers, suppliers, legislators, competitors, and government officials (Bates 2006, 4).

What are the responsibilities of a public relations practitioner? In the eyes of the Public Relations Society of America, a career in public relations includes an array of responsibilities including (prsa.org):

- Counseling an organization's management on the potential impact of directives, policies, or external influences on its operations.
- Safeguarding the reputation of an organization.
- Designing systems to support the internal and external communications activities of an organization, including crisis communication programs.
- Researching, creating, implementing, and evaluating multifaceted communications programs designed to inform the organization's publics about matters relating to an organization. Such programs may be directed to a variety of internal and external audiences including: employees, customers, suppliers, investors, and legislators.
- Developing and directing programs to support the organization's efforts to alter or influence public policy.
- Serving as a communications spokesperson for an organization where appropriate.

EXECUTIVE SUMMARY

Now that you have finished reading this chapter, you should be able to appreciate the history of the PR industry and be able to:

- Describe the early origins of the field dating back to Aristotle and Plato.
- Appreciate the influence of the industry's forefathers: Edward Bernays, Ivy Ledbetter Lee and Arthur T. Page.
- Realize the global evolution of the practice and the milestones made in the U.S. and Europe.
- Describe the significance of certain developments: trade associations, councils and standards of practice.
- Understand the influence of global events such as the World Wars, the Enron scandal and other unexpected developments in shaping advancements in the industry.

KEY TERMS

Arthur W. Page: Referred to as the pioneer of corporate PR and most famous for his work with AT&T. *p. 27*

Declaration of Principles: Lee's doctrine outlining how public relations should be conducted. *p. 25*

Editorial Services: Britain's first public relations agency. *p. 21*

Edward Bernays: Referred to as the father of PR, he developed many of the practices used in modern PR. *p. 22*

Engineering of Consent: Bernays famous article in which he outlines his beliefs about PR. *p. 22*

ICCO: Formed in 1988, it acts as the voice of PR agencies around the globe. *p. 31*

IPRA: Founded in the early 1950s, it was the first international public relations association. *p. 28*

Ivy Ledbetter Lee: Considered another pioneer in the field of PR, best known for his work with the Rockefeller family. *p. 25*

Krupp: Germany steel company that formed the world's first public relations department. *p. 21*

Public Relations Society of America (PRSA): Formed in 1948, it is the premier association for PR professionals in the U.S. *p. 29*

The Publicity Bureau: First public relations agency in the U.S. *p. 21*

DISCUSSION QUESTIONS

1. In your opinion, what one individual had the greatest influence on the PR industry? Why?
2. Do you think the advancements in the U.S. or Europe had a more significant impact? Why?
3. What was one part of the industry's history that surprised you? Why?
4. What lessons can modern day PR practitioners learn from the early influencers?
5. On balance, does it seem as if the industry has involved significantly since its early days or stayed the same?

CHAPTER 3
ETHICS AND PUBLIC RELATIONS

In 2020, Hollywood producers faced an ethical dilemma regarding the future of The Ellen DeGeneres Show after allegations surfaced of the mistreatment of the show's employees and guests.

From *Public Relations Principles: Strategies for Professional Success*, by Shawn T. Wahl and Michelle M. Maresh Fuehrer. Copyright © by Kendall Hunt Publishing Company. Reprinted by permission.

CHAPTER OUTLINE

Defining Ethics
The Importance of Ethics in Public Relations
Ethical Considerations
    The Ethics of Electronic Communication
Ethical Responsibility
    Adapting to the Audience
    Ethical Responsibility Strategies
Some Ethical Perspectives
    Religious Perspective
    Human Nature Perspective
    Dialogical Perspective
    Situational Perspective
Strategies for Professional Success
Executive Summary
Key Terms
Discussion Questions

CHAPTER OBJECTIVES

After studying this chapter, you should be able to:

1. Define the term ethics.
2. Identify the importance of ethics in your study of public relations.
3. Discuss ethical responsibility across communication contexts.
4. Apply ethics to political persuasion and adapting to the audience.
5. Explain the different perspectives of ethics in public relations and how each of them can be applied to real-life situations.

THE PRACTICE OF PUBLIC RELATIONS

> ### Ripped from the Headlines
>
> *In October of 2014, an independent study concluded that the University of North Carolina had engaged in one of the greatest cases of academic fraud in the history of the NCAA. Former federal prosecutor Kenneth Wainstein led an independent investigation that concluded that over 18 years at least 3,100 students took fake "paper classes." These classes required very little work and artificially inflated grades that helped some student-athletes remain eligible for money-making sports such as football and basketball (Ganin & Sayers, 2014). The fallout for the university has been immense; a university that once enjoyed a stellar reputation as a place where academics and athletics went hand in hand now has a stained reputation.*
>
> *As the university engaged in damage control following the scandal, UNC officials paid over $780,000 to a public relations firm to assist in regaining public approval and trust. The Edelman firm identifies itself as the largest public relations firm in the world, and had at least 14 employees assigned to work in response to the scathing report by Wainstein (Kane, 2014). The university had previously spent $500,000 on public relations related to the scandal.*
>
> Kenneth Wainstein, lead investigator into academic irregularities at the University of North Carolina at Chapel Hill, holds a copy of his findings during a news conference following a special joint meeting of the University of North Carolina Board of Governors and the UNC-Chapel Hill Board of Trustees in Chapel Hill, N.C.

As you continue your study of public relations, the previous example can serve as a critical indicator on how important public relations can be to people, institutions, and organizations. Having a negative public perception can decrease trust, public visibility, and in business can negatively affect the profitability of the organization. As you read this chapter, continually assess your own perception of how public relations affects you and others in your everyday life.

> *I've heard through the grapevine that my opponent has had numerous affairs while married to his wife!*
>
> *I've heard some studies have concluded this product causes cancer!*
>
> *We can say whatever we want in this debate; the constituents can't understand us anyway!*
>
> *Who cares if the information is misleading, so long as it swings public opinion our way?*

What do the above statements all have in common? The correct answer can be articulated in two words: ethical communication. Each of you encounters ethics and ethical choices in your life. Your values, beliefs, and morals help evolve your understanding of ethics. Many ethics, or codes of ethics, are universal, while others are strictly meant for particular individuals or cultures. In your study of public relations, you will inevitably encounter particular situations where your ethics will be tested concerning how you manage public opinion. To be an effective and credible public communicator, it is essential to follow a code of ethics that leads to honesty and transparency. First, think about this: Where do your ethics come from?

Let's face it. Understanding ethics is complicated. However, ethics is critical to your study of public relations. This chapter explores the connection between ethics and how we manage public opinion and craft our public relations strategies. In both your personal life and your professional career, you will be confronted with ethical issues and dilemmas concerning honesty and transparency between the organization you represent and the public. What should I do when information contradicts the values of my public relations platform? Is it OK to bend the truth to fit my public relations goals? Should I use inflammatory or distracting information to damage public relations platforms I don't agree with?

To study the effectiveness of public relations in both your life and your professional organization, it's important to place ethics at the core of your critical evaluation practice. The process of critically evaluating public relations messages is connected to ethical perspectives. You can think about ethical perspectives as a unique set of lenses that you may want to use to critically evaluate your discourse with the public. Many different lenses are

Ethical Perspectives: A unique set of lenses used to evaluate one's discourse with the public.

A code of ethics is the foundation for your interactions with the public.

available, and each one will allow you to see the world of public relations communication from different points of view. Similarly, each of the lenses covered in this chapter will encourage you to evaluate intercultural messages from different ethical points of view. Let's get more familiar with the term as connected to your study of public communication.

DEFINING ETHICS

When you hear the word *ethics*, what do you think of? Words such as *right*, *wrong*, *values*, and *principles* may come to mind. Put simply, ethics is a system of accepted principles that make up an individual's or group's values and judgments as to what's right and wrong. These "principles" can change from culture to culture or from group to group. Maybe you've heard of a code of ethics before. These are all different sets of principles that people hold themselves to or are held to by multiple organizations or groups. Take a moment to review the code of ethics held by the Public Relations Society of America (PRSA). This code establishes the importance of ethics in the study and practice of communication across contexts (see Figure 3.1).

> **Ethics:** Is a system of accepted principles that make up an individual's or group's values and judgments as to what's right and wrong.

> **Codes of Ethics:** Are all different sets of principles that people hold themselves to or are held to by multiple organizations or groups.

PRSA CODE OF ETHICS

The PRSA Code of Ethics applies to Public Relations Society of America (PRSA) members. Its purpose is to anticipate and accommodate ethical dilemmas. The Code uses factual examples of misconduct and the Code evolves as circumstances change.

The Code includes core values of PRSA members as well as the public relations profession and they are central to the integrity of the profession. The core values are: advocacy, honesty, expertise, independence, loyalty, fairness, and enhancing the profession.

Those who wish to become a member of the PRSA sign a pledge promising to conduct themselves professionally, according to the Code.

To see the full PRSA Code of Ethics, go to
https://www.prsa.org/AboutPRSA/Ethics/CodeEnglish/index.html#.Vh6xTH6rRhE

FIGURE 3.1: PRSA CODE OF ETHICS

Think for a moment about something you're a part of, perhaps a group or an organization. For example, maybe you belong to a religion, fraternity, sorority, sports team, or academic institution that provides a daily code of ethics for you. To properly understand ethics, you must have two abilities. The first is the ability to **distinguish**. To distinguish, you need to be able to decide what's right and wrong. The second ability is **dedication**. Dedication means committing to do what is right no matter the situation.

> **Distinguish:** The ability to decide what's right and wrong.

Imagine this scenario: You're supposed to meet with your professor to make up an exam due to an absence. You arrive at his or her office just a bit early, and the answer key is lying on the desk. Perhaps you're part of a church or religious organization that provides you with a code of ethics that assists you in choosing the right option. Maybe you signed an agreement with the university to honor the academic honesty policies. Regardless of the ethical code or codes you decide to honor or reject, ethics seem to play a role in almost every decision made throughout the day. In assessing this situation, you must use the two abilities we just listed. In your mind, you distinguish what is right and what is wrong; after completing the distinguishing process, you then decide to dedicate or commit yourself to the ethical decision or to reject it.

> **Dedication:** Committing to do what is right no matter the situation.

The definition of ethics includes the word *values*. **Values** are beliefs and attitudes we hold that can actually conflict with our ethical decisions. For instance, in the previous example, you may not be prepared for the test, and perhaps a low grade will cause you to fail the class or drop below the GPA you need to get accepted into graduate school. One of your values may be success, and a low grade on this exam could cause you to be unsuccessful. Thus, you may choose to violate your code of ethics to honor your values.

> **Values:** Beliefs and attitudes we hold that can actually conflict with our ethical decisions.

Now that you have a general understanding of ethics, let's not forget to connect this term to public relations. What comes to mind when you think of public relations? How do you communicate effectively and ethically with a public that might not share your organizational goals or values? What ethical criteria do you use when evaluating public communication? Do you consider ethics when you're crafting a public message? Would you consider yourself an **ethical communicator** or an **unethical communicator**? Ethical communicators value truthful information and public/social sensitivity. They want to communicate effectively and fairly with the public in a way that is both responsible and truthful. Unethical communicators will be insensitive, insulting, and ultimately ineffective communicators because of their lack of understanding and caring for the concerns and well-being for their respective publics.

> **Ethical Communicators:** Value truthful information and cultural sensitivity.
>
> **Unethical Communicators:** Insensitive, insulting, and ultimately ineffective communicators.

The value of having good grades can create an ethical dilemma with regard to cheating and plagiarism.

THE IMPORTANCE OF ETHICS IN PUBLIC RELATIONS

Ethics in public relations are critical to creating effective and trustworthy communication with both distinct groups and the public at large. A major area involving public relations communication pertains to the way the U.S. government (and modern Western democracies in general) communicates with other nations in the world. Public relations can be seen as a sort of balancing act between creating effective public relations platforms with both the national public and the international community as a whole. In the United States, democracy has achieved an almost sacred status and is generally considered a "universal" right. However, in some nations around the world, the transition and acceptance of modern democracy has been difficult, hostile, and even violent. Also, countries such as China reject Western democracy entirely, indicating that not all cultures hold democracy in the same esteem as the United States does. In this sense, it can be quite challenging to craft pro-democracy public relations platforms that appeal to both the native public and the global community. Scholar Monica Riccio (2011) discusses the evolution of democracy as a cultural ideal:

> The process of transformation and exaltation that the concept of democracy went through in the 20th century was punctuated and "promoted" by crucial historical steps. These led it to be a form of government which from "better" eventually turned into the only thinkable and feasible one. This process was accompanied by the progressive loss of the political weight of the concept, the concealment of its complexity and aporia, and finally its crystallization as a "universal value." (p. 74)

Ethics can often give us a broad internal government that keeps everyone accountable. However, this internal government must not be overthrown at any price. Many people are likely to remain ethical until it comes to the loss of their jobs or until they have a chance to gain money or favor. This might make us wonder, what good is an ethical system anyway?

The United States is known for valuing freedom; therefore, it's important that we respect the rights of all citizens. If we're all so diverse in our religious perspectives or values, then we must have a common code of conduct that doesn't tie directly to a religion or doctrine but, instead, relies on human decency. In this way, the United States tries to set guidelines for intercultural ethics that also apply to effective international public relations. No doubt, there's an ethical presence at your college or university. Think about your student handbook and review the current syllabus for this course you are

Developing a public relations platform that is considerate toward many diverse people and groups can be challenging.

taking related to public relations. What statements can you find that address being culturally sensitive when giving a public speech or presentation? What factors must you take into consideration when presenting a project or point of view in a diverse classroom? Something as simple as looking at your class syllabus or student handbook can give valuable insight into how critical ethics are with regard to public relations.

One of the central issues facing ethical public relations communications with an intercultural audience involves negative cultural transfer. Negative cultural transfer occurs when people take an ethnocentric view when engaging in public forums, thereby measuring or assessing their communication based on their own cultural understanding of truth, morality, and values. Intercultural communications scholar Xiaohong Wei (2009) discusses the impact our cultures have on our communication:

> The reasons why negative cultural transfer is one of the greatest obstacles to successful intercultural communication mainly lie in two aspects: (1) culture is deep-rooted; (2) culture is characterized by ethnocentrism. Culture is deep-rooted because most of culture is in the taken-for-granted realm and below the conscious level. Usually, the content of culture is consciously or unconsciously learned and transmitted from generation to generation. From birth, people are deeply influenced by their native culture. How they think and behave is guided by their native culture. With the development of economy and society, great changes may occur in such surface-structure cultural aspects as dress, food, transportation, housing, living habits and laws, etc., through innovation, diffusion and acculturation, but the deep structure of a culture such as values, ethics and morals, religious beliefs and ethics often resists major alterations.

As you can see, removing the ethnocentric viewpoint from your public relations communication is central to becoming an ethical communicator. Often, the media we consume (television, books, newspapers, Internet, etc.) are biased toward this idea that our particular culture is the pinnacle of truth, morality, and ethical behavior. This way of thinking can often lead to cultural misunderstandings and mistrust. Your first step as an intercultural communicator and public relations professional should be to open your mind to the beliefs and practices of other cultures and not to judge them based on your own culture's understanding of ethics.

Negative Cultural Transfer: Occurs when people take an ethnocentric view when engaging in intercultural public communication, thereby measuring or assessing their communication based on their own cultural understanding of truth, morality, and values.

ETHICAL CONSIDERATIONS

Many of you are probably thinking that by now you have a pretty good sense of ethical perspective. You probably understand the groundwork and many of the components. However, being ethical in public relations can become problematic if you do not have a proper understanding of the culture of the public you are addressing. Take a look at this example, known as the Teddy Bear Story, published by John Oetzel (2009):

> Gillian Gibbons is a British woman who was working in a Sudanese school as a teacher of young children. As part of the mandated government curriculum to learn about animals, Gibbons asked one of her students to bring a teddy bear to class. She asked the predominantly Muslim students to identify some names for the bear and then to vote on their favorite names. The voting was a way to introduce the students to democracy. The students, all around 7 years old, identified Abdullah, Hassan, and Muhammad as possible names. Ultimately, the vast majority chose Muhammad. The students took turns taking the teddy bear home and writing a diary, which was labeled "My name is Muhammad."

PR TIP

ARTICULATE YOUR VALUE PROPOSITION

According to Steven Hook, PhD, the easy formula to follow for just about any sales pitch is Problem-Solution-Action. There are too many sales pieces floating around that provide tons of information about a product but never get to the big close. Once you've identified the problem, you need to lead them directly down the path of solving the problem and how to accomplish that. Give your prospects the opportunity to say yes to your offer! Every web page should prominently display a "buy it now" button or a "contact us" link. The information you give should lead readers right where you want them to go.

SOURCE: http://www.10bestpr.com/tips/6-10/

Ethical Considerations: Can help walk you through the process of what you must ask yourself when you're trying to communicate with different audiences, or when you are trying to analyze the public communication of another person or organization.

Gibbons was arrested in November 2007 and charged with inciting religious hatred—a crime that is punishable by 40 lashes and 6 months imprisonment. The Prophet Muhammad is the most sacred symbol in Islam and to name an animal Muhammad is insulting to many Muslims. (p. 2)

In the previous story, many people would not consider Gibbons's classroom activity to be unethical; it was simply a cultural misunderstanding. However, this example indicates the ethical importance of researching your public thoroughly in order to be sensitive to the customs and traditions of the other culture. Use this story as a reminder that, while your intentions may be good, it is important to assess and be sensitive to any public before you begin your public relations campaign.

Ethical considerations can help walk you through the process of what you must ask yourself when trying to communicate with different audiences with which you hope to foster positive public opinion. You must always consider your motives, attitudes, integrity, and organizational values. You probably feel as though you're a fairly ethical person. Perhaps you don't cheat, steal, or lie. You speak politely and courteously to others. However, the interesting thing about public relations is that you often don't recognize when you are being insensitive or contradictory to another person's beliefs, but you more than likely recognize when someone is doing it to you. Therefore, the only thing you can do to stay on top of ethics is educate yourself on what you are doing and when you are doing it. Think about every conversation you've had in the past 24 hours. What questions were asked? Did you withhold information? Did you gossip? Did you tell the truth? At some point during the day, many of you have used an unethical tactic to get something from someone else (it can be as simple as exaggerating a story). Can you apply these ethical questions to public relations? What are some ways you can be unethical when communicating with the public?

Ethical considerations can save you time and stress. Think about these key elements to ethics at the beginning and end of each day. Hold yourself accountable regarding ethics. Check each conversation you have against your reflexive cycle to achieve ethical conversations and effective public communication. You'll be surprised at the level of respect others will have for you when you consider their feelings and needs by holding yourself accountable to doing what's right.

The Ethics of Electronic Communication

Think about your communication choices related to electronic communication. How can electronic communication be used to enhance public relations? What forms of electronic communication do you use to communicate with different publics and organizations? The preceding questions can be explored by assessing the presence of electronic communication in your life. Think about how you use social networking sites such as Facebook and Twitter to communicate, and how your communication can be perceived as a public relations campaign (for yourself) from an ethical perspective.

Earlier, when you were asked to use the reflexive ethics cycle, many of you probably considered just your face-to-face conversations. However, if you consider the strong reliance on technology today, it's important to apply the same ethical principles to electronic communication.

People from many different parts of the general public take topics in need of discussion, or controversial topics, and place them in electronic formats often termed *e-mail dialogues*—exchanges of messages about a particular topic using e-mail, blog space, and other electronic tools to encourage participation that will ideally lead to new ideas, planning, and sound decision making. These electronic exchanges are, at first glance, supposed to contain rational arguments for or against policies, proposals, and the like. E-mail dialogues can be useful and should not be avoided; however, there's a drawback to e-mail dialogues that many of you have already experienced. The dark side of these electronic exchanges is *electronic aggression*—a form of aggressive communication in which people interact on topics filled with emotionality and aggression (Quintanilla & Wahl, 2014). Topics that begin in an appropriate spirit can get nasty when people don't agree with the direction of the discussion or if particular language is used to disagree about a program or idea others support. People engaged in electronic aggression think their responses are persuasive. Unfortunately, these electronic exchanges filled with emotionality serve as daunting examples of incivility and unethical public communication today.

> **E-mail Dialogues:** Are exchanges of messages about a particular topic using e-mail, blog space, and other electronic tools to encourage participation that will ideally lead to new ideas, planning, and sound decision making.

> **Electronic Aggression:** A form of aggressive communication in which people interact on topics filled with emotionality and aggression.

Internet "flame wars" are distracting and can derail a public relations campaign.

The great thing about advances in new media is that you can send messages instantly and communicate at faster and faster rates each day. The downfall is that people often don't take the time to think before they "speak," or hit send. If you take some time to calm down during a heated conversation or electronic debate, you'll establish rational discussion rather than an aggressive dispute. However, you probably have heard of situations where hurtful or inappropriate electronic messages were forwarded to tens of hundreds of people to make a statement. It's important to be mindful when speaking to or about others in an electronically mediated message, because once you say it or type it, it doesn't go away.

How do you use electronic communication as a platform for public relations in your life? Think about how people use their cell phones or e-mail to communicate with others. Perhaps you've sent your significant other or friends text messages worded to initiate some sort of response. Maybe you've called someone and hidden your number. We often use technology to communicate with others for our own benefit, for instance, convincing your boss that you're sick through a text message or messaging others during a test to persuade them to share the answers. Whatever the cause, new media is often used in disturbing ways. It's important that, before you press the "send" button on any message, you apply the same ethical considerations when using new media as you do in face-to-face communication. Take a moment to evaluate your electronic communication from an ethical perspective (e.g., text messages, e-mail, Facebook, Twitter). Ask yourself if you're sensitive and ethical with people when you use electronic communication.

Think about your communication motives. Does anything need to change? Perhaps these ethical considerations could save you and others some grief and hurt. Each time you pick up your cell phone or turn on your computer, be mindful of how you go about getting your way when using electronic communication.

A recent example of unethical use of electronic communication occurred after the nuclear reactor meltdown in Japan that sent contaminated water into the sea. In 2011, rumors began circulating around the Internet that sea salt was no longer safe for consumption since it was contaminated by radiation. The rumor triggered panicked purchases of iodized salt in the United States and other countries, notably China. Supermarkets in many major Chinese cities soon found themselves with a salt shortage. In Korea, rumors spread that "radiation rain" could impact the country, and fake news stories encouraged the mass buying of iodized salt, seaweed, and other products to "resist radiation." This points to a similarity between Western and Asian cultures, in that the United States and other European countries have also had their fair share of Internet hoaxes. Scholar Xiaochi Zhang (2012) discusses this similarity:

> Especially from the above cases, the peoples from different cultural backgrounds, both the Asian people including Chinese people, Korean people and the Americans, appeared a confusing phenomenon that under the conditions of excessive "presses freedom," a large amount of false information has been spread while the information reflecting the truth cannot be communicated. Why? This is because the instinct to prevent potential danger has made people choose to accept more information that is closely related with their personal interests while the other information has been neglected. (p. 14)

The above passage indicates a fundamental need to be ethical and consider the repercussions of our communication. Regardless of whether we mean it as a joke or are actively trying to spread false information (please don't!), using electronic communication irresponsibly can have dire effects on countless people. Try to place yourself in the shoes of someone in the previous nuclear meltdown example; it can be easy to fall for a story like that, but such misinformation obscures clear, useful information and can cause irreparable harm to people's lives.

Ethics in Practice

Tim was recently hired onto a public relations firm that specializes in damage control for business organizations. For his first project, a bottling company had recently been exposed for failing to dispose properly of caustic chemicals that resulted as a byproduct of their manufacturing process. Despite evidence from an independent investigation, Tim's first action was to publicly announce that the findings were inaccurate; he presented a very dated study (which had since been thoroughly debunked) that showed the chemicals in question had no ecological or biological impact. His next actions involved spinning the story and trying to deflect blame onto the local and state government for failing to give the company proper warning about the chemicals being used in the plant. As a final measure, Tim organized a very misleading advertising campaign that either exaggerated or outright lied about the positive ecological projects the bottling company was engaged in within the local community. Although Tim had some immediate success in turning public opinion, his campaigns did not hold up to scrutiny and a local television station blasted the bottling company for trying to deflect blame and mislead the public. Tim was later fired for violating his company's code of ethics agreement.

QUESTIONS TO CONSIDER

1. What ethical considerations did Tim violate during his public relations campaign?
2. What other steps could Tim have taken that would have been more ethically responsible?
3. How would a more ethically sound approach aid in public perception, or at least public trust?
4. How critical is having a strict code of ethics in creating a successful public relations campaign?

ETHICAL RESPONSIBILITY

Now that you've covered the basics of ethics, let's focus on ethical responsibility. According to communication ethics scholar Richard L. Johannesen and his colleagues, **responsibility** includes the elements of fulfilling duties and obligations, being accountable to other individuals and groups, adhering to agreed-on standards, and being accountable to one's own conscience (Johannesen, Valde, & Whedbee, 2008). In public relations communication, there's at least one sender and (generally) very many receivers. While you have reviewed many responsibilities of the sender of a message, do you think the receiver of the message has ethical responsibilities, too?

With regard to ethical responsibility during public communication, it is important not to create your platform based on your own ideas of ethics, morals, and values. When we discuss using ethics in public relations communication, it does not necessarily mean finding loopholes to persuade others to join your way of thinking. Rather, it refers to the need to be considerate and understanding during your public communications. Scholar Stella Ting-Toomey (2010) discusses this situation:

> *Responsibility:* Includes the elements of fulfilling duties and obligations, being accountable to other individuals and groups, adhering to agreed-on standards, and being accountable to one's own conscience.

Many problematic cultural practices perpetuate themselves because of long-standing cultural habits or ignorance of alternative ways of doing things. Education or a desire for change from within the people in a local culture is usually how a questionable practice is ended. From a metaethics social ecological framework, making a sound ethical judgment demands both breadth and depth of culture-sensitive knowledge, context specific knowledge, and genuine humanistic concern. (p. 349)

From the above passage, it should be apparent that the goal of ethical communication in public relations has a goal beyond gaining public opinion or influence; it involves having knowledge of and concern for people of different cultures. That is not to say that public relations is not inherently the practice of trying to persuade; simply that it is important to be truthful, considerate, and knowledgeable when developing your campaigns and platforms. Many people can be deceiving or "shady" when participating in public relations. When you think of such people, politicians might come to mind. Many of you have probably heard jokes or quotes comparing politicians to used car salesmen or lawyers. In general, politicians aren't viewed as the most honest individuals in society. From Watergate to the Clinton sex scandal, Americans have seen their share of "dirty politicians." However, instead of focusing on the individual, focus on the ethical process of politics with respect to crafting

Public relations campaigns involving politics can find it incredibly challenging to be considerate of all audiences.

a political public relations platform. One of the many political processes is campaigning. Barack Obama didn't become the president of the United States on his own. It took a team of specialized public relations professionals representing him and constantly working on his public persona to get him into the White House. Sadly, appealing to the largest possible group of voters can lead to the repression of minority opinions and cultures. U.S. citizens who come from different cultures can find their deeply held beliefs thrown in their faces during elections. Campaigns are normally run through commercials that point out flaws in opposing candidates and their values. Because of this vicious format, people from different cultures or religious backgrounds may suddenly find themselves demonized or ridiculed based on their beliefs.

With so many types of communication and so many communicators in a campaign, it is almost impossible to monitor this notion of public relations ethics. Outside of the media, think of all the people involved with the campaign team—candidates, representatives, consultants, reporters, editors, and more. Each of these people who impact the campaign should be held responsible for following a strict code of ethics. However, they're all held responsible for portraying the candidate's image in an appealing manner in hopes of winning the election, which can sometimes encourage them to be insensitive or demeaning toward audiences different from the U.S. mainstream. This idea of ethics within politics or campaigns is difficult to enforce due to special interest and political action committees (e.g., Swift Boat Veterans, Human Rights Campaign, National Rifle Association), known for funding negative political campaign ads.

Adapting to the Audience

Many of you taking this course will probably have taken public speaking by now. Think back to the generic speeches some of your peers may have given. Often when people speak to an audience, they consider only their own personal opinions or values. However, at the extreme opposite end of this spectrum, other people try to please everyone in the audience. Questions about how far persuaders should go in adapting their message to particular audiences should also be associated with ethical responsibility (Johannesen et al., 2008).

Many politicians and business professionals struggle when they try to please everyone in the audience. You may sometimes have to step on a few toes or fall short of some people's expectations to remain ethically responsible in front of an audience. Some degree of adaptation for specific audiences in language choice, evidence, value appeals, organization, and communication medium is a crucial part of successful and ethical public relations communication. As a communicator, always be mindful of others' spiritual perspectives (if any), values, personal experience, families, and the like. You've probably seen speakers who are completely mindless of their audiences, as well as speakers who are willing to say anything to win the favor of their audiences. Both of these extremes are unethical and irresponsible.

Earlier in the chapter, we discussed how the ideal of democracy may not necessarily be shared across all cultures. China was used as an example of a country where Western-style democracy has not gained much popularity. Many politicians and media personalities make the unfair and inaccurate assertion that the Chinese government and people do not want freedom or the ability to speak freely. In practice, these public relations professionals are not taking into consideration the context, facts, and ideals of other groups in their discourse with the public. This is another example of unethical public communication. Scholar Rafael Capurro (2011) discusses this misunderstanding and what we can learn from it:

> What is the goal of this kind of analysis for intercultural debates on information ethics? First of all, to learn from each other. Western information societies can learn from Taoism and the spirit of the "Far East" not only on how to deal with blocking processes based on fixed moralities, exacerbating the primacy of direct speech. Information societies in the "Far East" might learn from direct speech, individual freedom and autonomy as correctives of an idealized harmony that might block social changes. In both cases we should be careful not to oversee the complexity and richness of our traditions including the difference itself between "Far East" and "Far West" that is nothing but a starting point for intercultural information ethics that should be both theoretical and empirical. (p. 43)

After reading the previous passage, it should be apparent that "intercultural information ethics" goes hand in hand with our discussions of ethics in public relations communication. The following section delves more into the ways we can use different ethical perspectives to become more effective intercultural communicators.

TOOLS FOR THE PUBLIC RELATIONS PROFESSIONAL

Read the questions below. When it comes to your communication choices, can you always answer "yes" to these questions? Can you think of examples for which you could not answer "yes"? As you read the passage below consider other communication strategies that would be more effective in this professional situation.

Lying: Are you telling the truth?

Secrets: Are you respecting the boundary placed around information by avoiding disclosure to others?

Integrity: Are you discerning right from wrong and explaining your reasoning for your decision? In other words, are you vocal about the ethics driving your decision (e.g., care and love, financial, respect for individual rights, equal for all)?

Aggressive communication: Are you communicating with others void of power abuse and aggression? Are you communicating with others in a dignified and respectful manner? Are you communicating with mutual respect and open dialogue?

Plagiarism (cheating): Are you communicating information that is authentic and not plagiarized? Is the source of information being credited appropriately?

1. Have you ever taken part in any of these communication behaviors?
2. If so, did you consider them unethical? Why or why not?
3. Did you consider them unprofessional? Why or why not?

SOURCE: Quintanilla, K. M., & Wahl, S. T. (2014). *Business and professional communication: Keys for workplace excellence* (2nd ed.). Thousand Oaks, CA: Sage. Page 19

Ethical Responsibility Strategies

Integrating ethical practices is critical to your daily interactions with others, and there are a few strategies you can use to incorporate ethical behavior in your daily routine. Basically, you should always be developing new ways to interpret a situation. One strategy is mindful reframing. **Mindful reframing** is described as "the mindful process of using language to change the way each person or party defines or thinks about experiences" (Ting-Toomey & Chung, 2005). Keep in mind that this practice is meant to be reciprocal; both parties should take an active role to keep the communication from becoming fragmented and ineffective. Think of mindful reframing as a reflexive

Mindful Reframing: The mindful process of using language to change the way each person or party defines or thinks about experiences.

practice, something you should be actively critiquing as your communication interaction occurs. A good way to practice might be to watch a television show or movie that involves communication between two or more political candidates and attempt to reframe the dialogue from several different perspectives in respect to public relations development.

Another ethical public relations strategy involves the use of **sustained dialogue**. The goal of sustained dialogue is to promote change in intercultural group relationships by moving the communication dynamic from negative to positive (Mollov & Schwartz, 2010). In our study of public relations, sustained dialogue can help public relations professionals better understand their public, and vice-versa. Basically, sustained dialogue is a method of relationship building that attempts to restructure the relationship from the ground up. Typically, this strategy is used whenever two different groups are in conflict. Critical to this strategy is the **contact hypothesis**. Scholars M. Ben Mollov and David Schwartz describe the contact hypothesis this way:

Sustained Dialogue: To promote change in public relations communication by moving the communication dynamics from negative to positive.

Contact Hypothesis: The theory that contact is not a means of altering public perception in group conflicts. Several conditions must be met in order for it to be effective.

For a global public relations organization such as the United Nations, how important is the idea of reframing in creating a healthy international dialogue?

The contact hypothesis developed initially by Allport (1954) and later enlarged upon by Amir (1969) maintains that contact in itself is not necessarily a means of bringing about perception change among groups in conflict, which can be a pre-requisite to relationship building. The contact hypothesis maintains that for such contact to have a positive impact several main conditions must be met: (1) equal status between the parties; (2) intimate as opposed to merely formal relations between the parties; (3) cooperative as opposed to competitive interactions; and (4) institutional support. (pp. 211–212)

As you can see, the principles of sustained dialogue and the contact hypothesis involve moving beyond formal dialogue and into a more intimate communication setting. Commonly, this strategy has been forwarded as a method to ease tensions in the current Israeli-Palestinian conflict, but this can easily be applied to your public interactions as well. Instead of using formal communication to alter public perception, it is sometimes better to change the relationship dynamic itself before launching a public relations campaign. Sustained dialogue enables public relations professionals and their publics to develop empathy for and understanding of the other that would otherwise not be possible.

SOME ETHICAL PERSPECTIVES

To get more familiar with ethics and its connection to your study of public relations, let's review a few different perspectives concerning ethics. These perspectives can be used alone or in combination with one another to help seek out the best ethical solution in certain situations. Think of these perspectives as being like a shelf full of eyeglasses at the eye doctor. Each different pair you try on causes you to see things around you a bit differently. As you read through these perspectives, try to see yourself in previous social situations from a different point of view.

Religious Perspective

Religious Perspective: Examines the relationship between us as humans and a higher power.

At one time or another, we have all landed on a television program or read a newspaper article that appealed to our beliefs. Many religious leaders have the reputation of appealing to people's psychological needs in hopes of gaining money or power. The **religious perspective** examines the relationship between us as humans and a higher power. Throughout the history of religion and media, there have been instances when spiritual leaders have stated that another religion is wrong or that its teachings and beliefs go against God's will. Florida pastor Terry Jones publicly encouraged followers to burn the Koran (the holy book of Islamic faith) on the 2010 anniversary of the 9/11 terrorist attacks.

Many times in life, we have to question the ethics of those who are communicating to us about another culture or belief. Is it acceptable to burn another faith's holy book? What are the pastor's motives? To assess Jones's appeal from an ethical perspective, let's consider Emory Griffin's ethics for Christian evangelism, established in 1976. To what degree could Jones's message be criticized as that of a "rhetorical rapist" who uses psychological coercion to force a decision to act (Johannesen et al., 2008)? This perspective is not to say that we should reject our religious views or values. However, in every communication situation, we have an ethical responsibility as senders and receivers. Therefore, we must be sure to notice when others may be appealing to our emotions with the goal of deceiving us. Are there other ethical standards of religious doctrine that you may be able to utilize in an instance such as this to evaluate Jones's entreaty to burn the Koran?

Developing positive public relations practices with respect to religion involves realizing some of the shortcomings that are inherent in using only one ethical perspective to view things. Part of becoming an effective public relations professional requires you to understand other ethical or religious perspectives and to use them to help frame your interactions. Scholar Satoshi Ishii (2009) offers two inherent weaknesses that exist in using only a Euro-U.S.-centric viewpoint in regard to religion:

> The first weakness is that their views and concepts of communication ethics supposedly derived from Ancient Greek philosophy, Judeo-Christianity, and the Western Enlightenment are academically Euro-US-centric, hegemonic, and imposedetic in nature. They commonly neglect to pay due respect to non-Euro-US-centric, particularly Asian, concepts and thoughts of communication and human relationship ethics. Their second weakness is that they ignore the traditionally latent impact of religion upon the foundation and development of ethical beliefs, values, and worldviews. Hence in promoting more interculturally trustworthy and sustainable communication ethics, it is crucial to complement

and enhance these two scholarly weaknesses with Asian religio-ethical philosophies and thoughts. (pp. 49–50)

As you can see from the above passage, we generate the most effective communication practices when we give ourselves the ability to understand communication from more than one viewpoint. Whenever we are exposed to other cultural practices that might seem backwards or barbaric, it is important to realize that many different cultures frame their concepts of morals and values from an entirely different religious perspective. Different religious institutions frame their relationships with the public based on ideologies that can contrast and even conflict with other religions at times. The next time you come across an international news story that leaves you appalled or angry, remember to be critical about the ethical and moral

Religions can be better understood by analyzing them from several different perspectives.

lessons inherent to different religious beliefs. Can you think of any morals or values you hold that could seem alien or brutal to someone from a different religious background?

Human Nature Perspective

What makes us human? This is a question many people ponder. Perhaps you've heard someone use the phrase, "I'm only human." What does this mean? Most often when people use this phrase, they are stating that they are prone to making mistakes and are declaring their imperfection. However, as humans we are often held accountable for our mistakes. We are judged, or we face consequences. Other mammals do not face trial or risk going to prison, so what is it about the human race that sets us apart? The **human nature perspective** states that we have an ability to judge, reason, and comprehend that far exceeds that of any other species. Therefore, we hold ourselves accountable to make good judgments and decisions. This is where our ethics come into play. You often hear parents say to their children that they are old enough to know right from wrong. These parents feel they have taught their children the ability to distinguish between good and bad; the children are expected to make good judgment calls from this point onward. Parents and guardians attempt to instill in their children values and morals similar to what you reviewed earlier in the chapter.

Throughout the past decade, we have seen leaders of our country and of the world commit unethical acts or fail to make ethical decisions. Perhaps this was going on all along, or perhaps social media such as Facebook, YouTube, and Twitter have just made footage and information of such events more widely accessible. We've seen the terrorist acts of 9/11, the hanging of Saddam Hussein, and even a shoe thrown at President George W. Bush during a press conference. We've seen companies shut down for discrepancies between the way they've handled their money and the information they gave customers about their money. We've seen the Federal Communications Commission tell musicians that their music cannot be played on the radio due to explicit and vulgar content. In each of these situations, humans have failed to make ethical decisions. The human nature perspective is both a gift and a curse. We are distinguished from other species, however, in that we are liable for our mistakes and misjudgments as humans.

Human Nature Perspective: States that we have an ability to judge, reason, and comprehend that far exceeds that of any other species. Therefore, we hold ourselves accountable to make good judgments and decisions.

As your individual global presence continues to increase, how important is the need for reflexive dialogue in your everyday interactions?

Dialogical Perspective

Dialogical Perspectives: Emerge from current scholarship on the nature of communication as dialogue rather than monologue.

Monologue: Is normally looked at as a performance or speech by a single person. Dialogue is a conversation between two or more people. Both are known as dialogical perspectives.

Dialogue: A conversation between two or more people.

Dialogical perspectives emerge from current scholarship on the nature of communication as dialogue rather than monologue (Johannesen et al., 2008). **Monologue** is normally looked at as a performance or speech by a single person. **Dialogue,** on the other hand, is a conversation between two or more people. Think about the way you handle yourself in a conversation with someone you like. You may be attentive and interested, even if the subject matter doesn't necessarily pertain to you; you have a general interest because you care about that person. Then, try to think of your last conversation with a person you don't like as much. How did you handle yourself in this conversation? In the dialogical perspective, we think of communication as a dialogue by considering the different attitudes we emit in a conversation. These attitudes can be those of hatred, prejudice, jealousy, inequality, or manipulation. On the other hand, the attitudes may be those of tenderness, compassion, interest, or love. Although we've just examined a few extreme ends of the spectrum, there are many different attitudes in each dialogue we encounter throughout the day. These dialogues are important because we must consider how to treat others ethically. In each social situation we encounter, we must consider our audience, even if it is an audience of one. This consideration of others and their feelings will help us remain ethical as we engage in conversations.

Let's take this same idea of communication as dialogue and apply it to public relations. If we engage in conversations with others and seek to manipulate them based on their misunderstanding of our platform, we are being unethical. People who have a hidden agenda or a desire to initiate a reaction through public relations are also acting unethically. It is important as we attempt to communicate with others in our dialogues that we do so by being sensitive and aware of their differences and also carefully assessing what meaning our words and nonverbal communication can convey. This act of public communication should not be manipulative or misleading.

Situational Perspective

The *situational perspective* examines every situation we encounter related to public relations. When we think of scenarios where public relations are involved, we often think of political campaigns, marketing campaigns, and advertisements. However, think about the different people represented in you city, state, nation, and the global community. Simply being from the same country does not mean that everyone shares the same needs and wants. Do you think you ever violate any ethical codes when persuading a friend to buy or rent a movie you would like to watch? Consider the concrete contextual factors to make a purely situational ethical evaluation.

> **Situational Perspective:** Examines every situation we encounter related to public relations.

STRATEGIES FOR PROFESSIONAL SUCCESS

In this chapter, we learned how to tie ethics into our study and practice of public relations. Through real-life examples and study of the text, we can see that being ethical in public relations is critical to success. However, it is not always an easy task to be ethically sound while doing your job in creating positive public perception. Author Jennifer Moyer offers several practical recommendations and guidelines for public relations professionals.

Pay attention to ethics before you need them.

Professional communicators should already be knowledgeable with the value systems of their organizations before those values are publicly called into question. Public relations professionals should begin studying ethics before any ethical problem needs to be addressed; doing so improves the decisions made in your public relations department (Moyer, 2011).

Know your own values.

Taking a thorough look at the personal values you hold and espouse will help you when being pressured by a supervisor, client, or someone else. Use these values and apply them to your organization's code of ethics. Matching your values with those of your employer will produce a solid relationship on which to build your professional career.

(continued)

(continued)

STRATEGIES FOR PROFESSIONAL SUCCESS

Engage in systematic and analytical means of contemplating ethical dilemmas.

The use of moral philosophy lends systematic and consistent methods of ethical analyses and decision making to the practice of public relations. Offering consistent reliable analyses is an incredibly useful means to enhance your personal credibility and that of your public relations organization.

EXECUTIVE SUMMARY

Now that you have finished reading this chapter, you should be able to

Define the term *ethics*:

- Ethics are the driving force of each of these lenses used to help you evaluate the ethical contact of public relations messages in your life.

Discuss how ethics are related to your study of public relations:

- You should become mindful of how to evaluate your approach and receptiveness to public relations campaigns and consider others as you grow in your role as a public relations professional. No matter if you're communicating via phone, computer, or face-to-face, you're always exposed to public relations in some form or another.
- Use ethical responsibility strategies such as mindful reframing and sustained dialogue.

Apply ethical perspectives to achieving professional success:

- You should understand the variety of ethical perspectives that might relate to public relations (e.g., religious, human nature, dialogical). Ethics in any public relations context serve as the primary foundation for professional success.

KEY TERMS

Codes of Ethics: Are all different sets of principles that people hold themselves to or are held to by multiple organizations or groups. *p. 40*

Contact Hypothesis: The theory that contact is not a means of altering public perception in group conflicts. Several conditions must be met in order for it to be effective. *p. 55*

Dedication: Committing to do what is right no matter the situation. *p. 41*

Dialogical Perspectives: Emerge from current scholarship on the nature of communication as dialogue rather than monologue. *p. 60*

Dialogue: A conversation between two or more people. *p. 60*

Distinguish: The ability to decide what's right and wrong. *p. 41*

Electronic Aggression: A form of aggressive communication in which people interact on topics filled with emotionality and aggression. *p. 47*

E-mail Dialogues: Are exchanges of messages about a particular topic using e-mail, blog space, and other electronic tools to encourage participation that will ideally lead to new ideas, planning, and sound decision making. *p. 47*

Ethical Considerations: Can help walk you through the process of what you must ask yourself when you're trying to communicate with different audiences, or when you are trying to analyze the public communication of another person or organization. *p. 46*

Ethical Communicators: Value truthful information and cultural sensitivity. *p. 41*

Ethical Perspectives: A unique set of lenses used to evaluate one's discourse with the public. *p. 39*

Ethics: Is a system of accepted principles that make up an individual's or group's values and judgments as to what's right and wrong. *p. 40*

Human Nature Perspective: States that we have an ability to judge, reason, and comprehend that far exceeds that of any other species. Therefore, we hold ourselves accountable to make good judgments and decisions. *p. 59*

Mindful Reframing: The mindful process of using language to change the way each person or party defines or thinks about experiences. *p. 54*

Monologue: Is normally looked at as a performance or speech by a single person. Dialogue is a conversation between two or more people. Both are known as dialogical perspectives. *p. 60*

Negative Cultural Transfer: Occurs when people take an ethnocentric view when engaging in intercultural public communication, thereby measuring or assessing their communication based on their own cultural understanding of truth, morality, and values. *p. 44*

Religious Perspective: Examines the relationship between us as humans and a higher power. *p. 56*

Responsibility: Includes the elements of fulfilling duties and obligations, being accountable to other individuals and groups, adhering to agreed-on standards, and being accountable to one's own conscience. *p. 50*

Situational Perspective: Examines every situation we encounter related to public relations. *p. 61*

Sustained Dialogue: To promote change in public relations communication by moving the communication dynamics from negative to positive. *p. 55*

Unethical Communicators: Insensitive, insulting, and ultimately ineffective communicators. *p. 41*

Values: Beliefs and attitudes we hold that can actually conflict with our ethical decisions. *p. 41*

DISCUSSION QUESTIONS

1. How important is ethical public relations not only at your job but in your everyday life as well?
2. Are there any current issues in your world that you think can be attributed to unethical public relations communication?
3. What are your ethical responsibilities when creating a public relations campaign for yourself or an organization?
4. How important is it to be reflexive when sending and receiving public relations messages?
5. What ethical perspective in this chapter resonates with you as you observe and evaluate public relations in your life?

CHAPTER 4
PUBLIC RELATIONS THEORY

In February 2010, Tiger Woods faced an enormous personal and professional crisis after telling the world about his infidelity and plans for the future.

From *Public Relations Principles: Strategies for Professional Success,* by Shawn T. Wahl and Michelle M. Maresh Fuehrer. Copyright © by Kendall Hunt Publishing Company. Reprinted by permission.

CHAPTER OUTLINE

Excellence Theory
News Framing Theory
Technology-Image Expectancy Gap
Corporate Apologia
Benoit's Image Repair Theory
    Image Repair Strategies
Strategies for Professional Success
Executive Summary
Key Terms
Discussion Questions

CHAPTER OBJECTIVES

After studying this chapter, you should be able to:

1. Understand Excellence Theory and its contributions to the public relations profession.
2. Understand News Framing Theory and how news framing impacts the practice of public relations.
3. Explain the Technology-Image Expectancy Gap's role in public relations.
4. Understand the role of Corporate Apologia in organizational crisis response.
5. Explain Benoit's Image Repair Theory and how it relates to PR.
6. Develop strategies for professional success related to public relations theory.

Ripped from the Headlines

In 2013, the documentary *Blackfish* premiered at the Sundance Film Festival and was picked up by Magnolia Pictures and CNN Films for wider release. The documentary's narrative focuses on Tilikum, an orca held in captivity at SeaWorld, who was involved in the death of three individuals including his trainer, Dawn Brancheau. Despite the criticisms the film received from the family of Brancheau (Garcia, 2014) and several of the trainers featured in the film—one said that the final film was "a complete 180" from what was originally presented to her (Davis, 2014), the film grossed $2.1 million in North American box offices (Box Office Mojo, 2013) and created an image controversy for the SeaWorld organization. Bands and singers such as Willie Nelson, Martina McBride, Cheap Trick, Heart, and the Barenaked Ladies cancelled their concerts at SeaWorld Orlando and Busch Gardens Tampa (Duke, 2013), SeaWorld announced a $15.9 million loss (Stock, 2013), legislation was proposed to ban keeping orcas in captivity in New York and California (Ball, 2014; Martinez, 2014), and Southwest Airlines ended its 26-year partnership with SeaWorld (Stout, 2014). This prompted SeaWorld to initiate a "Truth about Blackfish" campaign in an attempt to rebuild the reputation that this film tarnished.

The film *Blackfish* resulted in a massive public relations disaster for SeaWorld.

Even if you have not seen *Blackfish*, you can imagine how a documentary film that uses graphic footage and interviews with former trainers to accuse an organization, like SeaWorld, of animal cruelty could be persuasive. The effectiveness of this particular film in creating an image crisis for SeaWorld may be in part due to the frames used by the filmmakers and the news media when portraying SeaWorld's animal practices.

Kim and Cameron (2011) conducted a research study on the role of anger and sadness in the publics' response to crisis news framing. The results of their study indicate that emotional news frames (anger-inducing vs. sadness-inducing) affect the publics' response to a corporate crisis. Specifically, people who were made angry by the news had more negative attitudes toward the company. Consider the results of their study in connection with the *Blackfish* case. If moviegoers became angry at the images of animal mistreatment, animal captivity, and stories of how SeaWorld had prior knowledge of

Tilikum's violent nature, then it makes perfect sense that the public would have a negative attitude toward SeaWorld after watching the film. This knowledge is incredibly important for an organization like SeaWorld, as their crisis response will be evaluated based on their ability to empathize effectively with their angry stakeholders.

The *Blackfish*/SeaWorld case serves as an illustration of the importance of public relations professionals being familiar with public relations theory. In this case, knowledge of News Framing Theory would help SeaWorld's public relations practitioners make an informed decision about the type of crisis response and public relations efforts that they need to enact to restore their public image. As you read this chapter, you will be introduced to several public relations theories—including News Framing Theory—that will help you make educated choices in your public relations efforts.

EXCELLENCE THEORY

Excellence Theory is a general theory of public relations that resulted from a study on the best practices in communication management that spanned over a decade. The study included the incorporation of several theories of communication and public relations, survey research of 327 organizations, and interviews with individuals from 25 organizations (Grunig, Grunig, & Dozier, 2006). Funded by the International Association of Business Communicators (IABC), a team of six researchers (J. Grunig, L. Grunig, Dozier, Ehling, Repper, and White) sought to identify the characteristics of an excellent communication department, how excellent public relations makes an organization more effective, and the monetary value of excellent public relations (Grunig, 1992). The study resulted in ten generic principles of public relations excellence (Vercic, Grunig, & Grunig, 1996):

> Excellence Theory: A general theory of public relations that resulted from a study on the best practices in communication management that spanned over a decade.

Excellence Theory serves as an important contribution to the public relations field, especially as it pertains to exploring the characteristics of "excellent" public relations departments. Public relations professionals often have to make an argument for the monetary value of their work, and this theory provides an important foundation for being able to do so. Furthermore, as you enter the job market, it is important to work for an organization that values your work as a public relations professional. Using the principles of excellent communication departments, you may analyze the role of public relations at the organization at which you are applying to work. If the organization does

TOOLS FOR THE PUBLIC RELATIONS PROFESSIONAL

- *Involvement of public relations in strategic management.* Excellent public relations requires strategic communication with internal and external stakeholders.
- *Empowerment of public relations in the dominant coalition or a direct reporting relationship to senior management.* Public relations personnel, specifically senior communication managers, must have immediate communication access to an organization's powerful senior management.
- *Integrated public relations function.* All public relations functions should occur in a single department.
- *Public relations as a management function, separate from other functions.* Public relations must be its own department rather than playing a supporting role to other departments.
- *Public relations unit is headed by a manager rather than a technician.* Excellent public relations departments require a senior communication manager to direct public relations programs.
- *Two-way symmetrical (or mixed-motive) model of public relations is used.* Excellent public relations departments use two-way symmetrical public relations, balancing the interests of the organization and its publics.
- *Department with the knowledge needed to practice the managerial role in symmetrical public relations.* Excellent public relations programs staff individuals who are educated and active in professional associations.
- *Symmetrical system of internal communication.* Excellent organizations encourage employees to participate in decision-making and incorporate employee goals in their mission.
- *Diversity embodied in all roles.* Excellent public relations requires an organization and public relations professionals who are diverse in sex, race, ethnic, and cultural backgrounds.
- *Ethics and integrity.* Excellent public relations departments must operate in an ethical manner, especially when building credibility and relationships with the public.

Framing: The process of selecting some aspects of a perceived reality and making them more salient in communicating text in such a way as to promote a particular problem definition, causal interpretation, moral evaluation, and/or treatment recommendation for the item described.

not have a public relations department that is integrated with the management function of the organization, you may want to keep this in mind as you make a decision about your future with that organization.

NEWS FRAMING THEORY

Entman (1993) defined framing—within the context of a news story—as the process of selecting "some aspects of a perceived reality and mak[ing] them more salient in a communicating text in such a way as to promote a particular problem definition, causal interpretation, moral evaluation, and/or treatment recommendation for the item described" (p. 52). Framing may be done with the use of certain keywords, symbols, visual images, and metaphors. If you have ever heard that the news media has a liberal or conservative bias, chances are you have heard this from someone who has noticed the effects of framing on a particular news story.

The notion of framing, as a theory, was introduced by Goffman (1974) under the title of "Frame Analysis." Goffman argued that people interpret what is going on in their world through their primary framework. At the heart of News Framing Theory, as we understand it today, is the idea that the media influences how the public perceives certain issues by focusing attention on specific aspects of an issue and ignoring others (Durrant, Wakefield, McLeoud, Clegg-Smith, & Chapman, 2003; Hallahan, 2005). To understand the implications of news framing, consider the crisis in Ferguson, Missouri that was caused when an unarmed teenager named Michael Brown was shot by a police officer. The news media disseminated overwhelmingly violent images of officers in riot gear and vehement protestors looting from local businesses and setting off Molotov cocktails.

Gordts (2014) explained how framing impacted the public's perceptions of the Ferguson crisis, as many newspapers around the world "have published editorials that frame the events in the St. Louis suburb as evidence of a lingering racial divide in the United States" (n.p.). Some papers made connections between Brown's death and that of Trayvon Martin, a Florida teenager who was shot by a neighborhood watch volunteer in 2012. This has impacted the United States' image abroad, as the Chinese government's official news agency Xinhua "used the crisis in Ferguson as an opportunity to chastise the United States for violating human rights domestically while accusing foreign governments of infringing on people's rights" (n.p.).

News Framing Theory serves as a viable explanation for the way that public relations efforts can be framed by the news media, resulting in specific emotional responses and opinions from stakeholders. As both the Ferguson case and the *Blackfish* case that opened this chapter illustrate, a negative news frame can exacerbate crises. Furthermore, the importance of effective media relations is crucial in having public relations stories framed positively—although it does not guarantee the angle in which a story will be framed.

News Framing Theory: A theory that argues that the media influences how the public perceives certain issues by focusing attention on specific aspects of an issue and ignoring others.

The crisis in Ferguson, Missouri created a massive fallout for the U.S. government both domestically and abroad.

TECHNOLOGY-IMAGE EXPECTANCY GAP

Technology-Image Expectancy Gap: A theory that bridges technology and public relations and brings attention to an organization's vulnerability to crises based on a false sense of security created by technological advances.

Technology-Image Expectancy Gap theory bridges technology and public relations and brings attention to an organization's vulnerability to crises based on a false sense of security created by technological advances. According to Kazoleas and Teigen (2009), "this theory suggests that the marketing of technology, coupled with media coverage of technological advances, creates unrealistic expectations as to the ability of organizations to meet the needs of their stakeholders" (p. 416).

To gain a clearer understanding of the main premise of this theory, consider your exposure to technology on a daily basis. Think about how many times we take technology for granted. We assume that, when we purchase a product, it has been inspected for quality and will last for a long time. One look at the recalls.gov website will make us question the false sense of security that is created by technology. The author of this chapter visited recalls.gov while writing this chapter and found recalls for hundreds of products, including: hanging lamps, bed bug heat treatment systems, ATVs, hooded sweatshirts, child safety seats, vehicles, pesticide products, tires, boats, meat and poultry, and medical tourniquets.

This theory also posits that, because of the public's emphasis on technology, organizations believe that they must have a technological presence. Unfortunately, many organizations are not equipped to handle the expectations that come with technological presence. A memorable example occurred in 2013 when the Healthcare.gov website launched and subsequently crashed (see Figure 4.1). This technological failure violated the public's expectations for such a service and served as fodder for individuals who were already critical of the Affordable Care Act.

According to Kazoleas and Teigen (2009), this theory includes the following testable propositions:

1. "As technological advancements become more of a focus in a society, so will the generalized expectations that individuals will have regarding the uses of that technology" (p. 430).
2. "As technological advancements become more of a focus in a society, the media through the agenda-setting process will devote more coverage and discussion to technology and technology-based issues" (p. 430).
3. "As the media increase their coverage of technological innovations, the number of unrealistic expectations will also increase. This may be manifested by unrealistic expectations about the quality of products

CHAPTER 4: PUBLIC RELATIONS THEORY

Product recalls, such as eggs with salmonella, help intensify the technology-image expectancy gap.

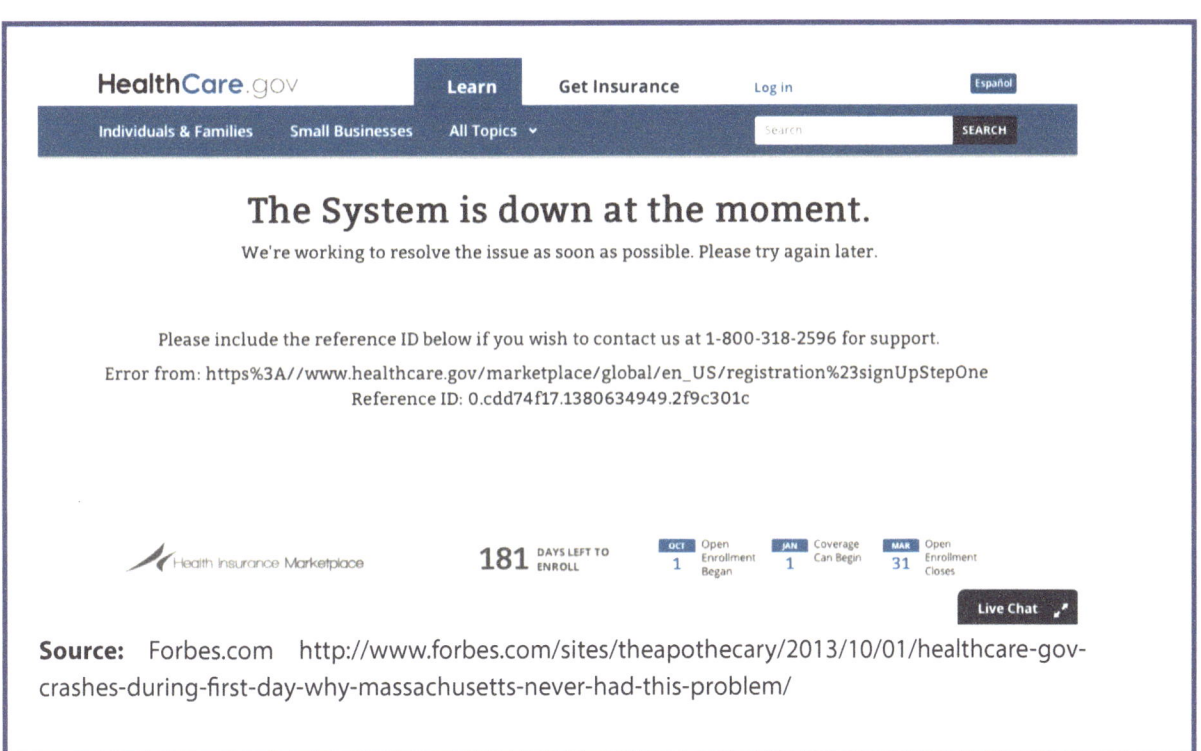

Source: Forbes.com http://www.forbes.com/sites/theapothecary/2013/10/01/healthcare-gov-crashes-during-first-day-why-massachusetts-never-had-this-problem/

FIGURE 4.1: ERROR MESSAGE ON HEALTHCARE.GOV WEBSITE

and services in general, and perhaps in the underassessment of risks in traditionally risk-laden activities" (pp. 430-431).
4. "As the media focus on technology increases, organizations (particularly those that are publicly-traded) will increase the emphasis of technology in their image-building, image-enhancing, and reputation-management strategies" (p. 431).
5. "As organizations increase their emphasis on technology as part of their image, the specific expectations regarding the quality of goods, products, services, and behavior will also increase" (p. 431).
6. "Organizations can moderate the expectancy gap by monitoring relevant publics' perceptions and expectancies, and by creating message strategies that are targeted at creating more realistic expectations of organizational abilities" (p. 431).

The Technology-Image Expectancy Gap is important to understand when communicating with stakeholders. We must be aware of the expectations that stakeholders have for our products, services, speed of communication, and the safety/security of our communicative channels. We must also understand the potential for technology to fail. This information is helpful in both crisis planning and response.

CORPORATE APOLOGIA

Apologia is a Greek word meaning "speech in defense." **Corporate Apologia** is a crisis communication theory about how organizations (specifically, corporations) use verbal or written defense to repair their image when they are faced with criticism. Hearit (2006) views humans as having an innate need to justify their behavior during unfavorable circumstances. In his theory, Hearit outlines five specific strategies for performing apologia. The first of these strategies is *denial*, or the claim that the organization has not committed any wrongdoing. This strategy is used when no public evidence exists that suggests that the organization has committed wrongdoing or when organizations must deny wrongdoing for liability reasons (Hearit, 2006). The second strategy is *counterattack*, or denying guilt of wrongdoing and arguing that the accuser (oftentimes, the media's coverage of a crisis) is at fault. *Differentiation* consists of an organization acknowledging some responsibility for a crisis but arguing that they are not fully liable. This often takes the form of a corporation distancing themselves from the behavior of an employee at a single franchise. A fourth strategy, *apology*, requires the organization to admit

---

Corporate Apologia: A theory about how organizations use verbal or written defense to repair their image when they are faced with criticism.

Denial: An apologia strategy that consists of an organization claiming that it has not committed any wrongdoing; also a posture in Situational Crisis Communication Theory that seeks to remove any connection between the crisis and the organization.

Counterattack: An apologia strategy that consists of denying guilt of wrongdoing and arguing that the accuser is at fault.

Differentiation: An apologia strategy that consists of an organization acknowledging some responsibility for a crisis but arguing that they are not fully liable.

Apology: An apologia strategy that consists of an organization admitting guilt and asking for the public's forgiveness.

guilt and ask for the public's forgiveness without a defensive approach to explaining their behavior. Finally, legal apologia requires an organization to form a response with their legal counsel, which usually maintains that an organization cannot currently comment on the situation because they are undergoing litigation.

The effectiveness of a corporation's apologia is contingent on their ability to complete the apologetic ritual. Hearit argues that this consists of an organization illustrating that their behavior is consistent with societal values, such as truthfulness and caring for the environment. Doing so requires a public statement of defense—even if it is ineffective—or else the public will be unable to move on from the crisis.

In 2014, the National Football League (NFL) faced a major crisis regarding its handling of players who commit acts of domestic violence. The case that started the crisis began when a graphic video surfaced of Ray Rice, now-former Baltimore Raven, punching his fiancée and knocking her unconscious. Reports claimed that the NFL had received the tape months before it surfaced online and that the NFL Commissioner, Roger Goodell, and the Ravens knowingly turned the other cheek and issued a light two-day suspension to Rice. In an attempt to enact corporate apologia, the NFL denied reports that they had received the video earlier. Unfortunately, this strategy did not help the NFL against the public's main criticism of the light punishment for players who have committed acts of domestic violence. The public did not care how much

Legal: An apologia strategy that requires an organization to form a response with their legal counsel.

Apologetic Ritual: A process that consists of an organization illustrating that their behavior is consistent with societal values and providing a statement of defense in order for the public to move on from a crisis.

Oil spills from private companies offer significant examples of corporate apologia in practice.

Ethics in Practice

Tammy works in the public relations department for a sports outfitting company. Recent allegations have been levied against her company, asserting that the company is guilty of hiring malpractice by firing employees who did not meet "standards of physical fitness." Public outcry began to build against the company for placing unfair standards of physical appearance as a hiring requirement for the organization. Upon thorough investigation of company records, Tammy discovered the allegations were accurate. Tammy began her public relations campaign by having the company assume responsibility for the actions, as well as requiring all hiring managers to attend a seminar on proper hiring techniques. The company then offered monetary restitution packages for all employees who were found to be unfairly fired. Tammy then urged the company to immediately begin a marketing campaign that encouraged physical fitness and sports activity for people of all fitness levels. Although public opinion remained low for a time, eventually the company recovered to a favorable public standing and the stigma from the scandal receded from the company.

QUESTIONS TO CONSIDER

1. What aspect of corporate apologia did Tammy successfully take advantage of, and why was it a useful strategy?
2. What public relations theory can be applied to the successful implementation of Tammy's public relations campaign?
3. If Tammy chose to deflect blame to a singular department or employee, how could that have backfired later on during the campaign?
4. What other steps could Tammy have taken to improve public perception of her company?

On July 8th in 2010, LeBron James announced his decision to join the Miami Heat by saying, "I'm going to take my talents to South Beach and join the Miami Heat" on an ESPN special called 'The Decision', resulting in significant backlash from his fans and the sports community.

information Goodell knew; rather, individuals like Terry O'Neill (president of the National Organization for Women) felt that "new leadership must come in with a specific charge to transform the culture of violence against women that pervades the NFL" (as reported by Volin, 2014). The public could not move on because the apologetic ritual had not been completed—the NFL had not shown that their behavior is consistent with societal values. As a result, the NFL began to take additional steps in an attempt to recover from this crisis. Goodell held a press conference and apologized, saying "I got it wrong with the handling of the Ray Rice matter and I am sorry for that. I got it wrong on a number of levels from the process that I led to the decision that I reached." The NFL has since partnered with the National Domestic Violence Hotline and the National Sexual Violence Resource Center and has been holding quarterly meetings focused on domestic violence (Rovell & Keneally, 2014; USA Today Sports, 2014).

BENOIT'S IMAGE REPAIR THEORY

Developed by communication scholar William L. Benoit, Image Repair Theory attempts to clarify the understanding of the strategies organizations and individuals use to respond to attacks on their reputation. Introduced in

Image Repair Theory: Developed by William L. Benoit, Image Repair Theory attempt to simplify the strategies organizations and individuals use to respond to attacks on their reputation.

In 2020, Prince Harry and Meghan Markle kicked off the year with a shocking announcement - they would step back from their senior royal duties, in what's since become known as Megxit.

the early 1990s, Image Repair Theory has been used by scholars to study an array of public responses, including those by politicians and athletes such as Tiger Woods and LeBron James as well as large multi-nationals organizations and celebrities such as Meghan Markle and Prince Harry. While there are other theories that examine message strategies used in a crisis, Benoit's theory is unique as it takes into account the specific messages used to defend an individual or an organization against a persuasive attack. The theory is also grounded in the basic premise that regardless of the complexity, communication transactions always have a purpose. Regardless of the exchange, there is always an end-goal ranging from simple asks to complex requests.

Image Repair Strategies

With the idea of the communication goal as the basis of his theory, Benoit purports there are fourteen different strategies individuals and organizations use to defend themselves when attacked. These strategies can be grouped into five categories-denial, evading responsibility, reducing offensiveness, corrective action and mortification.

Denial

The first of Benoit's five defense categories, the concept of denial occurs when an individual or organization publicly denies responsibility for a wrongdoing of which they have been accused. There are a few ways this can be done:

- **Simple denial:** The speaker denies responsibility for the act.
- **Shift the blame:** This strategy can be used in conjunction with a simple denial and involves trying to shift the blame for the act to another organization or individual.

Evade Responsibility

The second of Benoit's defense categories is based on the theory that sometimes individuals or organizations attempt to mitigate their level of responsibility for an act. This can be accomplished by employing one a few different strategies:

- **Provocation:** A speaker says the act was taken in response to another, improper act.
- **Defeasibility:** A speaker or organization cannot be held accountable because they did not have the proper information or possess the ability to control the actions.
- **Accident:** A person or individual cannot be held responsible as it was due to uncontrollable or unforeseen circumstances.
- **Good intentions:** When an individual or organization sets out to achieve a positive goal, and despite the error, is not assigned full blame for the incident due to the original intentions.

Reduce Offensiveness

The third of Benoit's defense strategies, occurs when a speaker tries reduce the offensiveness of the situation at hand. There are six ways to do this:

- **Bolstering:** Hoping to create positive feelings for the accused by talking about their better character traits.
- **Minimization:** Trying to lessen the gravity of a situation by suggesting the situation isn't as bad as it originally appeared.
- **Differentiation:** Attempting to lessen the severity of a situation by comparing it to another.
- **Transcendence:** A speaker or organization makes the case their actions, although erroneous, support a more important positive cause.

PR TIP

CAPTIVATING VISUAL DEMONSTRATIONS

The most important rule of public presentations focuses on presentation aids: If a visual presentation can stand alone, it is wrong. The problems with PowerPoint and Prezi are common, so consider these simple tips: 1. Do not simply use bullet points. Show what you have to offer. 2. Do not read off the screen. Know the value proposition. 3. Do not be overly technical or overly simplistic. 4. Attend a respectable workshop or seminar to learn the best practices of presentation aids.

SOURCE: http://www.10bestpr.com/tips/11-15/

- **Attack accusers:** An individual or organization publicly defames its critics with the hope of discrediting them.
- **Compensation:** An organization or individual offers to compensate those who have been mistreated as a result of the act.

Corrective Action

The fourth of Benoit's defense categories occurs when speakers promise to take specific steps to rectify the situation. Typically, two promises are made to the public:

1. Things will go back to normal
2. The act will never happen again.

Mortification

The fifth and final of Benoit defense categories happens when an individual or organization admits responsibility for the act and seeks forgiveness.

Using a combination of strategies often results in a higher degree of success. Very rarely do individuals or organizations employ only one tactic due to the gravity of the circumstances they are trying to combat. It is important to keep context of the situation and the needs of the effected individuals in mind when deciding how to respond to a situation.

STRATEGIES FOR PROFESSIONAL SUCCESS

In this chapter, you have learned several theories and strategies available to public relations professionals. When an organization or individual is accused of an erroneous action, the spokesperson addressing the public has arguably the most crucial role in damage control. Author W. Timothy Coombs offers several good practices for public spokespersons.

Avoid the phrase "no comment."

This language can be seen as evasive, and lead people to think the organization is guilty and trying to hide something.

Present information clearly by avoiding jargon or technical terms.

A lack of clarity can make people think the organization is purposely being confusing in order to hide or mislead the public.

Appear pleasant on camera by avoiding nervous habits that people interpret as deception.

(continued)

Have strong eye contact, avoid fidgeting or pacing, and limit disfluencies such as "Uhms" or "uhs." Lack of eye contact, language disfluencies, and nervous gestures are generally perceived as deceptive (Coombs, 2011).

Finally, brief all potential spokespersons on the latest crisis information as well as key message points the organization would like to convey to the public and stakeholders.

EXECUTIVE SUMMARY

Now that you have finished reading this chapter, you can

Understand Excellence Theory and its contributions to the public relations profession:

- Excellence Theory includes ten principles of excellent communication departments. These principles help make an argument for the monetary value of excellent public relations, as well as the steps that an organization must follow to have a successful public relations department. When you are searching for a job as a public relations professional, you may want to ensure that an organization practices "excellent public relations" before making a decision about your future with that organization.

Understand News Framing Theory and how news framing impacts the practice of public relations:

- News Framing Theory argues that the media influences how the public perceives certain issues by focusing attention on specific aspects of an issue and ignoring others. This theory explains how public relations efforts can be framed by the media and thus may result in specific responses from stakeholders. It also reiterates the importance of effective media relations.

Explain the Technology-Image Expectancy Gap's role in public relations:

- Technology-Image Expectancy Gap theory includes a set of 6 testable propositions that contend that technological advances bring a sense of false security to stakeholders and create expectations for organizations that are not realistic given that technology can fail unexpectedly. This is important to understand when making choices for public relations efforts, as we must ask ourselves: What expectations do stakeholders have? Does our organization have a contingency plan for moments when technology does not live up to these expectations?

Understand the role of Corporate Apologia in organizational crisis response:

- Corporate Apologia provides a framework for organizations in need of repairing their image during a crisis situation. This theory includes 5 strategies: denial, counterattack, differentiation, apology, and legal. One of these methods of verbal or written defense must be used in order for the public to move on from the crisis.

Define Benoit's Image Repair Theory:

- Explain the importance of Benoit's Image Repair Theory in PR and the five major defense categories: denial, evading responsibility, reducing the offensiveness of the event, corrective action, and mortification.

KEY TERMS

Apologetic Ritual: A process that consists of an organization illustrating that their behavior is consistent with societal values and providing a statement of defense in order for the public to move on from a crisis. *p. 73*

Apology: An apologia strategy that consists of an organization admitting guilt and asking for the public's forgiveness. *p. 72*

Corporate Apologia: A theory about how organizations use verbal or written defense to repair their image when they are faced with criticism. *p. 72*

Counterattack: An apologia strategy that consists of denying guilt of wrongdoing and arguing that the accuser is at fault. *p. 72*

Denial: An apologia strategy that consists of an organization claiming that it has not committed any wrongdoing; also a posture in Situational Crisis Communication Theory that seeks to remove any connection between the crisis and the organization. *p. 72*

Differentiation: An apologia strategy that consists of an organization acknowledging some responsibility for a crisis but arguing that they are not fully liable. *p. 72*

Excellence Theory: A general theory of public relations that resulted from a study on the best practices in communication management that spanned over a decade. *p. 67*

Framing: The process of selecting some aspects of a perceived reality and making them more salient in communicating text in such a way as to promote a particular problem definition, causal interpretation, moral evaluation, and/or treatment recommendation for the item described. *p. 68*

Image Repair Theory: Developed by William L. Benoit, Image Repair Theory attempt to simplify the strategies organizations and individuals use to respond to attacks on their reputation. *p. 75*

Legal: An apologia strategy that requires an organization to form a response with their legal counsel. *p. 73*

News Framing Theory: A theory that argues that the media influences how the public perceives certain issues by focusing attention on specific aspects of an issue and ignoring others. *p. 69*

Technology-Image Expectancy Gap: A theory that bridges technology and public relations and brings attention to an organization's vulnerability to crises based on a false sense of security created by technological advances. *p. 70*

DISCUSSION QUESTIONS

1. Consider the discussion of Excellence Theory in this chapter. What aspects of "excellent public relations departments" do you find necessary for your future employer to follow?
2. In addition to the implications of News Framing Theory presented in the chapter, what are some other effects that framing can have on public relations efforts/crisis communication?
3. In 2014, several retailers (Target, SuperValu, Home Depot, and Kmart) faced data breaches that may have exposed sensitive customer

information, such as debit card numbers, PIN numbers, e-mail addresses, and social security information, to hackers. Explain how these breaches relate to Technology-Image Expectancy Gap theory.

4. Consider the NFL/Ray Rice case presented in this chapter. Given your knowledge of apologia and the apologetic ritual, what should NFL Commissioner Roger Goodell have said/done differently to defend the NFL during this crisis?

CHAPTER 5
PLANNING AND STRATEGIC COMMUNICATION

Heidi Klum pours ice on Tim Gunn for the ALS Ice Bucket Challenge during the Project Runway Season 13 Finale Show during MBFW Spring 2015 on September 5, 2014 in NYC.

From *Public Relations Principles: Strategies for Professional Success,* by Shawn T. Wahl and Michelle M. Maresh Fuehrer. Copyright © by Kendall Hunt Publishing Company. Reprinted by permission.

CHAPTER OUTLINE

The Four-Stage Planning Process
Campaign Planning
    Planning
    Implementation
    Evaluation
Event Planning
    Initial Steps
    Speaker Considerations
    Tips for Hosting Impromptu Meetings
    Tips for Hosting Media Events
    Post-Event Pleasantries and Evaluation
Strategies for Professional Success
Executive Summary
Key Terms
Discussion Questions

CHAPTER OBJECTIVES

After studying this chapter, you should be able to:

1. Conduct the research necessary to engage in strategic communication for public relations campaigns, and event planning.
2. Understand the role of planning in each step of campaign development: planning, implementation, and evaluation.
3. Identify the steps that need to be taken to plan and evaluate public relations events.
4. Develop strategies for professional success in planning and strategic communication.

Ripped from the Headlines

Netflix, Inc. is an Internet television network with more than 44 million subscribers. In its 1997 inception, Netflix used a DVD rental by mail format. One decade later, the company introduced video streaming via the Internet, which became so popular that Netflix decided to rebrand and restructure their business model. In 2011, Netflix announced that it would be splitting its DVD by mail and Internet streaming services and would be charging a monthly fee for each one. This announcement infuriated customers, who would be charged up to a 60% increase if they chose to keep both features. Several months later, as a result of this backlash, Netflix CEO and Co-Founder Reed Hastings sent an e-mail message to customers. In his e-mail, Hastings apologized for the way that the company announced the separation of DVD and streaming services. Rather than showing that they listened to customers, Hastings used this e-mail to announce the launch of their new DVD by mail service, Qwikster. This debacle resulted in negative blog comments from customers (Bosker, 2011), the loss of 800,000 subscribers (Wagstaff, 2011), and a huge hit to the company's public image. Several weeks later, Netflix announced that it would be cancelling the Qwikster service before it ever truly launched (Bosker, 2011).

The actions taken by Netflix in the case described above led to a major crisis for the organization. The level of outrage expressed by customers when Netflix originally shared their plan to split DVD and Internet streaming indicates that Netflix representatives failed to proactively communicate their plans with their customers. The subsequent apology and product launch e-mail illustrates that Netflix did not listen to their customers' concerns nor did they learn from their original mistake. Consequently, this case is rife with errors that resulted from a lack of strategic communication and planning on the part of the organization's management and public relations team. Ultimately, the Netflix case reinforces the importance of planning and

CHAPTER 5: PLANNING AND STRATEGIC COMMUNICATION

The decision by Netflix to split their online streaming and DVD mailing services created a significant public relations disaster.

strategic communication in the field of public relations. An organization should not simply make a decision that will impact thousands of customers without engaging in a discussion with representatives of their public. Furthermore, an organization should not ignore its customers' concerns and assume that an idea is a good one just because an idea makes sense to the organization.

In any public relations endeavor, proper planning is necessary to determine whether a campaign or idea will be a success or failure. Additionally, a plan will ensure that there is consistency between the organization's mission and the potential action. It will guide budgetary decisions and provide a framework for measuring whether the action has met the goal(s) that it was designed to address. In the field of public relations, a lack of or improper planning can result in a negative public image, financial loss, environmental damage, physical injury, and—in the case of crisis management—death! Unfortunately, Becker (2010) notes that although planning is "one of the single most important functions of public relations," it "remains the single most neglected function" (n.p.). To reinforce the importance of planning in your life as a public relations practitioner, we will discuss various approaches to strategic planning for public relations. Upon reading this chapter, you will be able to conduct the research necessary to engage in strategic communication for public relations campaigns, and event planning.

THE FOUR-STAGE PLANNING PROCESS

All public relations programs—from image campaigns to crisis communication plans—require a four-stage planning process. These stages will be termed differently depending on the program, but consist of the same overarching elements: research, strategy, implementation, and evaluation. Research typically consists of collecting information that is pertinent to your organization and the issue or challenge at hand. In the strategy stage, you set goals and begin to formulate your public relations program based on the results of your research. Implementation requires putting strategies into action, and evaluation is an assessment of the effectiveness of your strategies in meeting your overall goals and objectives. It is important to note that these stages must be followed sequentially to ensure an effective outcome. Too often public relations practitioners fail to conduct research before implementing an idea, or cease to evaluate the effectiveness of their program to make adjustments for the future. Skipping stages is counterproductive and can lead to negative outcomes, such as wasted money or angry stakeholders. Furthermore, a public relations program should be constantly evolving, as the learning process never ends. As we continue this chapter, each of these stages will be discussed as they pertain to specific programs that you, as a public relations practitioner, will be required to create.

CAMPAIGN PLANNING

As a public relations practitioner, you will be responsible for creating a variety of campaigns. These **public relations campaigns** ultimately serve as a means for building a positive relationship between an organization and the public with the purpose of persuading the public to act, think, believe, or do something. The publics targeted by these campaigns can range from employees to customers, investors, media, and the general public. A well-planned public relations campaign is far more effective than advertising because of its focus on **mutual benefit** between the organization and the public, and the non-paid media recognition that it receives. On the other hand, an unplanned public relations campaign can result in disaster for the organization sponsoring the effort. For example, in 2014, the New York Police Department attempted to host a feel-good social media campaign, asking users to post photos of themselves with members of the NYPD on Twitter using #myNYPD. Unfortunately, this campaign backfired as individuals used the hashtag to post photos of police brutality instead (Harshbarger & Schram, 2014). A campaign that was meant to induce positive images of citizens' interactions with NYPD officers instead resulted in the mass sharing of violent images with negative implications for the NYPD.

The aforementioned example illustrates the importance of planning in creating a successful public relations campaign. As a public relations practitioner, you will need to engage in multiple forms of planning as you develop public relations campaigns. Bobbit and Sullivan (2013) introduced a three-step process for public relations campaign development: planning, implementation, and evaluation. Although the first stage is explicitly named "planning," the planning process is crucial in all three of these steps. For ease of understanding, this section of the chapter is organized around the steps proposed by Bobbit and Sullivan.

> **Public Relations Campaign:** A tool for building a positive relationship between an organization and the public with the purpose of persuading the public to act, think, believe, or do something.
>
> **Mutual Benefit:** The goal of all public relations efforts to benefit both the organization and the public simultaneously.

Planning

The first step in public relations campaign development is planning. Planning provides data-driven research upon which you may base your campaign strategy. Without conducting the necessary background research on your target audience, it is impossible for you to truly understand the problem/challenge at hand and the best strategy for addressing this problem. As a

PR TIP

STRATEGIC PLANNING

Data is the most important thing to include in strategic goal plans. Those who don't are on a one-way path with the destination being failure. Too often the data is what's missing in a plan. Chronological steps, milestone markers, metrics that measure improvement and audits along the way are all critical. The way to organize all the information is to use visuals. Create paretos, graphs, pie charts to get your progress mapped out. Dynamic computer-generated charts and interactive graphs serve to draw your audience in and get your message across.

SOURCE: http://www.10bestpr.com/tips/6-10/

result, you should conduct the following research in the planning step of your campaign:

- *Conduct background research on your organization*, including a discussion of the history of and services provided by the organization, the organization's competitors, the leadership structure of the organization, the Internet/social media presence of the organization, the public reputation of the organization, community service events that the organization sponsors or participates in, and the problems/challenges that the organization is hoping to solve with the present campaign.
- *Identify the target audience for your campaign*, and make an argument for why you are hoping to reach this audience, the demographics and defining characteristics of this audience, and the names of individuals who may be influential in persuading the audience.
- *Conduct primary research on your target audience*, with the explicit purpose of identifying their needs, perspectives, preference for receiving information, how the problem/challenge impacts them, and potential solutions for solving the problem.
- *Analyze the results of your primary research,* considering the statistics derived from quantitative research surveys and/or direct quotes from participants generated in qualitative research interviews or focus groups.
- *Develop campaign goals and objectives* based on your background and primary research.
- *Create key messages* that you would like for your audience to remember.

As you may have inferred while reading this list of planning requirements, the data that is collected in this portion of the campaign is used to make decisions for the entire campaign. Therefore, if you fail to research the needs and perceptions of your target audience, you will not be able to make informed decisions about the strategies that should be used in the next step of your campaign. Kentucky Fried Chicken's (KFC) Colonel's Scholars program is an excellent example of the benefits of conducting both background and primary research. KFC recognized a growing frustration among college students with being required to write an essay to be eligible for college scholarships. To address this problem, KFC decided to award a college scholarship based on a single 140-character Tweet. The winning tweet, "Hey Colonel! Your scholarship's the secret ingredient missing from my recipe for success! Got the grades, drive, just need cash!" resulted in a $20,000 college scholarship for 17-year-old Amanda Russell and more than 1,000 media placements, nine million social media impressions, and a 20% increase in Twitter followers for KFC (Black, 2011).

KFC's use of background and primary research allowed the company to create a better public image and online presence.

Implementation

The next step in public relations campaign development is implementation. This step typically consists of strategic planning for the messages that will be communicated in the campaign, as well as the logistical needs of the campaign regarding budgeting, staffing, and timing. The results of the background and primary research conducted in the first step should be used to make informed decisions about the appropriate strategy for the public relations campaign. When developing strategies for implementation, consider your answers to the following questions:

- How does the target audience feel about the problem and why do they feel that way?
- What media does the audience consume/find most credible?
- What solutions, if any, did the audience offer?
- What is the goal of your campaign?
- How does each potential strategy meet the purpose of public relations (little to no cost to organization, develops positive relationships, creates mutual benefit)?
- How might you integrate the messages that you would like for your audience to remember into each potential strategy?

Once you have answered these questions, you can begin to make strategic decisions for your campaign based on these results.

Choosing Channels

One of the biggest campaign decisions that must be made is selecting the communication channels that you will use to reach your target audience. There are a multitude of channels available to you, from traditional media (such as newspaper and radio) to interactive media (such as Facebook and Twitter); however, it may not always be effective to use certain channels. Your primary research from the first step of the campaign will be instrumental in choosing the appropriate channel for your message. Healthy Choice serves as a good example of selecting an appropriate channel based on the needs/preferences of the target audience. Healthy Choice conducted priority research and knew that their customer prefers using social media and has an interest in coupons. As a result, the company introduced a progressive coupon on their Facebook page. The value of the coupon started at $0.75 and would increase as people liked the page and signed up for the coupon. To announce the campaign, Healthy Choice used interactive media channels that complement social media, such as blogs, Facebook ads, and their brand's e-mail database. In just two weeks, the Healthy Choice Facebook page grew from 6,800 to 60,000 fans and received coverage in trade publications such as *Brandweek*. The coupon gradually increased in value, eventually becoming a "buy one get one free" offer (Black, 2011). In this example, Healthy Choice's focus on interactive media was instrumental in the success of their social media campaign. Healthy Choice would not have had as much success with their campaign if they had used a medium—such as the newspaper—that was not preferred by their target audience.

Establishing a Budget

The next consideration that must be made is in reference to the budget for your campaign. At the heart of public relations is the notion that we can create positive relationships with our public and generate positive media coverage without spending a lot of money. As a public relations practitioner, you will find that organizations have a variety of budget requirements and restrictions. A large corporation, for example, will have much more funding available for a public relations program than a nonprofit organization. Just because the funding is available to a larger corporation, however, does not mean that the organization will value public relations efforts and assign funds accordingly. These budgetary restrictions will need to be kept in mind as you formulate strategies for your campaign. One of the worst things that can happen in a public relations effort is to underestimate the cost of the program causing you to take short cuts or make an incomplete effort.

CHAPTER 5: PLANNING AND STRATEGIC COMMUNICATION

When developing your public relations strategy, you should create a comprehensive budget table that shows an itemized cost of the entire campaign. Potential expenses include personnel costs (such as the cost of hiring security for an event), program costs (such as the cost of catering for an event), and administrative costs (such as the cost of printing and mailing thank you cards to donors). For low-budget campaigns, such as in the case of nonprofit organizations, donated services and products are necessary. You should seek to secure pro bono donations, where a vendor provides products or services for free, or third-party donations, where a vendor charges full price for products or services, but a sponsor pays for these services.

When developing your budget, you should include information on how many units of an item need to be purchased, the cost per unit of each item, and whether an item will be paid for by the client or donated. It is also important to plan to spend at least 5-10% above the estimated cost of the campaign to account for inflation and other price changes. For a sample budget table, see Figure 5.1.

Pro Bono Donation: A vendor provides products or services for free.

Third-Party Donation: A vendor charges full price for products or services, but a sponsor pays for these services.

Creating a Calendar

In addition to the budget, every public relations campaign should include a comprehensive campaign calendar. This calendar should begin with your initial client interview and end with your evaluation. When designing the

Strategy	Item	Location	Unit Cost	#Units	Donated?	Cost
Website						
	Domain	1and1.com	$0.99/year	1	No	$0.99
	Web Host	1and1.com	$0.99/month	12	No	$11.88
	Design	XYDesignZ	$500	1	Pro Bono	$0.00
	Photos	Intern	$10.00/hour	2	No	$50.00
					Sum:	$62.87
					+ 10%	$6.29
					TOTAL:	$69.16

FIGURE 5.1: SAMPLE PUBLIC RELATIONS CAMPAIGN BUDGET

Street Team: A group of people who "hit the streets" to promote an event.

implementation portion of the calendar, you should include the name of each strategy that you will be implementing along with a list of steps that need to be taken to accomplish each strategy. If you are planning to have a street team—a group of people who "hit the streets" to promote an event—distribute flyers around the community to promote an upcoming concert, you will likely need to take the following steps:

- Design flyers
- Print flyers
- Assemble street team
- Distribute flyers

Let us imagine that our concert is going to be held on October 18. We will want to make some decisions about timing. Perhaps we want to promote the concert over the period of one month, which means that we will need to begin promotions on September 18. We can then work backwards to determine our other deadlines. Let us say that we need to spend at least two weeks locating street team members and that we want to have them in place at least 4 days before the promotion. This means that we need to be searching for street team members from September 1 until September 15. This will require that our flyers are printed by this date, but we may want to allot a few extra days in the event that something goes wrong. Depending on where the flyers are being printed, we may also want to consider the volume of work that will be done to ensure that we do not need to rush printing. This may require our flyers to be submitted for printing as early as August 25. Thus, our flyer design will need to be complete by this date. We should allot at least two weeks to designing the flyer to allow time for road testing the flyer with members of our target audience and making the necessary revisions. As a result, we may need to begin designing the flyer as early as August 11. Overall, we need to take each step over the course of two months. Imagine how this timetable may be extended if we were using the media to disseminate information about our concert. It is important to take media deadlines as well as other deadlines—such as securing permits—into account when designing your calendar.

Gantt Chart: A chart in which a series of horizontal lines illustrates the start and finish dates of planned work.

Ultimately, your campaign calendar serves as a timetable inclusive of key information on when each step needs to be completed and how long it will take to complete. Because of the ongoing nature of public relations planning, it is recommended that you use a Gantt chart to design your calendar. A Gantt chart is a chart in which a series of horizontal lines illustrate the start and finish dates of planned work. This type of calendar will provide you with a visual depiction of the work that needs to be done and is more accessible than a typical calendar. Gantt charts can easily be created in Excel or with SmartSheet (smartsheet.com) or by connecting your Google calendar to a service called Ganttify (gantt-chart.com). See Figure 5.2 for an example of a Gantt chart for the concert promotion example that was presented in this section. Note how some steps overlap each other and keep in mind that a public relations campaign for a concert would include quite a few strategies (such as radio announcements or guest spots) in addition to this particular promotion.

Assigning Staffing Duties

Once you have established a campaign budget and calendar, you should begin the process of planning the staffing for each step of your campaign. If you recall our discussion of researching the organization's employee hierarchy, you will remember that part of this research required identifying each employee's job duties. This part of the planning process will help you assign responsibilities to specific persons. In addition to these assignments, you should indicate whether assignments might change in the future. For example, in the concert event promotion mentioned above, you will be recruiting a street team. Street team members may change in future concert promotions, so we will want to identify this possibility to prepare for future recruitment. Special considerations should be made for planning recruitment of staff (such as hiring interns), available budget for compensating staff (if applicable), and any approvals that will need to be made (such as a manager signing a document). Budgetary and calendar adjustments may need to be made once you have planned for the staffing of each campaign strategy.

Evaluation

The final step in public relations campaign development is evaluation. We will talk in greater detail about the specifics of Measurement and Evaluation in Chapter 7. Here we will briefly discuss it as it related to the overall planning process. Ideally, a formative evaluation should be conducted before and during the implementation phase to ensure that the campaign is well received by the target audience. Adjustments may need to be made during the campaign to maximize the effectiveness of the campaign. However, a summative evaluation is necessary at the conclusion of the campaign to assess whether the goals and objectives that were set in the first step of the campaign were met. The summative evaluation should include:

Formative Evaluation: An evaluation that is conducted before and during the implementation phase of a public relations campaign to ensure that the campaign is well received by the target audience.

Summative Evaluation: An evaluation that is conducted at the conclusion of a public relations campaign to assess whether the goals and objectives that were set in the first step of the campaign were met.

Task Name	Aug 10							Aug 17							Aug 24							Aug 31					
	S	M	T	W	T	F	S	S	M	T	W	T	F	S	S	M	T	W	T	F	S	S	M	T	W	T	F
1. Design Flyer																											
2. Submit Flyer for Printing																											
3. Search For Street Team																											
4. Street Team Promotion																											

FIGURE 5.2: SAMPLE GANTT CALENDAR

- A simple summary restating the goals and objectives of the campaign.
- A description of the methods (such as focus groups, interviews, surveys, social media analysis) used to evaluate whether the goals and objectives were met.
- A discussion of the results of the evaluation.
- A visual representation of the results of the evaluation (such as pie charts to represent statistical data).
- An argument for the effectiveness of the campaign.
- A description of what the organization can learn from the campaign, especially surprising trends, attitudes, or challenges.
- Concluding remarks with suggestions for the future.

An evaluation is a necessary step of the public relations campaign process, and it is crucial in being able to communicate the value of public relations to organizations and the public. Although public perception is an essential component to building trust between organizations and their publics, many CEOs and organizations fail to make public relations a priority. To convince organizational management of the importance of public relations, practitioners must be prepared to show them the tangible (and sometimes intangible) results of their efforts. According to Gonring (2004), this may be done with

> a greater sharing of results. PR leaders must…demonstrate outcomes. Showcasing these skills to help someone else meet a business goal will get noticed. And sharing stories of the successes and lessons learned with other business leaders will help foster better working relationships. Non-PR types need to see the link between PR outputs and business outcome. (p. 15)

EVENT PLANNING

As a public relations practitioner, you will find yourself hosting events on a regular basis. Regardless of the demographic, the public typically deems

CHAPTER 5: PLANNING AND STRATEGIC COMMUNICATION

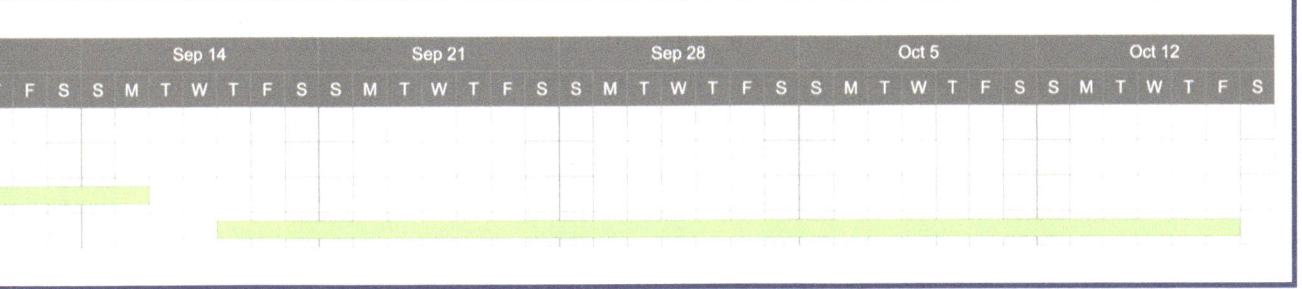

face-to-face communication as more credible than mediated communication. An event is an effective means of establishing trust and building/maintaining a relationship with your public. Public relations events take many forms. Events may be used to communicate important information and respond to questions (such as a news conference during a crisis event), solicit input and make decisions (such as a town hall meetings to discuss a controversial decision), create awareness (such as a grand opening event for a new branch of your business), celebrate or recognize people or achievements (such as a ceremony honoring community leaders), share services with the public (such as a tour of facilities), fundraise, train employees, obtain media exposure, and serve the community (such as a clothing drive for a fire victim). As with all public relations functions, planning is essential to the success of any event.

Planning your first event will likely be a healthy mixture of excitement and stress. As you become seasoned at planning events, you will find yourself developing relationships with vendors. These relationships will eventually lead you to work repeatedly with certain businesses and individuals and will help you to limit the amount of time it takes to organize an event. To help you reach this stage of event planning, you should begin building a file that identifies all of the components that are necessary for hosting various events. Consider including the following information in your file:

- Contact list for local and trade media that includes names, addresses, phone numbers, e-mail addresses, and social media handles for each contact
- Contact list for frequently invited participants such as upper management, employees, customers, and dignitaries
- Contact list and detailed information about catering services, entertainment options, photographers, videographers, and vendors, including a description of facilities, photos of facilities, meal and beverage options, associated costs, tax and service charges, contract information, and insurance requirements
- Liability laws and other regulations for the state where you are holding your event Permit, insurance, and security requirements for the use of local facilities

Initial Steps

Although there are many types of events, preparing any successful event requires similar steps during the planning process. The first step that needs to be taken is to identify the purpose of the event. Ask yourself what you are specifically trying to accomplish. What do you want attendees to think, do, or feel as a result of the event? Your purpose will be a key factor in making decisions about the event and will also be a message that needs to be communicated to your target audience of potential attendees. The next step should be to choose the audience for your event. Make sure that you can easily identify the reason each person is being invited. An important rule is to invite people who can help you achieve your desired outcome (such as individuals who can donate time, money, or services if locating potential sponsors is your goal), individuals who can influence others to help you achieve your goals, people with specific expertise (such as a chemist during a press conference for a refinery explosion), anyone who may be directly affected by decisions made by your organization (such as stockholders for a meeting about a potential business merger), local dignitaries, employees and their families, media, customers, and individuals who contributed to the success of the organization or the event.

Once you have created your invitation list, it is important to conduct an audience analysis of these individuals. Ask yourself what the participants' expectations will be for the event. Consider the public relations event that we discussed in Chapter 1 regarding CHRISTUS Spohn Health System's proposal to demolish Memorial Hospital. Some additional information about this case is the fact that CHRISTUS Spohn Memorial Hospital is a 70-year-old hospital in need of a major (approximately $400 million) renovation. In its place, CHRISTUS Spohn prepared a $325 million plan to build a primary care clinic adjacent to the Memorial Hospital location. The clinic would cost approximately $20 million to $25 million to build and the rest of the funding would be spent to make changes to another local hospital in the system (Hendricks, 2014). As you know, this proposal faced an onslaught of negative reactions from the public, which led to CHRISTUS Spohn's decision to host a series of town hall meetings to provide the public with an opportunity to ask questions and engage in a discussion about the proposed changes. When planning these town hall meetings, CHRISTUS Spohn's public relations practitioners had to consider the possible attitudes and expectations of individuals who would be attending the meetings. Clearly the overall reaction would be negative and defensive, and the expectation would be that they would have an opportunity to share their feelings and influence the decision-making process. It is important to identify and meet these expectations, as a violation of expectations could lead to a potential crisis in this type of situation.

Your next step should be to consider the messages that you would like the event to communicate about your organization and/or the initiative. Do you have a particular theme in mind? The police department in the chapter author's hometown recently hosted a fundraiser event with the purpose of benefiting their nonprofit Crime Stoppers program. To tie into the detective theme, they held a murder mystery dinner. This event was open to the public and featured local judges playing characters in the fictional murder mystery. The theme of this event was strongly tied to the purpose of the organization, and advertisements about the event included information about the number of crimes that were solved because of the public's use of the Crime Stoppers service. The consistency between the event theme and the organizational goals undoubtedly played a contributing role to the success of the event.

Charity events such as marathons are often used to raise money and awareness for diseases.

Once you have established your purpose, analyzed your audience, and considered key messages/themes that you would like to communicate to your audience, you should review your budget. Consider your budget range—do you have a fluid budget or are you restricted to a certain amount of money that can be spent? You should begin to research all of the necessary components to the event and check this against your budget allowance. Certain decisions may be made based on this information. For example, a smaller budget may not be conducive to hosting a formal gathering with a plated dinner or celebrity speaker.

Finally, you should develop a contingency plan to prepare for any potential problems that may arise. If your event is outdoors, what will you do if it rains? If your speaker is flying into town from another state, what will you do if their flight is delayed or cancelled? Part of your contingency plan should be a crisis plan for preventing and responding to potential problems that may arise. If there are children present, consider potential issues that could arise. For example, children could become separated from their parents. Develop a plan for preventing this issue—perhaps having color-coded wristbands with their parents' name and phone number. Also consider what will need to be done if the crisis is unpreventable. Let us consider a child who tears off their wristband and becomes lost. What will we need to do? Who will we need to contact? If the media comes to request an interview, what do we need to say? Following each of these steps will ensure that you have given ample time to preparing for the basic needs of your event.

CHAPTER 5: PLANNING AND STRATEGIC COMMUNICATION

Placing the tables in a U-shape during training sessions allows for greater communic ation between individuals.

TOOLS FOR THE PUBLIC RELATIONS PROFESSIONAL

Event Planning Checklist

Event planning is a complex venture. Entire books and courses have been developed to cover the ins and outs of this subject. The depth of this information is beyond the scope of this book, but the author of this chapter has devised the following checklist to help jumpstart your planning process:

- Who will be invited?
    - Identify your target audience
    - Create a list of individuals to invite
    - Identify the expectations of your target audience
    - Sign invitations and disseminate information to potential attendees
    - Consider the costs associated with your invitation/advertisement methods
- What message do you wish to communicate?
    - Make a decision about whether a theme is necessary
    - Determine the formality of the event (formal or informal)
- What type of instructing information needs to be given to attendees?
    - Make sure that the attendees know the purpose, formality, cost, dress code, time, date, and location of the event
    - Include any necessary information about transportation, potential traffic difficulties, alternate routes, hotels, parking, and associated costs

(continued)

THE PRACTICE OF PUBLIC RELATIONS

- Where will the event be held?
  - Consider your needs along with the advantages and disadvantages of hosting the event indoors, outdoors, on-site, off-site, and out of town
- When will the event take place?
  - Consider the advantages and disadvantages of hosting the event during the morning, afternoon, and evening
  - Consider the advantages and disadvantages of hosting the event during the week and on the weekend
  - Consider whether the event needs to correspond with a specific time of year or holiday
- What time will the event be held?
  - Consider the attention span and daily commitments of your target audience
  - Prepare a detailed schedule of events to ensure that your event is not longer than necessary
- What criteria will the venue need to meet?
  - Budgetary preferences/restrictions
  - Preferred date and times
  - Number of guests that can be accommodated
  - Number and size of rooms
  - Rules for set-up and dismantling
  - Services provided by the venue (such as catering)
  - Condition of restrooms
  - Lighting (such as dim lighting to be able to see a projected image on a screen)
  - Heating and cooling considerations
  - Insulation against room noise and other distractions
  - Parking facilities and costs
  - Booking, cancellation, deposit, and payment policies
  - Restrictions on decorations (such as not being able to use open-flame candles)
  - Insurance and other legal/regulatory requirements
  - Take note of any "hidden" costs associated with staffing, set up, etc.
- Will refreshments and/or food be served?
  - Consider having refreshment breaks for a lengthy event
  - Consider having coffee, tea, and plenty of water for most events
  - Make decisions about whether alcoholic beverages will be served and if they will be waiter-served or served by the bottle or drink
  - Consider asking guests about dietary restrictions and/or food allergies, but let them know that you may not be able to accommodate all of their needs
  - Consider a special menu for children (such as chicken nuggets)
  - If serving prepackaged food, inquire about having an ingredients label for individuals with food allergies

(continued)

- Talk to the catering manager about the number of individuals attending, the percentage of meals they will overset, and what happens to uneaten food
- Take note of the costs associated with refreshments, food, and restricted/special menus
● Will you need entertainment?
  - Select entertainment that fits the occasion, such as a speaker, music, performance, games, or videos
  - Take note of the costs associated with entertainment
● What equipment and materials will you need?
  - Consider the technology that you may need, such as an LCD projector, projection screen, laptop, sound system, and microphone
  - If you will be having a speaker, consider additional equipment that you may need, such as a stage, raised platform, and podium
  - If the event is large, make sure that you have at least one available restroom for every 50 people
  - If the event is outdoors, you may need to rent portable toilets
  - Consider your decorative needs, such as centerpieces, flowers, chair covers, and tablecloths
  - Take note of the costs associated with renting or setting up these materials
● What type of ambiance would you like to establish?
  - If you would like to encourage interaction and participation among meeting attendees, use a round table
  - If you are holding a training session, place the tables in a U-shape
  - If you will be engaging in decision-making, have the tables set in a rectangle and have the leader seated at the head of the table.
  - If you would like to encourage socializing, use round tables that seat 6, 8, or 10
  - Consider whether you will need to seat participants strategically
● What safety and liability precautions will need to be taken?
  - If you are hosting an event with children, you may need to have parents fill out an information form (with information such as allergies and medical conditions) and possibly a permission form or liability waiver
  - If you are engaging in any potentially dangerous activity (such as hosting a celebrity football game for charity), you also need to have a liability waiver
  - Consider whether your venue requires security personnel
  - Make sure that you (and your guests) know where the fire exits are located
  - Take note of any costs associated with hiring security personnel
● What are your staffing needs?
  - Consider the steps that need to be taken to plan for the event (such as researching venues, designing invitations, printing invitations, sending thank you cards) and identify who will be in charge of completing these tasks

(continued)

- Consider whether your event will need an emcee, greeters, session leaders, or other employees or volunteers
- Take note of the costs associated with staffing
● How will you guarantee that you are protected against contractual issues?
  - Make sure that you see what you will be getting before you sign a contract. This includes venue, room, and restroom appearance, food and drink tastings, sample speeches or musical playlists, etc.
  - Ensure that you have copies of signed and dated agreements for any service that you are requesting and/or paying for (you will likely have a venue contract, catering contract, security contract, and entertainment contract at the least)

Speaker Considerations

Many public relations events are built around a speaker. When a speaker attends an event that your organization is hosting, it is an implicit endorsement of your organization. Thus, it is crucial for you to ensure that the speaker's experience is positive and that they feel that their time was appreciated. Remember that good news travels fast, but bad news travels faster. If the speaker has a negative experience with your organization they will likely share this information with others, which may affect your ability to secure other speakers in the future. To create a pleasurable experience for your speaker, you should adhere to several guidelines. Before the event, you should share with them the purpose of the meeting, the length of time that they will be asked to speak, and whether there will be a question and answer (Q&A) period. You should make them aware of the formality of the event (especially in terms of requested attire), arrangement of the room, as well as the technology that will be available to them for use during their presentation. You should also alert them of any information that should be included in the presentation, subjects that should be avoided, the names of VIPs who will be in attendance, and any media event requirements (such as being available for television and newspaper interviews).

Once you are in the process of securing the speaker for your event, you should inquire about any fees (such as honorariums, or speaker fees) that they might charge for their attendance at the event. Some speakers will speak for free, as long as their travel and lodging arrangements are made and paid for by the organization hosting the event. Furthermore, you should inquire about their audiovisual (AV) requirements and any other requests or needs. If the speaker chooses to book their own flight, you should ask for a copy of their travel itinerary so that you can track their arrival. If their flight is delayed or cancelled, you may need to enact your contingency plan.

Ensuring your speaker is prepared is critical to an event's success.

To properly promote the speaker prior to the event, you will want to ask them for a biographical sketch, high-resolution and low-resolution digital portraits (usually a professional headshot), other promotional materials, and permission to videotape and audiotape (if necessary). You should let them know your plans for these materials, which will likely include publication on your organization's website, social media, press releases, and other promotional advertisements. On the day of the event, you should be prepared to escort the speaker to any off-site media interviews and facilitate opportunities for them to meet any dignitaries who are in attendance.

Immediately after the conclusion of the event, it is a good idea to make sure that your speaker has arrangements for returning to their hotel, the airport, and/or home. You should also send a handwritten thank you card to the speaker no more than 72 hours after the event. If the speaker was not given a gift as part of the event, you may also choose to send flowers, a gift card to a coffeehouse, or another small token of appreciation from the organization.

Tips for Hosting Impromptu Meetings

The reality of public relations is that an unexpected crisis event or negative reaction to an organization's announcement *will* occur to every organization at some point. Despite any uncertainty that you may have during this type of situation, planning remains the key to navigating such events with success. If this type of situation occurs in your organization, it is likely that you will need to host an impromptu meeting—of employees, citizens, and/or media—to communicate important information to your stakeholders. The following tips should be followed to properly plan an impromptu meeting for crisis and non-crisis situations. Crisis planning and the field of crisis management will be explored in Chapter 12.

Non-Crisis Meetings

- Gather all of the necessary information.
- Develop a list of topics that need to be addressed.
- Set an agenda that allots time to sharing information and additional time for interaction.
- Keep the meeting short and focused.

Crisis Meetings

- Convene the crisis communication team.
- Gather all of the necessary information and confirm that you have *facts*.
- Designate a spokesperson(s).
- Ensure that the spokesperson has several key messages, or talking points, to share.
- Prepare a statement that states the facts, expresses the organization's position and conveys a sympathetic and proactive tone.
- Provide timely information to all stakeholders before speaking to the media.
- Instruct all members of your organization to refer the media/public to the spokesperson(s).
- Select additional experts to speak, if necessary.

Tips for Hosting Media Events

Part of building a positive relationship with the media may include inviting the media to visit your organization's facilities. Media events could take the form of a tour with the purpose of showing the media completed renovations or additions to the building that houses your organization's offices. A news conference may also draw the media to your organization. Additionally, if you are hosting an event on the premises, you will strive to have journalists

Ethics in Practice

Cody is a public relations executive for a bottling plant in a major city. Recently, one of his company's trucks overturned on the highway, causing an accident that killed three people. Initial reports suggested that the truck driver was working long hours and became drowsy behind the wheel. Deciding that his company needed to make a public announcement, Cody scheduled an impromptu meeting with several local media outlets. Prior to the meeting, Cody neglected to discuss his talking points with the rest of his PR team and to inform stakeholders what information would be presented at the media event. Going solely off the newspaper report, Cody began the meeting by asserting that his company had followed all guidelines concerning driver safety and there was no indication that the company driver was even at fault. When confronted with a police report that indicated the driver had indeed fallen asleep at the wheel, Cody went on the defensive and refused to offer a company statement regarding the accident. The resulting public outcry led to calls for the company to leave the city and possibly pay the families for damages. As the situation continued to spiral out of control, Cody was fired from his position as the company brought in an outside consulting firm to begin damage control.

QUESTIONS TO CONSIDER

1. Before the initial meeting, what key mistakes did Cody make during the planning process?
2. What were the issues regarding the initial tone of Cody's message to the public?
3. What other information should Cody have sought before making his statement?
4. What steps must the company take now in order to win back the public's trust?

---

present for a story. Inviting the media to visit your facility will require careful consideration of the journalists' needs and schedule requirements. The media has a powerful influence on your organization's representation to the public, so you must persuade them to take time out of their busy schedules to attend your media event. The best way to do this is to show them what makes your event is timely and newsworthy.

Planning a media event requires preparing a press kit—or, more importantly, reviewing an existing press kit—for distribution, training spokespersons on how to talk to the media, making sure that spokespersons are available on the day of the event to respond to media inquiries, requesting that the CEO (or other members of management) give an informative presentation to the media, and having employees assist with providing tours of the facility on the day of the event. Once the event has concluded, you should send thank you notes to all attendees and share the results of these efforts with the members of the organization.

Media events, such as news conferences, offer key opportunities to build public relations.

Post-Event Pleasantries and Evaluation

Akin to the evaluation required of public relations campaigns, an event that your organization hosts should also include an evaluative assessment. One of the most common methods for evaluating the success of an event is to collect participant feedback. A simple evaluation form (no more than 5-10 questions) can be created to assess the event and gather suggestions and general comments. This form may be distributed at the event and participants may be given time to fill it out and return it to you. Participants should be asked to refrain from writing any identifying information on their forms. Once the feedback has been collected and analyzed, you should use the feedback to improve future events. From a relationship-building standpoint, it is helpful to send an e-mail message to participants to let them know how you will be making adjustments to future events based on their feedback.

In addition to evaluation, you should spend time communicating pleasantries after an event. Handwritten thank you notes, small tokens of appreciation, or direct phone calls of thanks to attendees will go a long way in securing attendance at future events. Furthermore, if you received donations of money, goods, or time, the results of those efforts should be communicated to the participants. It is important to be open and transparent with all public relations efforts, especially those that involve monetary contributions. If you hold a charity fundraiser, you should be ready to send a letter of thanks to participants that includes the total amount of money raised and how the funds were used (such as the name of the specific charity or charities that benefited from the funds and information on how those charities used the money, if possible). For example, the author of this chapter is a member of her local Rotary club. The club hosts an annual event that serves as a fundraiser for the club. Soon after the event, the club's leadership distributes a newsletter and posts information on their website and social media accounts about the amount of money raised at the event and how the money is used. Typically the money is used to fund two of the club's projects: scholarships for students attending the local university, and purchasing materials to build wheelchair ramps for local citizens in need.

STRATEGIES FOR PROFESSIONAL SUCCESS

In this chapter, we have learned how to conduct the research necessary to engage in strategic communication for public relations campaigns, crisis communication plans, and event planning. Campaign development requires public relations professionals to understand the importance of planning the initial campaign, implementing the plan once it has been researched, and evaluating the overall results after the campaign is over. Ville Tuominen and Albert Eckert, the authors of *The Campaign Handbook*, offer several tips for strategic campaign planning.

Establish a Clear Objective

A large number of campaigns fail because of vague objective setting. Having a small but well-built campaign with a clear objective is much more preferable than a large uncertain campaign with unclear objectives.

Keep the Campaign Positive

Positive campaigns are generally better than negative ones; they are more effective in convincing supporters who have not yet formed an opinion and are generally safer. Trust and influence must be built up over a period of time.

Keep the Campaign Flexible

Campaigns must be flexible as the campaign grows or shrinks. Uncontrolled growth can be as damaging as shrinking the scope of your message. Ensure that the structure of your campaign is equipped to handle fluctuations in growth or shrinkage.

http://campaignhandbook.gef.eu/planning-strategically/

EXECUTIVE SUMMARY

Now that you have finished reading this chapter, you can

Conduct the research necessary to engage in strategic communication for public relations and event planning:

- Public relations campaigns consist of a three-step process that involves planning, implementation, and evaluation.
- Event planning requires five steps: identifying the purpose of the event, choosing and analyzing the audience for your event, considering the messages that you would like the event to communicate about your organization, reviewing your budget, and developing a contingency plan for potential problems.

Understand the role of planning in each step of campaign development: planning, implementation, and evaluation:

- Planning is involved in each of the three steps of campaign development. In the planning step, background research is conducted, the target audience is identified, primary research on the target audience is conducted, the results of this research are analyzed, and campaign goals and objectives are developed based on the results of this research.
- In the implementation step, planning specifically focuses on developing strategic messages that will be communicated during the campaign and considering the logistical needs of the campaign such as budgeting, staffing, and timing.
- In the evaluation step, research is conducted to ensure that the campaign is well received by the target audience and to assess whether the goals and objectives that were set in the first step of the campaign process were met.

Identify the steps that need to be taken to plan and evaluate public relations events:

- There are many steps that occur in the planning process for events. Some of the key areas of planning include creating an invitation list; developing messaging; identifying what instructing information needs to be given to attendees; selecting a location, time, date, and venue for the event; making choices about food, beverages, and entertainment; creating ambiance at the event; reserving necessary equipment and materials; identifying staffing needs; taking safety and liability precautions; and preparing contracts.

KEY TERMS

Formative Evaluation: An evaluation that is conducted before and during the implementation phase of a public relations campaign to ensure that the campaign is well received by the target audience. *p. 93*

Gantt Chart: A chart in which a series of horizontal lines illustrates the start and finish dates of planned work. *p. 92*

Mutual Benefit: The goal of all public relations efforts to benefit both the organization and the public simultaneously. *p. 87*

Pro Bono Donation: A vendor provides products or services for free. *p. 91*

Public Relations Campaign: A tool for building a positive relationship between an organization and the public with the purpose of persuading the public to act, think, believe, or do something. *p. 87*

Street Team: A group of people who "hit the streets" to promote an event. *p. 92*

Summative Evaluation: An evaluation that is conducted at the conclusion of a public relations campaign to assess whether the goals and objectives that were set in the first step of the campaign were met. *p. 93*

Third-Party Donation: A vendor charges full price for products or services, but a sponsor pays for these services. *p. 91*

DISCUSSION QUESTIONS

1. What ethical issues should be considered when formulating a public relations campaign?
2. What research techniques might you use to find out what your target audience thinks about an organization?
3. What channels exist for disseminating public relations messages to the public?
4. Why is evaluation essential in ensuring that public relations is viewed as a credible profession?
5. In today's economy, many individuals are cutting back on the amount of money that they spend attending events. How might you attract participants to a charitable event? What steps would you take to promote your event? What strategies would you use to entice participants to donate time or resources to your cause?

CHAPTER 6
PUBLIC RELATIONS WRITING AND SOCIAL MEDIA

Ellen DeGeneres, Jimmy Kimmel, Ryan Seacrest at the Hollywood Walk of Fame Ceremony for Ellen Degeneres at W Hollywood on September 4, 2012 in Los Angeles, CA. All three celebrities have a huge social media following.

From *Public Relations Principles: Strategies for Professional Success,* by Shawn T. Wahl and Michelle M. Maresh Fuehrer. Copyright © by Kendall Hunt Publishing Company. Reprinted by permission.

CHAPTER OUTLINE

News Releases
- Standard News Releases
- Broadcast News Releases

Social Media News Releases (SMNRs)

Media Information Documents
- Backgrounders
- Fact Sheets
- Pitch Letters
- Media Advisories
- Media Kits
- Electronic Press Kits (EPKs)

Writing for Television and Radio
- Video News Releases (VNRs)
- Public Service Announcements (PSAs)

Writing for the Internet
- Online Newsrooms
- Blogs

Writing for Social Media
- Social Media Strategies
- Measuring Social Media Engagement

Strategies for Professional Success

Executive Summary

Key Terms

Discussion Questions

CHAPTER OBJECTIVES

After studying this chapter, you should be able to:

1. Know the difference between five types of news releases.
2. Write news releases for standard, broadcast, and social media distribution.
3. Create and organize media information documents, such as backgrounders, fact sheets, pitch letters, media advisories, media kits, and electronic press kits.
4. Write VNR and PSA scripts for television and radio.
5. Create content for online newsrooms and blogs.
6. Compose social media posts that engage your public.
7. Develop strategies for professional success in public relations writing and social media.

Ripped from the Headlines

On February 11, 2014, residents of Bobtown, Pennsylvania awoke to an early-morning explosion that—according to one resident—"sounded like a jet engine going 5 feet above your house" (Born & Hamill, 2014a). The explosion occurred at a Marcellus Shale natural gas well owned by Chevron. The same well had been previously criticized for causing water contamination and other issues in Pennsylvania (Begos, 2014). The blast injured one worker and killed another: 27-year-old Ian McKee (Born & Hamill, 2014b). Five days later, Bobtown residents received a letter of apology from Chevron Appalachia Community Outreach that included a coupon for a free large pizza and two-liter soda at Bobtown Pizza with an expiration date of May 1. Several photos of these letters were uploaded to social media and resulted in feelings of outrage from the public. More than 12,000 people from the Netherlands to San Francisco signed a petition demanding that Chevron apologize for insulting residents by offering them coupons for free pizza after such a devastating crisis (Colaneri, 2014).

The case outlined above illustrates the importance of having effective writing skills when working in the field of public relations. Although the individual who wrote the letter of apology to Bobtown residents did not commit a spelling or grammatical error, she or he still demonstrated poor writing skills. Writing for public relations requires more than the ability to construct sentences—it also requires awareness, or an understanding of how your writing is going to affect your public and their perception of your organization. Rather than appearing sympathetic to the fact that an employee was killed in an explosion that occurred at a well that they owned, Chevron seemed to minimize the accident by offering a pizza coupon to the community.

Writing occurs in every step of the public relations process, from researching your priority audience for a campaign to apologizing during a crisis like the Bobtown explosion. Regardless of the channel you are using to communicate with your public, your message will always begin with the written word. Consequently, employers will expect job candidates to demonstrate that they have effective writing skills and that they know how to format public relations documents, such as news releases, for a variety of channels. Therefore, in this chapter, we will explore the various types of writing required of public relations professionals. Upon reading this chapter, you will be able to construct public relations documents with clearly stated messages for a variety of channels.

NEWS RELEASES

Standard News Releases

A **news release (or press release)** is a form of written communication released to the media with the purpose of making an announcement with the intent of it being turned into a news story. The goal of the public relations practitioner is to distribute a news release that attracts media attention and gains positive placement in a medium that reaches their target audience. To accomplish this goal, you should place yourself in the role of a journalist. First, think about the audience that you wish to reach with your message. What channels (i.e., newspapers, magazines, television stations) reach that audience? If you wanted to announce that your organization will be holding a charity fundraiser at a local country club, you would not send a news release to a national news network such as ABC; rather, you would sent it to your local news station(s) and newspaper(s).

Second, you should consider the type of stories that are typically run in each channel and ask yourself whether your announcement fits that mold. A news station that does not have a segment dedicated to financial information may not be the best place to submit your news release announcing your organization's quarterly earnings. For a nominal fee, services such as MuckRack (MuckRack.com) and Press Pass (PressPass.Me) can help you locate journalists and identify the type of stories they cover by beat, media outlet, and region. Furthermore, **news wire services**, or commercial fee-based news release distribution services, such as PR Newswire (PRNewswire.com) can make distribution more affordable

> **News Release (or Press Release):** A form of written communication released to the media with the purpose of making an announcement with the intent of it being turned into a news story.

> **News Wire Services:** Commercial fee-based services that distribute news releases to credentialed journalists.

Press releases are best used to gain media attention.

Media Relations: Developing positive working relationships between an organization and the media.

as they do the work of delivering the release to credentialed journalists and bloggers.

Finally, consider the ways that you could facilitate the journalist's job. This is an important aspect of media relations, or developing positive working relationships between your organization and the media. Having effective media relations will help you gain positive coverage in the future, and may ensure that you receive fair coverage during times of crisis. To have optimal media relations when submitting a news release, you should write your release using a format that can easily be published without modification. This requires knowledge of the style that is typically used in the specific channel you are submitting your release to and may require that you submit multiple versions of the same news release to editors across different channels. Your news release should also include key elements such as a catchy headline and photographs that will get the attention of the journalist and the audience. You must also keep a list of your media contacts with notes about their schedules and deadlines so that you can choose an ideal time to submit your news release. It is also helpful to keep in mind that new media has changed the way that news releases are distributed. Journalists receive thousands of news releases via e-mail every day.

Many of these submissions are deleted simply because they do not meet style guidelines or are not newsworthy stories for that particular medium. Following the steps above, along with developing a face-to-face working relationship with journalists, will increase your likelihood of having your story disseminated by the media.

Types of News Releases

The first step in crafting a news release is to identify the type of news release that you will need to write. All news releases share a common format, but the emphasis of the information within the release will differ across types. Specifically, there are five types of news releases:

A *general news release* covers information occurring in an organization that is of interest to local, regional, national, or international media. This is the most common type of news release distributed to media outlets. A general news release may be used to announce that your organization will be opening a new location, or that one of your employees has won an award. The rule of thumb for this type of news release is that it should proactively share information that casts a positive image on your organization.

A *product news release* is used to distribute information about specific products. This type of news release may be used to announce the launch of a new product or version of a product; to distribute important news, such as product safety recalls, to consumers; or to share other milestones, such as awards or recognitions, that are pertinent to a product. This type of news release often places an emphasis on product specifications—such as the slim design of the new Apple iPhone—and is most effective when a photo of the product is included.

A *launch news release* is intended to generate publicity about an upcoming launch. This news release can be used to announce the start of a new company or organization, a new website or redesigned logo, or a campaign. At the time this chapter was written, AT&T had issued a launch release to inform the public of the latest feature in their DriveMode app—Parental Alerts. The release contained information detailing how the feature works along with a link to a YouTube video that contains a visual depiction of instructions for using the feature.

A *financial news release* is used to distribute financial information about your organization to shareholders and financial media. This type of news release may detail specific information about quarterly and fiscal year earnings and

General News Release: Covers information occurring in an organization that is of interest to local, regional, national, or international media.

Product News Release: Distributes information about specific products, the launch of a new product or version of a product, important news about a product, and other milestones that are pertinent to a product.

Launch News Release: A news release that is used to generate publicity about an upcoming launch, the start of a new company or organization, a new website or redesigned logo, or a campaign.

Financial News Release: Distributes financial information about an organization to shareholders and financial media.

other changes that may impact an organization's financial standing, such as the acquisition of another company, or changes in the organization's board of directors. It is important that financial news releases are distributed at least quarterly (if not more often) and with transparency in mind.

An *event news release* details information about an upcoming event and is distributed with the intent of making the event known to the public. When writing this type of release, you should clearly communicate the 5 W's: who, what, when, where, and why. The focus should be on making this information easily accessible to the journalist, so using bullet points to outline the details of the event will enhance the readability of this type of release.

Event News Release: Details information about an upcoming event and is distributed with the intent of making the event known to the public.

Financial news releases are especially important in the business world.

News Release Format

An effective news release requires a *narrative*, or story, that can easily be edited by journalists for inclusion in their media channels. All news releases should be formatted following the guidelines set forth by the *Associated Press (AP) Stylebook*. The *AP Stylebook* covers rules for abbreviation, capitalization, grammar, numerals, punctuation, and spelling. It also includes a formula for writing photo captions; a key of editing symbols used by proofreaders; a

Narrative: Structuring the contents of a news release to tell a story that can easily be edited by journalists for inclusion in their media channels.

reference section for business and financial news; terminology, statistics, and rules commonly referenced by sports reporters; and an overview of legal and ethical issues in journalism. The *AP Stylebook* is updated annually, so you must be prepared to renew your subscription each year to stay current.

In addition to the *AP Stylebook* guidelines, you should also understand the key elements of a news release. As the public relations practitioner, each release should begin with your contact information. Specifically, your phone number, e-mail address, and social media handle should be included in the contact information block. You should then include a header that communicates when the story should be published. If you would like a story to run immediately, you should include a header that says "FOR IMMEDIATE RELEASE"; if you would like your story to run on a specific date in the future, the header should say "FOR RELEASE ON [DATE]." Next, your release should have a headline, or a title previewing the content of your story. Your headline should be between 60 and 80 characters (not including spaces) and should be tight, or void of unnecessary words. Consider the following headline: "Belgian Parliament adopts a bill that extends the right to euthanasia for minors." Are there any words that could be removed or condensed to make this headline tighter while still communicating the same message? How about "Belgian Parliament passes bill on child euthanasia"? Learning to write tight headlines is an important practice, as it increases journalist and reader interest, and makes your headline more Tweetable/Google searchable. Your headline needs to be catchy, making your audience want to continue reading the story or click the link that accompanies the social media post to your story. Reading headlines to stories that are run on various print and social media publications can help you identify best practices for generating audience interest.

The next element of a news release is the dateline, or information regarding the origin of the news release. The dateline should include the city name in uppercase letters, the abbreviated state name, and the full date of issue (including the year) followed by an en dash "—." The *AP Stylebook* identifies 8 states that should not be abbreviated (Alaska, Hawaii, Idaho, Iowa, Maine, Ohio, Texas, and Utah), and 30 cities in the United States that do not need to be followed by the name of their respective states (Atlanta, Baltimore, Boston, Chicago, Cincinnati, Cleveland, Dallas, Denver, Detroit, Honolulu, Houston, Indianapolis, Las Vegas, Los Angeles, Miami, Milwaukee, Minneapolis, New Orleans, New York, Oklahoma City, Philadelphia, Phoenix, Pittsburgh, St. Louis, Salt Lake City, San Antonio, San Diego, San Francisco, Seattle, and Washington). State abbreviations in AP style also differ from those used in postal zip codes. See Table 6.1 for a list

Contact Information: The inclusion of a public relations practitioner's phone number, e-mail address, and social media handle in a news release.

Headline: A title previewing of the content of a news release.

Tight: Refers to writing a headline that is void of unnecessary words.

Dateline: Information regarding the origin of a news release.

Lead (or Lede): The opening sentence of the news release that serves as the hook to entice the journalist to run the release.

of AP state abbreviations. The dateline should appear in the first line of the body of the release preceding the introductory sentence. For example, "LINCOLN, Neb., July, 14, 2014—First sentence of body."

The **lead (or lede)**, or the opening sentence of the news release, should directly follow the dateline. Upon distribution of your news release, the lead will serve as the hook to entice the journalist to run your release. Should the journalist choose to run your story, the lead becomes the hook to entice the reader into your story. The lead should answer the five W's: Who, What, When, Where, and Why and, along with the remainder of the news release, should be written in third person. The words "you," "we," or "I" should appear only in a quotation attributed to a specific person.

Immediately following the lead is the body of your news release. When writing the body of the news release, you may find that you have several areas where a long block of text appears. In this situation, it is both acceptable and helpful to use a bulleted list to break this information up to make it easier to read. It is also important to incorporate storytelling into the body of the release by including quotations from specific individuals. Quotations should be written in the present tense to make the news release timely, unless it is clear that the story occurred in the past.

The last paragraph of a news release is the **boilerplate**, or a description of the organization discussed in the release. A boilerplate should include a summary of the company's history, mission, and practices. It may also include the company's phone number and website and social media information. A subhead such as "About [Organization Name]" should be used to separate the boilerplate from the body of the news release. At the conclusion of the boilerplate, a traditional **close** symbol "###" should be centered at the bottom of the page. This indicates that the news release has ended.

Ideally, your news release should be approximately 400 words; however, a more detailed and serious

Alabama	Ala.
Arizona	Ariz.
Arkansas	Ark.
California	Calif.
Colorado	Colo.
Connecticut	Conn.
Delaware	Del.
Florida	Fla.
Georgia	Ga.
Illinois	Ill.
Indiana	Ind.
Kansas	Kan.
Kentucky	Ky.
Louisiana	La.
Maryland	Md.
Massachusetts	Mass.
Michigan	Mich.
Minnesota	Minn.
Mississippi	Miss.
Missouri	Mo.
Montana	Mont.
Nebraska	Neb.
Nevada	Nev.
New Hampshire	N.H.
New Jersey	N.J.
New Mexico	N.M.
New York	N.Y.
North Carolina	N.C.
North Dakota	N.D.
Oklahoma	Okla.
Oregon	Ore.
Pennsylvania	Pa.
Rhode Island	R.I.
South Carolina	S.C.
South Dakota	S.D.
Tennessee	Tenn.
Vermont	Vt.
Virginia	Va.
Washington	Wash.
West Virginia	W. Va.
Wisconsin	Wis.
Wyoming	Wyo.

FIGURE 6.1: AP STATE ABBREVIATIONS

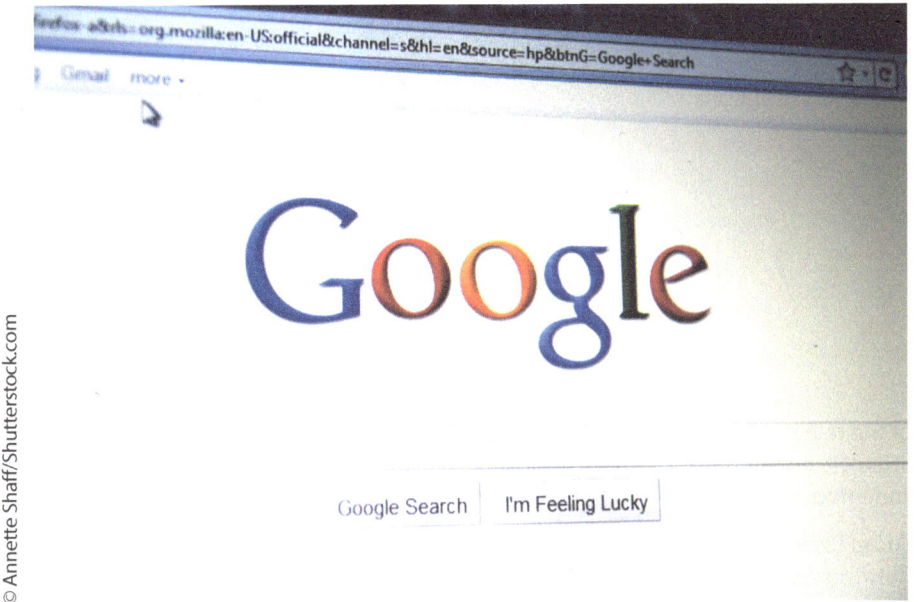

PR professionals need to know how to create keywords that will allow news releases to pop up on search engines like Google.

Boilerplate: A description of the organization that is discussed in a news release.

Close: A symbol "###" located at the center of the bottom of a news release and "#####" at the center of the bottom of each radio spot, indicating that document has ended.

Search Engine Optimized (Seo) Keywords: Hyperlinked words within a news release.

announcement may be up to 800 words in length. The word length requirement is inclusive of all of the text in your release—from the headline to the close. It is also important to check your spacing to ensure that you have only used one space after punctuation. Search Engine Optimized (SEO) keywords or hyperlinks within your news release should also be included, with at least 1 link per 100 words. Additionally, relevant photos, videos, infographics, and logos should be included with the news release. Images and videos are more likely to be published and shared. If you are submitting your news release to a journalist via e-mail, include the images in the body of the e-mail if possible—if not, include a link to a website that hosts the images or video (such as Flickr or YouTube) along with a description of the content. Never upload images or news releases as an attachment, as many journalists will not open them for fear of downloading a computer virus. Finally, include your headline (or a five- or six-word condensed version of your headline) as the subject of your e-mail to gain interest. For a sample news release template, see Figure 6.1.

Broadcast News Releases

Writing a news release for broadcast television is, in many ways, similar to writing a news release for written communication. The key difference is that you must

---

Company Name

Address

Contact: [Your Name]

Your Phone Number

Your E-mail Address

Your Social Media Handle

RELEASE HEADER

HEADLINE

Dateline – Lead. The body of the release should be written with the introduction answering the five W's. Releases that are not submitted via e-mail should be double-spaced starting with the lead. The start of each paragraph should be indented.

The next paragraph can be used to provide more information about the story/announcement. Specific quotes can be inserted and attributed to important people relevant to the story. Longer pieces of text can be broken up using bullets, especially when communicating instructional information such as recall information during a product recall crisis.

About [Organization]

The final paragraph is your boilerplate. Include company information here. When you reach the bottom of the first page, let the reader know if more will follow (indicated using the symbol "–more—") or if you are at the end of the release ("###"). The appropriate symbol should be featured at the center of the bottom of the page.

FIGURE 6.1: SAMPLE NEWS RELEASE TEMPLATE

Clear: Ensuring that the audience understands a message the first time that they hear it.

Concise: Communicating a message using few words.

Conversational: The tone that should be used when writing broadcast news releases.

write for the ear instead of for the eye. Writing for the ear requires adhering to the six C's of broadcast writing: clear, concise, conversational, complete, and current (Rahorn, 2006). Clear writing ensures that the audience understands the message the first time that they hear it. Being concise requires communicating a message in few words. When we discussed writing a tight headline by eliminating excess wording, we were making the message concise. Writing for the ear should also be done in a conversational tone, meaning that you communicate with your public much the same way that you would communicate with a friend. Your message should also be complete by answering the five W's that you must answer when writing any news release. In any news release, the content must be current—the timeliness of a story is crucial to its coverage. Finally, you must ensure that your news release is correct, or free from error.

Broadcast News Release Format

A broadcast news release will include most of the elements required of an online or print news release. Your contact information should appear at the top of the page. Your header should specify the date or date range in which your message should be run. For a one-time release, "FOR IMMEDIATE RELEASE" can be used; however, messages that should be run several times should be presented in a range, such as "Begin October 21, 2014 – End October 31, 2014." A headline should also be included, but your release does not need a dateline. Datelines are not necessary in broadcast releases because they will not be read on air. The location where the story originates should be clear in the narrative contained in the lead. The remainder of the release should be written the same way that it will be read by a broadcast journalist. Quotations should be paraphrased, and a boilerplate is not necessary unless you would like to include a means for gathering more information. As you review your broadcast news release, ask yourself whether the broadcast journalist or the public may need additional information. If the answer to this question is yes, revise your release to include such information. For a sample broadcast news release template, see Figure 6.2.

Complete: Answering the five W's (who, what, when, where, and why) in a news release.

Current: The timeliness of a news release.

Correct: Ensuring that a news release is free from error.

Company Name

Address

Contact: [Your Name]

Your Phone Number

Your E-mail Address

Your Social Media Handle

Release Header

    The body of the release should be written with the purpose of answering the five W's. This should be done using a narrative format that follows the structure used by broadcast journalists in their reporting.

    Paraphrased quotes can be attributed to important people relevant to the story. Text can be broken up using bullets, especially when communicating instructional information such as tips for preparing for a hurricane.

    Information on the organization being discussed can be included but does not need to be done as a formal boilerplate. When you reach the end of the release, you should include the close symbol at the center of the bottom of the page.

###

FIGURE 6.2: SAMPLE BROADCAST NEWS RELEASE TEMPLATE

SOCIAL MEDIA NEWS RELEASES (SMNRS)

Social Media News Release (Smnr): Uses social media tools to distribute information about an organization and simultaneously encourage public engagement with its content.

The purpose of the social media news release (SMNR) is to use social media tools to distribute information and simultaneously encourage public engagement with its content. Social media platforms are rife with opportunities to connect with diverse audiences and generate collaboration and interaction. As such, a SMNR must be designed as a multimedia warehouse of information that provides journalists and bloggers with all of the information that they need to write and share a news story. Journalists and bloggers benefit from the SMNR's tangible format as they can easily "cut through the clutter" to select the information that they are interested in. The general public also benefits from the SMNR's interactivity, as it encourages two-way communication between the organization and the public. SMNRs are designed to be distributed through social media, so it is ideal for an organization to have an online newsroom, or a website designed to provide information about an organization with the purpose of increasing accessibility for journalists. Specific details on how to create an online newsroom will be discussed later in this chapter.

Online Newsroom: A website designed to provide information about an organization with the purpose of increasing accessibility for journalists.

Social Media News Release Format

Akin to the standard news release, a social media news release should include a headline, introductory paragraph, supporting facts, and quotations from the CEO/company executives or customers. In addition to these elements, SMNRs also require photo, video, or audio to be embedded into the release. One of the most effective ways to do this is to upload photos and videos to hosting websites, such as Flickr and YouTube, and embed the link to these sites within your news release. Search Engine Optimized links should also be included within the content of the news release to link to sites that contain background information or other relevant stories. A link to the company's RSS feed, or repository for subscribing to all releases from the company, should also be provided. RSS feeds can easily be created using a variety of free or paid programs such as RSS Builder or FeedForAll, which allow you to create RSS files to upload to your website or podcast feeds to upload to iTunes. Digital tags to link to sites like Technorati or Digg may also be included to track the spread of your SMNR and identify who is discussing areas of interest. Links to the organization's social media sites and relevant topic hashtags—such as #Sasquatch2014—should also be included. Finally, options allowing users to post, blog, share, bookmark, comment, or contact the organization should also be included. For a sample social media news release template, see Figure 6.3.

Rss Feed: A repository for subscribing to all releases from an organization.

© Yuriy Vlasenko/Shutterstock.com

RSS feeds allow individuals to subscribe to all releases from a particular company.

[Organization's Logo] Date

Headline

Introductory paragraph summarizing the information contained in the release. This should be done in a narrative format.

Additional factual information should be provided in the following paragraphs (approximately 3-5 paragraphs).

This can be presented using bullets for lengthier information or statistics.

Relevant quotations should also be embedded in this section.

Remember to include links for search engine optimization.

About [Organization]

The boilerplate goes here. Links can be provided to the company's main website, etc.

Contacts

Name

Job Title

Phone Number

E-mail Address

[Company Website Link]

Multimedia

[Image]

[Image]

[Image]

Featured Video

[Embedded Video]

Tags

[Tag]

[Hashtag]

[Organization] RSS Feed

[RSS Feeds]

Sharing

[E-mail, Print, G+1, Twitter, Facebook, LinkedIn, Gmail, etc.]

FIGURE 6.3: SAMPLE SOCIAL MEDIA NEWS RELEASE (SMNR) TEMPLATE

MEDIA INFORMATION DOCUMENTS

Backgrounders

Backgrounder: An in-depth informational document that provides background information on a specific issue.

A **backgrounder** is an in-depth informational document that provides background information on a specific issue. The target audience for backgrounders typically consists of reporters, speechwriters, editors, journalists, and ad copywriters. Backgrounders typically accompany news releases and supply background information that is not found in the news release and may be included in a media kit or used to prepare talking points for an interview. To write an effective backgrounder, several guidelines should be followed.

A backgrounder should be about four pages in length, but should not be written to fulfill a page number. As with all public relations documents, concise writing is preferred. The document should begin with a brief statement about the subject of the accompanying news release presented as a headline in uppercase letters. Consider the backgrounder released by the Saint Louis Zoo in 2013 in reference to an existing swamp that opened in June 2004. The headline of the backgrounder reads: "EDWARD K. LOVE CONSERVATION FOUNDATION CYPRESS SWAMP."

The next paragraph should consist of a historical overview of the issue, including a description of the major events leading up to it. If you must consult other sources to write this section, be sure to include the appropriate citations within the text formatted in adherence with the *AP Stylebook*. The historical background should be followed by the significance of the issue at hand and the implications of the subject. This section should consist of informative and factual information. The Saint Louis Zoo backgrounder includes a description of the Zoo's Cypress Swamp, which features 16 species of North American birds that thrive in cypress swamps along the Mississippi River, and the importance of swamps to the vitality of certain animal species (Saint Louis Zoo, 2013).

Other formatting considerations for backgrounders include adding underlined subheadings to enhance the readability of a text-heavy document. Backgrounders that are more than one page in length should include the "—more—" symbol centered at the bottom of each page until the document is at the end. The close symbol should be centered at the bottom of the final page.

Fact Sheets

A **fact sheet** is an informational document used to communicate general information about an organization, product, or service. Fact sheets are typically one to two pages in length and are often distributed alongside a news release or media kit. As a result, the fact sheet should contain information that elaborates on the information that is presented in the accompanying documents.

Components that should be included in a fact sheet include the contact information for the organization. This information should be located in the upper left corner of the document. If a company letterhead is used, this step may be removed. Next, the contact information for the public relations practitioner should be located on the upper right corner of the document. A triple space should be inserted and then the name of the subject should be centered in uppercase letters. A double space should be entered and "Fact Sheet" should be typed in the center and underlined.

The body of the fact sheet should include underlined headings with pertinent information below each heading. Consider the headings included in The Public Relations Society of America's (PRSA) fact sheet: Overview, Mission, Membership, Initiatives, Organizational Structure, PRSA Foundation, College of Fellows, PRSSA, Conferences, Awards, Publications, Leadership, and Headquarters (The Public Relations Society of America, 2014). All of this

Fact Sheet: An informational document used to communicate general information about an organization, product, or service.

Fact sheets should be simple, concise, and generally one to two pages in length.

information can be used to provide the public with information about the PRSA in interviews, news stories, and news reports. Finally, as you conclude your fact sheet, if the document is longer than one page, "—more—" should be in the center of the bottom of each page. At the end of the fact sheet, the close symbol should be centered.

Pitch Letters

Pitch Letter: A brief letter that is sent to journalists to pique their interest in a story.

A *pitch letter* is a brief letter that is sent to journalists to pique their interest in your story. Pitch letters often accompany a news release, backgrounder, media advisory, or media kit. These letters are typically 3-5 paragraphs in length and should not exceed one page. Standard business letter formatting should be used with the public relations practitioner's name and contact information at the top of the letter. A headline, like those used in news releases, may be used for these letters but it is not necessary. You may begin your letter by formally addressing the journalist. When you are writing the journalist's name, double check that you have spelled it correctly.

Akin to the format for a news release, the first paragraph of your pitch letter should be your lead. It should introduce your story and provide a hook that will make the story interesting to the media. Consider a statement like, "On February 26, the world record for the largest living sun will be broken." This statement piques the interest of the reader while also describing a newsworthy event that will take place at a charity event. The remainder of the first paragraph should include the five W's. Subsequent paragraphs should explain the relevance of the story. For example, a testimonial may be used when pitching a story about a product. If we are pitching the world record story, these paragraphs could detail how the world record is part of a charity run/walk event designed to raise money for a local school that serves children with developmental disabilities. We could emphasize that this is the only school of its type in the city and that the school is nonprofit and relies on public support to function. In your pitch letter, it is important to emphasize *relevance*, or the importance of the information to your target audience.

Relevance: The importance of information to your target audience.

The final paragraph should include your contact information. Depending on the type of pitch you are sending, you may also need to include instructing information about how the journalist can reach relevant parties. If you are pitching an interview with a visitor to your organization, for example, you should detail their availability for an interview as well as information on how to attend their presentation. Pitch letters for a particular product or service should include an invitation to try a sample of the product or service, as well as your contact information. For a sample pitch letter, see Figure 6.4.

Media Advisories

A **media advisory** alerts the news media to an upcoming news event with the intent of having them attend. Media advisories should be sent to journalists several days (no more than one week) before the event and should be followed

Media Advisory: Alerts the news media to an upcoming news event with the intent of having them attend.

Contact: [Your Name]

Your Phone Number

Your E-mail Address

Your Social Media Handle

[Optional Headline]

Dear [Name of Journalist],

On [date] distinguished Communication researcher, [Researcher's Name], will be presenting a keynote address at [University] as part of the University's COMM Week. The presentation will be held in [Location] at [time] and is open to the public, free of charge. A book signing will follow the presentation.

[Researcher's Last Name], Professor in the Department of Communication Studies at [University] is an award-winning researcher in the areas of [areas]. In [Month/year], [Researcher's Last Name] was invited by the Consortium on Social Science Associations to give a Congressional Briefing on issues of [area] in Washington, DC. [Researcher's Last Name] was also instrumental in establishing one of the country's first courses in the discipline of Communication on [area]. She specializes in training health professionals about [area].

[Researcher's Last Name] will be available to discuss her research on [Date]. If you would like to book her for an interview, just call the number above. You are also invited to attend the presentation on [Date]. I will be in touch within the next few days to discuss a possible interview.

Sincerely,
[Your Full Name]

FIGURE 6.4: SAMPLE PITCH LETTER

FOR IMMEDIATE RELEASE

Contact: [Your Name]

Your Phone Number

Your E-mail Address

Your Social Media Handle

[Date]

Free Health Screenings

[Background information on the importance of health screenings in our local community; perhaps a discussion of the rising cost of health insurance and the fact that the upcoming screenings are free.] The [Name of Organization] will be offering a day of free health screenings at [Location], [Date].

WHO: Licensed physicians who are members of the [Name of Organization]

WHAT: A day of free health screenings, open to the community

Services to be offered include: pulmonary function tests, hearing tests, skin exams, varicose vein screening, dental screenings, blood sugar/glucose testing, diabetes testing, vision testing, HIV testing, spinal screening, asthma device demonstration, blood pressure testing, iron screenings, cholesterol screening, post-mastectomy support, compression garment demonstration, mammogram screening, immunizations, athletic physicals, children's identification cards, and CPR training.

WHERE: [Location], [Address], [Cite, State]

WHEN: [Time] to [Time], [Date]

WHY: The event will highlight the importance of preventive health screenings for children, women, and men in our community.

[Full Name], [Job Title] of [Name of Organization] will be available throughout the day for press interviews.

For more information, contact [Full Name, Title] at the phone number or e-mail address above.

FIGURE 6.5: SAMPLE MEDIA ADVISORY

up with a phone call. The advisory should be redistributed one day before the event as a reminder. Typically, media advisories are one page in length and are written using an outline format, making it quick and easy for the journalist to identify the necessary information.

The media advisory should begin with the public relations practitioner's contact information and a headline. The first paragraph should include a brief summary of your event with a description of the purpose of the event and why the event is relevant to your target audience. Then, the five W's of an event should be covered in outline format. Finally, a description of how interviews can be set up between a spokesperson and the media should be included, along with contact information that can be used by reporters before or after the event. For a sample media advisory, see Figure 6.5.

Media Kits

A media kit (also referred to as a press kit) is an information packet about an organization, public figure, or product. Media kits are typically distributed at news conferences, product launches, and promotional presentations. In addition to journalists, media kits may also be created to target potential investors and consumers. With this in mind, each kit should be designed with the target audience in mind and should only contain information that is relevant to that audience. The overarching goal of distributing a media kit is to gain interest, provide background information about an organization, address questions, and make a lasting impression.

Your media kit should be enclosed in a folder with a cover that includes the name of the organization and the purpose of the media kit. You should also have a label with the name of the journalist and their publication/news agency on the cover of the folder. The contents of the folder may include several of the following informational items:

- Table of Contents
- News Release
- Backgrounder
- Fact Sheet
- Company Brochures/Newsletter/Annual Report

PR TIP

CULTIVATE MEDIA PARTNERSHIPS

In the same way that a band is louder than one guitar, media partnerships can be more effective than a single publicist. That's why it makes sense to use the many different media outlets that are at your disposal, including print media, radio, television, etc. Join forces with as many as you can. Give them something of interest that they will want to showcase: a brand new company launch, interesting study findings, a merger of two prominent companies. Be sure to add photos, snappy quotes, good descriptions and they'll want to share your message.

SOURCE: http://www.10bestpr.com/tips/6-10/

Media Kit (or Press Kit): An information packet about an organization, public figure, or product.

- Product/Service Reviews
- Recent Publications/Articles
- Captioned Photographs
- Audio/Video Files
- List of Frequently Asked Questions

When compiling materials for a media kit, remember that journalists receive a great deal of information on a daily basis. To get noticed, you must package your materials professionally and find unique ways to catch their attention. When distributing kits to the media, make sure that all members of the media receive a copy of the kit. Kits should be mailed to journalists who were not present at the event that your kit covers. It is also wise to follow up with recipients of the media kit to provide an opportunity for them to ask questions, schedule interviews, and solicit additional information. This will improve your media relations and your opportunity for publicity. Most importantly, you should always keep several copies of your media kit on your person, readily available for requestors.

Electronic Press Kits (EPKs)

Electronic Press Kit (Epk):
A digital version of a media kit.

An **electronic press kit (EPK)** is a digital version of a media kit. This format has quickly become the standard for media kit distribution because it requires less time and effort to update and is more cost-effective than printing glossy photos and color copies of documents. EPKs can be distributed via the Internet (such as an organization's online newsroom), USB flash drive, or DVD. An EPK should include many of the same items as a media kit, but should also include high-resolution graphics, multimedia (such as videos or audio), active links, and interactivity. Informational components, such as news releases or backgrounders, should be linked to a downloadable portable document format (PDF) version. Ultimately, you must consider your target audience's expectations for digital documents. Most individuals prefer infographics to text when it comes to online communications. As such, your EPK is more likely to catch your audience's attention if you can make it stand out graphically such as portions of *Entrepreneur Magazine*'s EPK.. This document is made available from a specific link on their main website and links to a downloadable PDF file. The following list is a link to this example along with other sample EPKs that may serve as templates for your creativity:

- http://www.entrepreneur.com/mediakit/pdf/2013-entcommediakit.pdf

- http://mediakit.fastcompany.com/resources/FC_MediaKit.pdf
- http://www.menshealthmediakit.com/downloads/
- http://thechive.files.wordpress.com/2012/04/thechive_mediakit-4-16-12.pdf

WRITING FOR TELEVISION AND RADIO

Video News Releases (VNRs)

A **video news release (VNR)** is a video segment that is designed to look and sound like a news report but is created entirely by a public relations practitioner. VNRs can be designed with an informational and/or persuasive purpose and are often used to promote products and services. For example, on February 7, 2012, Walmart released a VNR promoting their "Great For You" food labeling initiative. The VNR is just under two minutes in length and includes footage of shoppers browsing products in the aisles of a Walmart store, commentary about the increasing difficulty of identifying healthy products in stores, and a discussion of Walmart's resulting initiative of adding "Great For You" labels to products that meet certain criteria. In the video, we see the SVP of Sustainability discussing the initiative, as well as a male "reporter" (an individual employed by Walmart) wearing a suit and walking down an aisle while discussing the initiative. You have probably seen this or other video news releases on the local or national news. It is common for journalists to air VNRs that are produced by public relations practitioners to fill 30-, 60-, and 90-second holes in newscasts.

Producing documents, such as VNRs, for television requires the public relations practitioner to have a level of knowledge that goes beyond the scope of a typical public relations course. Additional coursework in media, screenplay writing, video production, cinematography, or editing will be helpful for learning how to create scripts and shoot and edit video footage for the VNR. In its most basic form, you should focus on visualizing how a news report should look and sound. Spend time watching other VNRs to identify patterns—such as walking down an aisle of a store when discussing a product—that can be emulated in your release. Once you have visualized your script, you may write a **script treatment**, or an informal draft of a television spot. A script treatment for a VNR should be approximately 1-2 pages in length and describe what you envision seeing and hearing in the release. A sample script treatment can be seen in Figure 6.6.

Video News Release (VNR): A video segment that is designed to look and sound like a news report but is created entirely by a public relations practitioner.

Script Treatment: An informal draft of a television spot.

TOOLS FOR THE PUBLIC RELATIONS PROFESSIONAL

Script Treatment: [Organization Name] "VNR Name"

Client: [Organization Name]

Prepared By: [Your Name]

Opening shot of gang graffiti painted on neighborhood fences and local business buildings.

(Voice over:) GRAFFITI COSTS AMERICAN COMMUNITIES OVER $8 BILLION PER YEAR. IT HURTS EVERYONE BY DECREASING PROPERTY VALUES, DRIVING AWAY BUSINESS, AND SENDING A MESSAGE THAT A NEIGHBORHOOD IS DANGEROUS.

Cut to close-up of a neighbor's hand as she paints over the graffiti on her fence.

(Voice over:) THIS DOES NOT HAVE TO BE A PROBLEM THAT PLAGUES OUR COMMUNITY. THE [CITY] POLICE and CRIME STOPPERS HAVE TEAMED UP TO SPONSOR A NEW PROGRAM CALLED "CLEAN SWEEP."

Cut to bust shot of [Officer's Name], Sheriff of [Police Department] standing near his police car.

(Transcript of [Officer's Name]'s remarks:) "The reason that graffiti does not get cleaned up quickly is because the responsibility is placed on the home or business owner to clean it up. Many people cannot afford to encumber the cost of paint and paintbrushes on a regular basis."

Cut to extreme long shot of a group of officers and young adults cleaning graffiti.

(Transcript of [Officer's Name]'s remarks:) "The Clean Sweep program is funded by a state grant and provides the police department with funding for the supplies needed to clean graffiti and an internship program for Criminal Justice students. When your home or business is tagged, you can file a report with us and we will put your name in a database. Each weekend, a group of Criminal Justice students and local officers will visit the locations on the database to clean the graffiti, free of charge."

Cut to exterior of graffiti-free buildings.

(Voice over:) IF YOU HAVE BEEN THE VICTIM OF GRAFFITI CRIMES, THE POLICE DEPARTMENT WOULD LIKE FOR YOU TO REPORT THE CRIME AT [WEBSITE] OR [PHONE NUMBER].

Fade

FIGURE 6.6: SAMPLE SCRIPT TREATMENT

When writing a script treatment, you should provide directions for the visual elements of the video (such as the camera opening to a scene of children playing flag football in the afternoon) and labels for voice-overs (such as an individual discussing heat exhaustion in children). All spoken language should appear capitalized with the exception of quotations provided by individuals. You should also include appropriate terminology for audio elements, camera directions, camera movement, and transitions. The following is a list of terminology and acronyms that may be used in your script treatment:

- **Ambient Sound:** Naturally occurring sound.
- **Bust Shot:** A shot of a person from the chest up.
- **Close-Up (CU):** A shot of a person from the neck up.
- **Cut:** A quick change from one shot to another.
- **Dissolve:** A gradual change from one image to another.
- **Dolly In/Out:** Moving the camera in a straight line toward or away from object.
- **Extreme Close-Up (ECU):** A shot that focuses on a specific aspect of the head or neck, such as the eyes or mouth.
- **Extreme Long Shot (ELS):** A shot of a person in the distance.
- **Fade:** A gradual change to a black background.
- **Long Shot (LS):** A shot of an entire person that fills the screen.
- **Medium Shot (MS):** A shot of a person from the waist up.
- **Music Under:** The volume of the music is lowered.
- **Music Up:** The volume of the music is raised.
- **On Camera (OC):** Indicates a narrator that appears on camera.
- **Pan Right/Left:** Moving the camera head to the right or left.
- **Sound Effects (SFX):** Any sounds that accompany the video.
- **Tilt Up/Down:** Moving the camera head up or down.
- **Truck Right/Left:** Moving the camera right or left, parallel to object.
- **Voice-Over (VO):** Indicates a narrator that does not appear on camera.
- **Wipe:** An effect where an image is "wiped" from the screen and another appears in its place.

Once your script treatment is complete, you may begin to write your **shooting script**, which is a completed script that will be used to produce your video news release. The goal of the shooting script is to have a complete guideline for shooting your VNR. Everything from camera movement, audio, narrative, timing, and transitions should be included in your shooting script. Your shooting script should have two columns, one labeled "VIDEO" and the other labeled "AUDIO." The video column should contain camera directions and camera movement, transitions, and descriptions of the imagery that will be

Shooting Script: A completed script that is used to produce a video news release.

THE PRACTICE OF PUBLIC RELATIONS

PRODUCTION: [Name of VNR]

PRODUCER: [Name of Production Company or PR Practitioner]

VIDEO	AUDIO
Camera opens to shot of a fence filled with graffiti. Camera PANS RIGHT, showing the length of the graffiti on the fence. CUT to close-up of neighbor's hand painting over graffiti on fence	NARRATOR: GRAFFITI COSTS AMERICAN COMMUNITIES OVER $8 BILLION PER YEAR. GRAFFITI HURTS EVERYONE AND IS EVERYONE'S PROBLEM. IT DECREASES PROPERTY VALUES, DRIVES AWAY BUSINESS, AND SENDS A MESSAGE THAT A NEIGHBORHOOD IS DANGEROUS. THIS DOESN'T HAVE TO BE A PROBLEM THAT PLAGUES OUR COMMUNITY. THE [CITY] POLICE AND CRIME STOPPERS HAVE TEAMED UP TO SPONSOR A NEW PROGRAM CALLED "CLEAN SWEEP."
CUT to BUST SHOT officer	OFFICER: "Clean Sweep is funded by a state grant and serves as an internship program for Criminal Justice students.
CUT to shot of online reporting tool CUT to exterior of graffiti-free buildings	When your home or business is tagged, you can file a report with us and your name will go into a database. Each weekend, the city police and Criminal Justice students will join together to clean the graffiti at the database locations, free of charge."
CUT to shot of phone number and website on blank screen. FADE	NARRATOR: IF YOU HAVE BEEN THE VICTIM OF GRAFFITI, REPORT THE CRIME IMMEDIATELY AT [WEBSITE] OR [PHONE NUMBER]

FIGURE 6.7: SAMPLE SHOOTING SCRIPT

visible in the video. The audio column should contain the music, sounds, and narration that will be present in the film. Your document should contain page numbers, as well as the name of the organization and the producer of the VNR. For a sample shooting script, see Figure 6.7.

Public Service Announcements (PSAs)

"This is your brain. This is your brain on drugs. Any questions?"

"Friends don't let friends drive drunk."

The quotes listed above are familiar to many of us. These phrases are widely recognized because of their appearance in well-known public service announcement campaigns. A **public service announcement (PSA)** is an audio or video message, sponsored by a nonprofit organization, disseminated by the media free of charge with the purpose of raising awareness or calling a public to action. Common PSA topics include obesity, compulsive gambling, gang prevention, heart attack warning signs, animal adoption, drunk driving, and texting and driving. The National Highway Traffic Safety Administration (NHTSA) and the Ad Council sponsor a public relations campaign titled "Stop the texts. Stop the wrecks." Part of their campaign includes a PSA called "Stairs." This 30-second video starts with footage of a young woman texting on her cell phone while she walks upstairs. She falls, her phone flies out of her hand, and everyone laughs. This is followed by a black screen with white lettering that reads, "NOT EVERYONE SHOULD TEXT AND WALK." The camera then cuts to a clip of a young woman texting while driving. As she is looking down to type a message, a woman and child are crossing the street. The driver slams on her brakes and the audience is left to presume that she hit the woman and child with her car. The screen then fades to black with lettering that reads, "NO ONE SHOULD TEXT AND DRIVE." The next message shows the name of the campaign and is followed by a screen that says, "How will you stop texting and driving? Tell us at StopTextsStopWrecks.org" along with the logos for the Ad Council and NHTSA.

Public service announcements are generally meant to serve the community and public at large.

Public Service Announcement (PSA): An audio or video message, sponsored by a nonprofit organization, disseminated by the media free of charge with the purpose of raising awareness or calling a public to action.

Spot Announcement: A script that is sent to radio announcers to be read live on air.

As-Recorded Spot: A pre-recorded radio message.

Hook: A word or phrase that captures attention.

PSAs are generally inexpensive to create, as the only cost incurred to the organization is the cost of production. PSAs are aired free of charge because the Federal Communications Commission (FCC) requires that television and radio media serve "the public interest." This interest is served by airing PSAs. To streamline the process, public relations practitioners should send PSAs that are ready-to-air. In other words, producing a PSA video for television is necessary. When it comes to radio, however, a spot announcement can be sent to announcers to be read live on air as opposed to an as-recorded spot, or pre-recorded message.

When creating a PSA, several guidelines should be followed to ensure that your PSA is selected for coverage by the media. First, you must keep in mind that you only have a few seconds to reach your audience. The typical time for a televised PSA spot is 30 seconds or less, and the standard lengths for radio spots are 10 seconds (10-25 words), 15 seconds (30-35 words), 20 seconds (40-50 words), and 30 seconds (60-75 words). Because of this, you should ensure that your PSA is simple and covers one key point. The writing should include a hook, or a word or phrase that captures attention. A hook may be in the

---

[Organization Name]
[Organization Address]

"NAME OF SPOT": 20 SEC. LIVE RADIO SPOT

ARE YOU FEELING MORE TIRED THAN USUAL? DIABETES IS THE SEVENTH LEADING CAUSE OF DEATH IN THE UNITED STATES. THE [NAME OF ORGANIZATION] WOULD LIKE TO REMIND YOU TO HAVE YOUR DOCTOR CHECK YOUR BLOOD SUGAR.

#####

(station call letters) AND THE [NAME OF ORGANIZATION] CARE ABOUT YOUR HEALTH. IF YOU ARE EXPERIENCING BLURRED VISION, DRY MOUTH, INCREASED HUNGER OR THIRST, FATIGUE, OR UNEXPLAINED WEIGHT LOSS, HAVE YOUR DOCTOR CHECK YOUR BLOOD SUGAR.

#####

ABOUT TWO HUNDRED AND EIGHT THOUSAND AMERICANS UNDER AGE TWENTY ARE ESTIMATED TO HAVE DIABETES. REMIND YOUR LOVED ONES TO HAVE THEIR DOCTORS CHECK THEIR BLOOD SUGAR. A MESSAGE FROM [ORGANIZATION NAME].

#####

FIGURE 6.8: SAMPLE SPOT ANNOUNCEMENT

form of a startling statistic or a catchy phrase such as the Texas Department of Transportation's slogan, "Drink. Drive. Go To Jail." Your PSA should include a request for a specific action from the public, such as reporting litterers. A radio PSA should begin with the name of the sponsoring organization, whereas a televised PSA should end with the sponsoring organization's name and/or logo. For a televised PSA, make sure that the phone number and web address is on the screen long enough for viewers to write it down (approximately 8 seconds). You may also consider designing a website or dedicating a portion of your main website to the campaign.

Spot announcements for radio are typically sent in packages of two, three, or four. The formatting should include the name and contact information for the organization in the upper left corner followed by the title and length of the spot underlined and capitalized. Multiple spots may appear on one page for 10 to 20-second spots; however, 30-second spots should appear on separate pages. The text for the spot should be double-spaced. A close symbol "#####" should appear at the bottom center of each spot. The format of as-recorded spots, however, varies from station to station, so it is a good idea to call each station to ask for their formatting requirements. See Figure 6.8 for a sample spot announcement template.

WRITING FOR THE INTERNET

Online Newsrooms

The results of two media surveys conducted by *PRWeek* and *PR Newswire* highlight the fact that journalists are being required to take on more work with fewer resources, and that public relations practitioners can ease this burden with the creation of online newsrooms (PRNewswire, n.d.). As we discussed earlier in this chapter, an online newsroom is a website designed to provide information about an organization with the purpose of increasing accessibility for journalists. A standard online newsroom should include:

- Contact information for your organization's media contact(s).
- A backgrounder or fact sheet.
- Links to news releases organized in reverse-date order, and an archive of past releases.
- A list of upcoming events.
- Links to press coverage in reverse-date order, and an archive of past coverage.

- Biographies for the organization's management personnel.
- Links to other downloadable content such as brochures, newsletters, and annual reports.
- Downloadable high-resolution and low-resolution JPG photos.
- Infographics, charts, graphs, and other relevant graphics.
- Streaming video or audio.
- Downloadable presentations.
- A "Frequently Asked Questions" (FAQs) section.
- Links to all of the organization's social media profiles.
- RSS feeds.
- An opt-in e-mail section.
- A search bar, allowing individuals to search for information by keyword.

It is also important to note that the online newsroom should be kept simple. Refrain from using any graphic or video file extensions or scripts that take a long time to download or may not be downloadable unless a particular program is installed on the user's computer. You should always include both high- and low-resolution photos for journalists, and all content that appears in the newsroom should include social media buttons for quick and easy sharing. These buttons can easily be added using a free tool like ShareThis.

Nikon's online newsroom (found at http://www.nikonusa.com/en/About-Nikon/Press-Room/index.page) is visually appealing and includes all of the necessary elements. The newsroom contains a search bar that allows users to search news releases by date and category. A "Media" link contains company podcasts and videos. A photo gallery allows users to download low-and high-resolution versions of product images. A "Featured Pro" section contains photos and information about employees. The most recent news stories about Nikon appear on the page with a link to download or share the content. A large yellow circle stands out to the user, prompting them to links that read "Subscribe," "Contact," "RSS," and a search bar to "Search the Press Room." Finally, a row of social media links appears at the bottom of the website. All of this information is well organized, aesthetically appealing, and easily accessible to journalists who visit the newsroom.

Blogs

Blog (or Weblog): Journal-type entries used to build relationships or generate conversation.

A blog (or weblog) provides organizations with the opportunity to post journal-type entries to build relationships or generate conversations. One of the most important characteristics of public relations is two-way communication, which is the primary function of a blog. Many organizations have blogs but do not use them to their full capacity. A blog writer should go beyond posting information about the organization's achievements, views, opinion, or innovations—rather, a blog should be the start of a conversation. Starbucks' blog "My Starbucks Idea" is a global marketplace of ideas. The company blogs about ideas for new drinks, food items, merchandise, music, technology, atmosphere, and community service ideas and readers build on the ideas with comments. The blog includes a list of ideas that were proposed by the public and are currently under review, reviewed, in the works, or implemented. Examples of implemented ideas include designing a cup contest, bicycle racks at store locations, Verismo pods in bulk, grilled cheese sandwiches, and a variety of Chai teas.

Blogs are especially useful for creating two-way communication for a large group of individuals.

Guidelines for Blogging

When writing a blog post or commenting on another person's/company's blog, it is important to craft a message that can be easily comprehended by a reader who is scanning the page. Many blog readers do not take the time to read an entire lengthy post, so clarity is important. Other strategies for enhancing comprehension include the use of bullet points, short sentences, short paragraphs, few key points, bold or italicized lettering to emphasize important information, headings, photos, and search engine optimized keywords.

Bloggers should also take time to follow rules for spelling, grammar, and avoiding plagiarism. Content that does not belong to an organization—such as a quotation or photograph—should be posted with the permission of and credit to the author. Blogs should also be conversational in tone with an invitation for discussion. You should also make sure that you take the time to read comments that are left by others and respond accordingly. The opportunity for two-way communication is useless if bloggers do not take the time to interact with their publics.

Ethics in Practice

Ellie is a recent college graduate beginning her first job as PR blogger for a small manufacturing company. Since her company uses many volatile chemicals for manufacturing that the public might not be familiar with, Ellie decided to begin her blog by offering a discussion forum for residents to voice their concerns and learn more about the chemicals being used in their community. Ellie began by offering very dense, scientific information about the chemicals being used, as well as very long-winded explanations for their environmental impact. Many responders on the blog complained that the information was not very clear and did little to address the community's major concerns about public health and safety. When asked by a responder about disposal techniques, Ellie simply posted a link to a federal regulatory agency, saying that the information was somewhere in the link. As criticism grew for her blog not offering relevant information, Ellie decided to ignore the complaints and focus on another aspect of the manufacturing company in her posts. After receiving numerous complaints about the lack of information or two-way communication, Ellie's company decided to relieve her of her duties and have another person take over the company blog.

QUESTIONS TO CONSIDER

1. What simple tenets did Ellie break when managing her company blog?
2. What were the major problems with Ellie's writing style and response format?
3. When creating a blog for PR purposes, what should be the primary concern when interacting with respondents?
4. What steps should Ellie's company take to rectify the situation?

WRITING FOR SOCIAL MEDIA

Over the years, social media has presented a unique challenge when it comes to public relations writing. While most traditional forms of public relations writing consist of one-way information dissemination, this strategy is not effective on social media. In other words, social media should not be used strictly to share information about your organization or promote a product or service. Social media messages should be centered on facilitating two-way communication between the organization and its public with an overarching goal of relationship building. To enhance trust and relationship building, you (as a social media content manager) should ask questions, answer questions, use a person's name when responding to one of their questions, use your first name when responding to a person's question, provide instructing information when problem solving is necessary, facilitate communication between "fans" of your page, and share relevant photos and videos.

Social Media Strategies

Facebook and Twitter are presently the two most commonly used social media platforms. Although each app requires its own formatting rules (such as Twitter's 140-character limit), the type of post that you share will be similar across platforms. When composing social media messages, remember that the majority of posts should be engaging or sharing other people's content (as long as it is relevant to your industry), fewer messages should be about your organization and its values, and the least number of messages should be dedicated to persuading your public to take an action. The following list contains an additional set of ideas for the type of information that you should share on social media:

- Posts from your organization's blog.
- Press coverage of your organization.

There are many different factors to consider when creating a social media strategy.

- News articles on relevant topics.
- Other people's or organizations' relevant content.
- Stories/photos/videos/statistics about your organization's positive impact on the community.
- Photos from "behind the scenes".
- Facebook groups for specific events.
- Photos from events.
- Stories about your organization's members/employees.
- Posts about an upcoming event or campaign with a unique hashtag created for Twitter.
- Event announcements.
- Other announcements.

Measuring Social Media Engagement

We will talk more about the specifics of creating a comprehensive social media measurement and evaluation program in the next chapter. In this section, we will explore issues relative to engagement. The goal of all social media posts by an organization or public figure should be to maximize social media engagement, or "the cumulative effect of your online content in getting your audience's attention" (Ionescu, 2012). Kaushik (2011) identified four measures for quantifying social media engagement using the following key performance indicators (KPI):

- Conversation Rate = # of Audience Comments/Replies Per Post
- Amplification Rate = # of Shares/Retweets/Share Clicks Per Post/Tweet/Video
- Applause Rate = # of Favorite Clicks/Likes/+1s Per Post
- Economic Value = Sum of Short and Long Term Revenue and Cost Savings

Most of the data necessary for the KPI equations can be found using existing programs or apps such as HootSuite, Facebook Insights, Google Analytics, All My +, Crowdbooster, and TrueSocialMetrics. For example, Facebook's Insights tab appears on all business pages, free of charge. This tab includes specific information about engagement, including the number of likes, comments, shares, post clicks, and post reach, as well as demographic information about your "fans." Insight information is presented visually and is easy to understand. It can also be easily analyzed to identify patterns of the types of posts that create the most engagement. As an example, the author of this chapter is currently a page administrator for her University's Facebook page for Public Relations

Social Media Engagement: The cumulative effect of your online content in getting your audience's attention.

Key Performance Indicators (KPI): Measures for quantifying social media engagement.

minors. When reviewing the post insights, it is clear that the posts that result in the most engagement are those that solicit feedback from participants ("Did you know that many businesses are looking at Klout scores when hiring candidates? Comment and let us know how you feel about that."), those that announce employment opportunities, and those that share photos/videos of our alumni in their professional lives. Social media engagement data is invaluable to public relations practitioners because (1) it allows us to identify ways to increase our engagement and establish an effective social media presence, and (2) it serves as an important argument for the worth of employing public relations practitioners.

STRATEGIES FOR PROFESSIONAL SUCCESS

In this chapter, we have learned the differences between the types of news releases as well as how to write news releases for standard, broadcast, and social media distribution. Because social media has become increasingly popular (as well as free to distribute in many formats), knowing how compose social media posts that engage your public is crucial to any business or organization in modern times. Writer and blogger Susan Payton outlines several key strategies for creating relevant and engaging blog content.

Keep it short, sweet, and customized

It is imperative that you explain why readers need to care about your brand. Especially if you would like other bloggers to discuss and/or promote your brand, you must make sure they find it compelling for them and their other readers. Blanket press releases with no customized information are not going to engage individuals to care about your organization.

Tie it together

Blogger outreach can be woven into your wider public relations strategy. If you find your information posted on another blog, tweet it, repost to your Facebook page, and share it on bookmarking sites. You want to solidify relationships for future partnerships.

| Understand the importance of blogger outreach

People generally trust other consumers (bloggers) more than they trust traditional news releases. If you are successful in gaining credibility and trust with independent writers and bloggers, the public will in turn perceive your message to be more credible and engaging.

http://mashable.com/2010/04/23/blogger-outreach-pr

EXECUTIVE SUMMARY

Now that you have finished reading this chapter, you should be able to

Know the difference between five types of news releases:

- *General news releases* cover information that is of interest to local, regional, national, or international media. This is the most common type of news release.
- *Product news releases* distribute information about specific products, the launch of new products or versions of a product, and important news about products.
- *Launch news releases* are designed to generate publicity about an important launch of a new company, website, logo, feature, or campaign.
- *Financial news releases* distribute financial information about an organization to shareholders and financial media.
- *Event news releases* detail information about upcoming events with the intent of making the event known to the public.

Write news releases for standard, broadcast, and social media distribution:

- Effective news releases must adhere to the Associated Press (AP) Stylebook. They require contact information, a header, a headline, a dateline, a lead (or lede), a narrative, a boilerplate, search engine optimized (SEO) keywords, and a close symbol.
- News releases should be clear, concise, conversational, current, and should answer the five W's (who, what, when, where, and why).
- Social media news releases should also incorporate photo, video, audio, links to the organization's RSS feed and social media sites, and options for interactivity.

Create and organize media information documents, such as backgrounders, fact sheets, pitch letters, media advisories, media kits, and electronic press kits:

- Backgrounders should begin with a brief statement about the subject of the accompanying news release, a headline, a historical overview of the issue, and the implications of the subject. Underlined subheadings may also be used.
- Fact sheets should include contact information for the organization and public relations practitioner, the name of the subject, underlined headings, and pertinent information about the organization.
- Pitch letters should be written using standard business letter formatting and should include contact information, an optional headline, the journalist's name, a lead (or lede), establishing relevance, and an invitation for the journalist.
- Media advisories should begin with contact information, a headline, and be written using an outline format that answers the five W's.
- Media kits and electronic press kits should be designed with the target audience in mind and should include a variety of materials including a table of contents, news release, backgrounder, fact sheet, company brochures or newsletters, photos, etc.

Write VNR and PSA scripts for television and radio:

- Video news release and public service announcement script treatments should be 1-2 pages in length and should contain information about the audio and visual elements of the message.

- PSA scripts should be between 10 and 30 seconds for a radio announcement and 30 seconds or less for a televised announcement. The script should include the name of the sponsoring organization, include a hook, cover one key point, and include a call to action.

Create content for online newsrooms and blogs:

- Online newsrooms should include contact information, backgrounders or fact sheets, links to news releases, lists of upcoming events, links to press coverage, biographies, downloadable content, photos, infographics, video, audio, frequently asked questions, and a link to all of the organization's social media profiles.
- When writing a blog, it is important to start a conversation with readers. It is important to craft an easily comprehensible message and use bullet points, short sentences, short paragraphs, key points, and other means of emphasizing important information.

Compose social media posts that engage your public:

- Social media messages should be centered on facilitating two-way communication between the organization and the public. The majority of posts should be engaging or sharing other people's content, fewer should be about the organization, and even fewer should be about persuading the public to take action.
- Potential messages include posts from your organization's blog, links to press coverage of your organization, articles about relevant topics, stories that show your organization's positive impact on the community, photos from behind the scenes, event announcements, stories about your organization's members, etc.
- Engagement can be measured using key performance indicators (KPIs) such as conversation rate, amplification rate, applause rate, and economic value.

KEY TERMS

Ambient Sound: Naturally occurring sound. *p. 133*

As-Recorded Spot: A pre-recorded radio message. *p. 136*

Backgrounder: An in-depth informational document that provides background information on a specific issue. *p. 124*

Blog (or Weblog): Journal-type entries used to build relationships or generate conversation. *p. 138*

Boilerplate: A description of the organization that is discussed in a news release. *p. 119*

Bust Shot: A shot of a person from the chest up. *p. 133*

Clear: Ensuring that the audience understands a message the first time that they hear it. *p. 120*

Close: A symbol "###" located at the center of the bottom of a news release and "#####" at the center of the bottom of each radio spot, indicating that document has ended. *p. 119*

Close-Up (CU): A shot of a person from the neck up. *p. 133*

Complete: Answering the five W's (who, what, when, where, and why) in a news release. *p. 121*

Concise: Communicating a message using few words. *p. 120*

Contact Information: The inclusion of a public relations practitioner's phone number, e-mail address, and social media handle in a news release. *p. 117*

Conversational: The tone that should be used when writing broadcast news releases. *p. 120*

Correct: Ensuring that a news release is free from error. *p. 121*

Current: The timeliness of a news release. *p. 121*

Cut: A quick change from one shot to another. *p. 133*

Dateline: Information regarding the origin of a news release. *p. 117*

Dissolve: A gradual change from one image to another. *p. 133*

Dolly In/Out: Moving the camera in a straight line toward or away from an object. *p. 133*

Electronic Press Kit (EPK): A digital version of a media kit. *p. 130*

Event News Release: Details information about an upcoming event and is distributed with the intent of making the event known to the public. *p. 116*

Extreme Close-Up (ECU): A shot that focuses on a specific aspect of the head or neck, such as the eyes or mouth. *p. 133*

Extreme Long Shot (ELS): A shot of a person in the distance. *p. 133*

Fact Sheet: An informational document used to communicate general information about an organization, product, or service. *p. 125*

Fade: A gradual change to a black background. *p. 133*

Financial News Release: Distributes financial information about an organization to shareholders and financial media. *p. 115*

General News Release: Covers information occurring in an organization that is of interest to local, regional, national, or international media. *p. 115*

Headline: A title previewing of the content of a news release. *p. 117*

Hook: A word or phrase that captures attention. *p. 136*

Key Performance Indicators (KPI): Measures for quantifying social media engagement. *p. 142*

Launch News Release: A news release that is used to generate publicity about an upcoming launch, the start of a new company or organization, a new website or redesigned logo, or a campaign. *p. 115*

Lead (or Lede): The opening sentence of the news release that serves as the hook to entice the journalist to run the release. *p. 117*

Long Shot (LS): A shot of an entire person that fills the screen. *p. 133*

Media Advisory: Alerts the news media to an upcoming news event with the intent of having them attend. *p. 127*

Media Kit (or Press Kit): An information packet about an organization, public figure, or product. *p. 129*

Media Relations: Developing positive working relationships between an organization and the media. *p. 114*

Medium Shot (MS): A shot of a person from the waist up. *p. 133*

Music Under: The volume of the music is lowered. *p. 133*

Music Up: The volume of the music is raised. *p. 133*

Narrative: Structuring the contents of a news release to tell a story that can easily be edited by journalists for inclusion in their media channels. *p. 116*

News Release (or Press Release): A form of written communication released to the media with the purpose of making an announcement with the intent of it being turned into a news story. *p. 113*

News Wire Services: Commercial fee-based services that distribute news releases to credentialed journalists. *p. 113*

On Camera (OC): Indicates a narrator that appears on camera. *p. 133*

Online Newsroom: A website designed to provide information about an organization with the purpose of increasing accessibility for journalists. *p. 122*

Pan Right/Left: Moving the camera head to the right or left. *p. 133*

Pitch Letter: A brief letter that is sent to journalists to pique their interest in a story. *p. 126*

Product News Release: Distributes information about specific products, the launch of a new product or version of a product, important news about a product, and other milestones that are pertinent to a product. *p. 115*

Public Service Announcement (PSA): An audio or video message, sponsored by a nonprofit organization, disseminated by the media free of charge with the purpose of raising awareness or calling a public to action. *p. 135*

Relevance: The importance of information to your target audience. *p. 126*

Rss Feed: A repository for subscribing to all releases from an organization. *p. 122*

Search Engine Optimized (Seo) Keywords: Hyperlinked words within a news release. *p. 119*

Script Treatment: An informal draft of a television spot. *p. 131*

Shooting Script: A completed script that is used to produce a video news release. *p. 133*

Social Media Engagement: The cumulative effect of your online content in getting your audience's attention. *p. 142*

Social Media News Release (SMNR): Uses social media tools to distribute information about an organization and simultaneously encourage public engagement with its content. *p. 122*

Sound Effects (SFX): Any sounds that accompany the video. *p. 133*

Spot Announcement: A script that is sent to radio announcers to be read live on air. *p. 136*

Tight: Refers to writing a headline that is void of unnecessary words. *p. 117*

Tilt Up/Down: Moving the camera head up or down. *p. 133*

Truck Right/Left: Moving the camera right or left, parallel to object. *p. 133*

Video News Release (VNR): A video segment that is designed to look and sound like a news report but is created entirely by a public relations practitioner. *p. 131*

Voice-Over (VO): Indicates a narrator that does not appear on camera. *p. 133*

Wipe: An effect where an image is "wiped" from the screen and another appears in its place. *p. 133*

DISCUSSION QUESTIONS

1. Why is writing such an important skill for public relations practitioners to have?
2. What are some reasons that journalists ignore many news releases?
3. Should a news release be completely unbiased?
4. What are some ways that a public relations practitioner can develop effective media relations?
5. How has social media changed the public relations profession?
6. What are some advantages and disadvantages of the Internet/social media for public relations practitioners?

CHAPTER 7
PR MEASUREMENT AND EVALUATION

A measurement and evaluation module of a PR campaign has become a critical component. The challenge is striking the optimal balance between measuring impact versus supporting corporate objectives.

CHAPTER OUTLINE

Early roots of PR Measurement and Evaluation
PR Measurement in the 21st Century
The Barcelona Principles
Importance of PR Measurement and Evaluation
Developing a Program Framework
    Speak with Your Client
    Design the Campaign Program
    Programs Depend Upon the Client
Specific Elements of Measurement and Evaluation
Timeline for Measurement and Evaluation
Essentials for Measurement and Evaluation
Measuring and Evaluating Social Media Campaigns
Designing a Social Media Measurement Program
    Step 1: Establish Program Goals
    Step 2: Design a Measurement System
    Step 3: Launch the Program
    Step 4: Track Your Results
    Step 5: Tweak and Repeat
Strategies for Professional Success
Executive Summary
Discussion Questions
Key Terms

CHAPTER OBJECTIVES

After studying this chapter, you should be able to:

1. Define the concept of measurement and evaluation in the public relations arena.
2. Identify the importance of measurement and evaluation in your study of public relations.
3. Realize the critical role measurement and evaluation plays in managing public relations campaigns.
4. Understand how to apply measurement and evaluation tools to a public relations campaign.
5. Appreciate the difference in the measurement and evaluation of traditional media versus social media.

Ripped from the Headlines

In 2012, The Victoria and Albert (V&A) Museum in London happened upon a unique opportunity when granted permission to assemble an exhibit on the life of British rock sensation David Bowie. The museum was allowed to use artifacts from the David Bowie Archive in the exhibit. Their hope was to increase their total number of patrons to 230,000 over six-months, as well as attract new types of visitors and secure revenue through the purchase of advance tickets for the event. The exhibit opened at the V&A in March 2013. To promote the exhibit, the museum used specific techniques to track the success of the PR campaign relative to other marketing tactics. It used market research to understand media consumption of different audiences, connected PR and earned media efforts to the museum's business objectives and identified the total audience reach by linking sponsor mentions to its own market research.

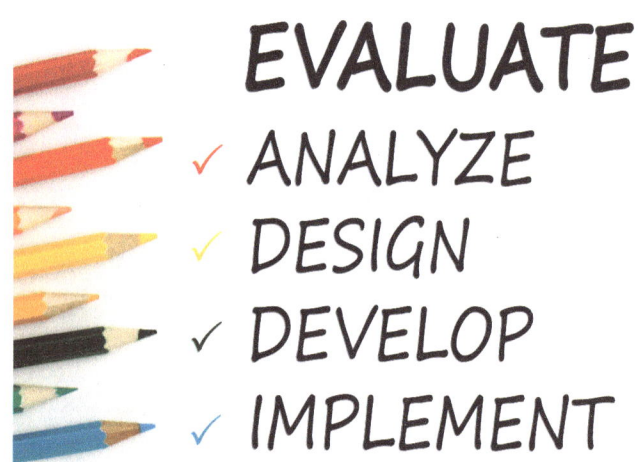

The result? Specific PR tactics such as the press launch event and corresponding media campaigns provided a significant boost to advance ticket sales. The museum also successfully expanded its reach to new audiences across the UK and abroad. Overall, the exhibit exceeded target expectations by 36%, with 27% of the attendees being first time guests and 24% coming from outside the U.K. The museum itself also benefited from the exhibit with more than 10,000 individuals purchasing memberships to the V&A.

SOURCE: International Association for the Measurement and Evaluation of Communications (AMEC).

The case outlined above showcases how PR techniques can be effectively used to promote communication campaigns, both domestically and abroad. It also illustrates how PR technqiues can be broken out and measured independently relative to other program elements. Now that you have learned how to plan a public relations campaign and create supporting content, it is important to understand how to measure and evaluate the success of it in the marketplace.

EARLY ROOTS OF PR MEASUREMENT AND EVALUATION

In the early 2000s, with the pervasiveness of web-based media and the increasing influence of social media, it was clear the public relations industry was entering a new dimension. Gone were the days when the success of a public relations campaign was defined by the number of column inches of editorial coverage in the daily newspaper or total audience reach of the publications that picked up a release. Such techniques date back to the early days of public relations with *The Publicity Bureau* in Boston in the early 1900s (Cutlip 1994). To gauge the success of the firm's work for the railroad companies, the Publicity Bureau used a system called the "The Barometer." Created by the Publicity Bureau, this technique involved tracking the attitudes

of editors and the media's use of the firm's materials. Media outlets were then categorized as being either "Good" or "Bad" depending upon their expressed opinion toward the railroad industry (Cutlip 1994, 21). It was this work that laid the foundation for today's measurement and evaluation techniques.

Early measurement companies were commonly referred to as cuttings agencies, with their sole purpose being to monitor press coverage for clients. But, it was not until the early 1930s when Arthur W. Page, who introduced opinion research widely at AT&T, that a formal system for measuring and evaluating the success of public relations campaigns was developed. In 1932 and 1933, AT&T, under Page's direction, conducted two studies tracking the success of its news dissemination to the media. Page used the number of company mentions in the media outlet and the resulting total of column inches of coverage as metrics of success (Griese 2001). This marks the first time an organization used a structured framework to measure the success of its public relations efforts.

By the end of the 1930s, measurement and evaluation methods were increasing in popularity across the United States, notably by government agencies (Lee 2006). The city of Toledo, Ohio, for example, monitored and interpreted its media publicity. "Ninety-one per cent of more than 72,000 clippings, representing newspaper circulations totaling more than one and half millions, were regarded as favorable to the city's interests" (Bachelor, 214). In Europe, the practice of PR measurement and evaluation also started to increase in popularity. For example, in the United Kingdom, governing bodies from cities and municipalities tracked coverage in local newspapers for opinions of their actions (Hill 1937).

PR MEASUREMENT IN THE 21ST CENTURY

Despite these early successes it was only in the early 2000s, PR measurement and evaluation became a mainstay of the modern PR program. A survey of public relations industry professionals in the late 1980s revealed they "lacked confidence to promote evaluation methods to employers and clients" (Watson 2001). Fast-forward a few decades, things have certainly changed for the better.

In 2010, a group of PR practitioners from 33 countries met at a conference in Barcelona, Spain, organized by the International Association for Measurement and Evaluation of Communication (Margee 2010) resulting in the creation of

CHAPTER 7: PR MEASUREMENT AND EVALUATION

> ### The Barcelona Principles 2.0
> 1. Goal-setting and measurement are an integral part of any public relations program.
> 2. Measuring communication outcomes is recommended over simply measuring outputs.
> 3. The effect on overall organizational performance can and should be gauged where possible.
> 4. Media measurement requires the use of both quantitative and qualitative techniques.
> 5. Advertising Value Equivalents (AVEs) cannot effectively measure the value of public relations.
> 6. Social Media must be measured and evaluated consistently with other media channels.
> 7. Measurement and evaluation should be conducted in a way that is replicable, transparent, and valid for all steps in the process.
>
> **(SOURCE:** International Association for the Measurement and Evaluation of Communication)

The Barcelona Principles, a set of seven guidelines to measure the efficiency of PR campaigns. It marks the first time a comprehensive framework for measuring and evaluating the effectiveness of public relations campaigns was released (*PR News*, 3/29/18). These principles provide basic guidelines for public relations practitioners to use in judging the effectiveness of their programs. An updated version of these guidelines was released in 2015, *The Barcelona Principles 2.0* (see box below).

In addition to the Barcelona Principles, other organizations have developed frameworks and best practices to support effective measurement and evaluation of PR programs. In 2011, PRSA and the American Statistical Association (Source: PRSA) joined forces to assemble a best-practices guide focused on the inclusion of statistics in PR campaigns. It highlights their value and purpose in supporting a program. PRSA partnered with the Institute for Public Relations (IPR) to create a database of resources PR practitioners can use to effectively demonstrate the tangible value of their work (Source: PRSA). The Institute for Public Relations' Management Measurement Commission assembled an online resource bank of information regarding measurement standards and evaluation best practices (Source: IPR).

In June 2011, the AMEC released a paper entitled, "Valid Metrics for PR Measurement: Putting the Principles into Action." Using the Barcelona Principles as the framework, the AMEC outlines its guidelines for designing and implementing effective PR measurement and evaluation models. Recently, the AMEC launched its "Interactive Integrated Evaluation Framework" (amec.org) to help PR practitioners create effective and credible measurement tools. As noted by the AMEC, "We wanted to make something that took users on a clear measurement journey from planning and setting SMART

Barcelona Principles: A set of seven guidelines to measure the efficiency of PR campaigns developed by the IAMEC

objectives, defining success, setting targets though to implementation and the measurement and evaluation itself. Most importantly, we wanted to find a mechanism that would help credible and meaningful measurement pervade the industry" (amec.org). We will explain this framework in greater detail later in the chapter.

IMPORTANCE OF PR MEASUREMENT AND EVALUATION

Despite these resources, many public relations professionals still face an uphill battle when it comes to measuring and evaluating the success of a client's campaign. As noted by Amit Jain in a July 2014 article in *PR Week*, "The Communications industry finds itself groping the dark when it comes to identifying the outcomes of PR and corporate communication and its value to an organization" (Jain 2014). The main challenge is traditional media relations is only one element of a modern public relations campaign. Today, public relations practitioners are implementing strategies and engaging in tactics traditionally done by marketers or advertisers. Public relations efforts are part of a company's larger communication program, making it much more challenging to measure and evaluate its individual contribution to a campaign.

Regardless of the challenges posed to public relations professionals, the measurement and evaluation of public relations campaigns is increasingly important. Organizations want to see results and understand the value associated with them. The measurement and evaluation component of a campaign should not be created after the campaign is launched but, instead, in conjunction with its overall framework.

DEVELOPING A PROGRAM FRAMEWORK

Speak with Your Client

Before you can think about designing a program, you have to speak with your client. The meeting happens after the client signs a contract with the primary focus being an overview of their business, followed by a Q&A session.

In addition to discussing the fundamentals of the business, be sure to cover the following areas:

1. **Metrics:** You cannot read your client's mind, so it is important to ask their definition of success. Is it the number of times their story appears in the media, the number of retweets they receive, or the number of products they sell? After you ask the "What," be sure to follow up with the "Why?" As noted by Matt Kucharski and Heidi Wright in their article, "For Best PR Results, Follow the 3 O's of Metrics: Outputs, Outtakes & Outcomes" a successful measurement program "should be a continuous effort used to adjust or alter a program to improve its effectiveness. It's not a performance review—it's a diagnostic."

    Metrics: The criteria used to measure the success of a program or campaign.

2. **ROI versus Something Else:** In addition to understanding your client's metrics, it is important to discover their idea of a successful campaign. Is it based on making their money back—media-generated versus cost to support the efforts—or an intangible asset such as reputation or perceived leadership (Kucharski and Wright 2012)?

    ROI: Return on Investment.

PR practitioners need to ask clients the tough questions

Detailed conversations with clients will lead to the development of an effective measurement and evaluation program.

The AMEC Framework

3. **Definition of Value:** As noted by Kucharski and Wright, there are three types of value: monetary, utility, and brand. Ask your client how they value public relations and its role relative to the overall success of the organization.

    - Monetary Value: Cost of a campaign versus revenue generated from it.
    - Utility Value: Improvements resulting from campaign efforts.
    - Brand Value: Enhancements or degradation of the organization's reputation.

> Monetary Value: Cost of a campaign versus revenue generated from it.
>
> Utility Value: Improvements resulting from campaign efforts.
>
> Brand Value: Enhancements or degradation in an organization's reputation.

Design the Campaign Program

After working with your clients to answer these questions, this next step is the design of the public relations program including the measurement and evaluation component. The AMEC provides a road map for the design of such a program.

1. **Set SMART Objectives:** An objective is something with a measurable impact. A SMART objective can be viewed as a specifically defined objective, the idea of which has been circulating in the business community for decades. It was used by Peter Drucker in 1995 and by G.T. Doran in 1991, but it is unclear who first coined the term (CMI, March 2011). The acronym **SMART** stands for: specific, measurable, achievable, realistic, and timely. Each is defined as the following:

    - Specific—Clear description of what is expected.
    - Measurable—Definition of progress and associated timeframe.
    - Achievable—Attainable goals based upon resources and landscape.
    - Realistic—Focus on the long-term goals and associated outcomes instead of short term tactics.
    - Timely—Timeframe to support measurement framework.

    The three to five objectives you establish with your client should support the focus and goals of the campaign at hand. You cannot assume all objectives can apply to all programs.

> SMART objectives: Refers to the idea of a specifically defined objective that stands for: Specific, Measurable, Achievable, Realistic and Timely

2. **Determine Logical Inputs:** Inputs are items such as the target publics of the campaign, as well as the strategic PR plan to support it. The plan includes such things as situation analysis, strategies, tactics, resources, and budget.

> Inputs: Items such as the target publics of the campaign, as well as the strategic PR plan to support it.

3. **Establish Activities:** In this context, activities are the work that goes into supporting a strategic plan—field testing, market research, materials production, and tactics implemented. This includes a combination of tactics leveraging all aspects of the PESO model: paid, earned, shared, and owned opportunities.

4. **Track Outputs:** Using both qualitative and quantitative methods, this is where you evaluate the results of the activities. You are looking for who and what reacted to the campaign's techniques. Examples include: number of retweets of a social media post, frequency of product/service reviews, attendance at an event, media coverage of an announcement, or response to an advertisement.

5. **Observe Outtakes:** The outtakes are the response targeted publics have to campaign techniques. As explained by the AMEC, "How attentive were they to the content, what was their recall, how well understood is the topic, did the audience engage with the content or did the audience subscribe to more information" (AMEC).

6. **Interpret Outcomes:** With outcomes, you look to measure the effect of a campaign on the targeted publics. These effects usually come in the form of changes of opinion, awareness, attitude, and understanding.

7. **Judge the Impact:** In this final step, you try to understand the overall effect a campaign has on a client's business. At this time, the objective is to see if the campaign results in overall organizational improvements such as reputation, client or supplier relationships, sales, donations, or policy changes.

Programs Depend Upon the Client

When designing a measurement and evaluation metric, it is important to realize there is no one way to do it. PR practitioners need to remember their client's needs and definition of success, then put together the program to support it. Regardless of the program's design, there are three areas that are scrutinized: campaign objectives, program effectiveness, and budget (Wilson, Ogden, and Wilson 2019, 219). At the end of the day, the most important thing to any client is positive coverage of a campaign across targeted outlets. If they see the coverage, they are happy, and if not, they question the value of the campaign.

Executives who understand the value of public relations are more supportive of it.

In addition to justifying the cost of a campaign, effective measurement and evaluation programs help executives realize the overall value of the public relations function. As noted by PRSA, in organizations where the executives understand and appreciate the concept of public relations, the effectiveness of campaigns is even greater. Executives who believe in public relations appreciate the positive effect it can have on a business in everything from raising its profile in the marketplace to navigating a crisis, to supporting a CSR program (Source: PRSA). For those who truly believe in public relations, the value of a multifaceted program outweighs the financial costs associated with it.

SPECIFIC ELEMENTS OF MEASUREMENT AND EVALUATION

Now that we have talked about the importance of a program and explored the AMEC's framework, we will zero in on the four critical elements of measurement and evaluation: outputs, outtakes, outcomes, and impacts. They are defined as follows:

THE PRACTICE OF PUBLIC RELATIONS

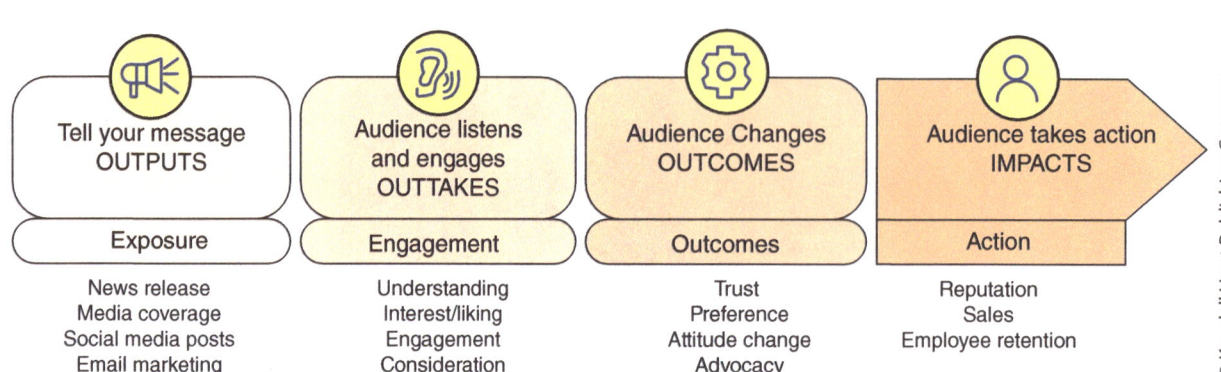

Communication objectives: How we communicate

© Kendall Hunt Publishing Company. Adapted from AXIA.

Outputs: The results of campaign activities

Outputs: *Anything you proactively distribute that communicates your message, as well as the resulting media coverage.* This could be anything from a press release to social media post to a Tweet to a speech. By tracking where the news gets picked up and the public's reaction to it, you can gauge whether the campaign has been successful in reaching the right people (Source: Faith PR).

Outtakes: The response targeted publics have to campaign techniques.

Outtakes: *The interpretation of your messages in the marketplace.* Your goal is to judge whether messages were received by the target audience and if they resonated with them. This can be measured in a variety of ways, including: tracking how messages were interpreted by news media, reading responses to social media posts, and viewing the number of retweets (Faith PR).

© DreamStockIcons/Shutterstock.com

Outcomes: *The change in attitude or behavior resulting from a campaign.* This involves observing the actions targeted audiences took as a result of exposure to the campaign. The complexity can vary based upon the campaign's focus—sometimes it is easy if the goal is simply to increase sales of a product. Other times, it can be more challenging if you are looking to alter a change in behavior or an individual's way of thinking (Faith PR).

Impacts: *The effect a PR campaign has on an organization's overall business objectives.* Specifically, how a PR effort either positively or negatively influences an organization's key metrics. This can be complicated as it often varies between organizations. It can include anything from the number of products sold,

160

to the organization's reputation in the market, to the legislative success it has in influencing local, state, or federal governments (Wilson, Ogden, and Wilson 2019, 219).

As noted by the team at the Faith PR, "Measuring allows for analysis into your customer base and target markets, it can dissect what PR is working and, more importantly, what isn't and shows to your customer; that if you're willing to react positively—you are making changes to benefit them."

Outcomes: The effect of a campaign on the targeted publics.

Impacts: The overall effect a campaign had on a client's business.

TIMELINE FOR MEASUREMENT AND EVALUATION

When building the measurement and evaluation program, it is important to keep in mind everything cannot be measured at the same time. In fact, measurement and evaluation should have a timeline similar to that of the program's execution:

- **Outputs** are judged in the initial phases of a public relations campaign. When measuring and evaluating outputs, the most important question to ask: *Did the campaign's message get exposed to the targeted audience?* (Ochieng 2018).
- **Outtakes** are reviewed in the initial weeks of a program. When evaluating outtakes, be sure to consider: *Does the target audience understand the purpose of the campaign?* In determining this, you want to consider what did the audience say or do as a result of seeing the campaign? This can be done by tracking the audience's engagement, looking at the number of shares and tracking comments (Ochieng 2018).
- **Outcomes** are evaluated at the end of a campaign or at the halfway point, depending upon the length of program. The primary question you want to answer: *What was the result of the campaign?* For a public relations program, this might mean a measurable change in knowledge, attitude, or behavior. It could also focus on one aspect of the PR effort such as social

media or an influencer program (Ochieng 2018). Outcomes are difficult to measure relative to the other Os, because they are hard to track. Kucharski and Wright offer a three-step approach for measuring outcomes:

- **Step 1: Conduct research prior to launch to establish a benchmark:** It is impossible to show the impact a campaign has on attitudes or behaviors, if you don't understand the baseline.
- **Step 2: Establish clear and quantifiable objectives:** The more precisely you can define the objectives, the greater the likelihood you will be successful. Use specific numbers rather than vague terms and establish a time frame.
- **Step 3: Measure the success of the overall program, not just the tactics.** You want to judge the overall impact of the program, rather than just the distribution of a release.
- **Impacts** are also measured at the end of a campaign. The big question to ask here: *How did the PR campaign contribute to the organization's overall business objectives?* This is also a tough factor to measure but possibilities include: reputation, sales, or donations (Wilson, Ogden, and Wilson 2019, 219).

Each of the three Os is going to be specific to your client. It is important to discuss each in detail prior to development of the program. If clients don't participate in defining of each of these items, they are more likely to question the results if they aren't what they expected (Kucharski and Wright 2012).

ESSENTIALS FOR SUCCESSFUL MEASUREMENT AND EVALUATION

The more specific and quantifiable the tools you use to measure and evaluate the success of a PR campaign, the more credible and irrefutable the results will be. That being said, there are a couple of things to keep in mind:

- **Remember the Basics:** As noted by Raleigh Cavey at Empower in his June 2019, *PR Week* article, "Too often, measurement is retroactively gathered when pulling together campaign reports. It may seem obvious, but it's worth repeating: ask yourself from the very beginning, 'What is the most important metric?'" Including tactics such as brand awareness surveys to establish benchmarks at the beginning of a campaign is vital for proving success.

- **Partner with Clients and Colleagues:** Work with your client to establish objectives and metrics as it will improve the likelihood they will appreciate the results. Also, leverage the experience of colleagues as their war stories could become your successes if you can learn from their mistakes. As explained by SEO expert Ben Sprangler, "holistic integration makes every channel work harder. So, start by asking your colleagues in web development what keyword and search opportunities are out there. Then, tailor your comms and content with these keywords in mind" (Cavey 2019). Ask professionals from other areas how integration of their measurement techniques into yours could help showcase results.
- **It's About the 2Qs: Qualitative and Quantitative:** When measuring success, qualitative or qualitative just won't do it. You need to use a combination of both techniques. As explained by Kieran Fagan, VP of communications at CVS Health, "There's a difference between measuring and counting" (Cavey 2019). You cannot base the success of a campaign on statistical results, it needs to include observed behavior or verbal feedback. Numbers without insightful context do not provide meaning, and qualitative feedback without numbers do not prove business results. It is essential to incorporate tools that capture both perspectives in the campaign's measurement component or else you risk leaving your client with many unanswered questions.

Successful measurement programs strike a balance between quality and quantity.

MEASURING AND EVALUATING SOCIAL MEDIA CAMPAIGNS

How does social media measurement differ measuring traditional media? Greatly. For one thing, you can measure the results of a campaign almost instantly. It is also vastly different in many other ways. To start, let's review the two ways of doing it:

- **Ongoing Analytics**—Provides continual monitoring of a campaign with daily delivery of results. This system of monitoring is good for tracking the changes in opinion about a company and its brand over the long term.

- **Campaign-focused Metrics**—Involves monitoring of a campaign before its launch and after its completion. This type of monitoring provides insights on the influence of deliberate, targeted marketing initiatives and specific to the campaign it is supporting.

Most social media measurement programs involve a combination of both techniques. As with all communication outreach efforts, it is important to design the measurement and evaluation program before launching it (Davis 2012). We touched on social media measurement in the last chapter as it relates to the creation of content. Now, we will look at the nuances of designing a measurement and evaluation campaign specific to social media.

DESIGNING A SOCIAL MEDIA MEASUREMENT PROGRAM

Step 1: Establish Program Goals

Similar to the design of a measurement and evaluation platform for a public relations program, the first step in designing a social media measurement program is to determine the goals. Approach it the same way you would in determining your public relations goals, speak with your client. In this discussion, be sure to ask the following questions:

- What do you hope to achieve through the launch of a social media campaign?
- Which social media channels do you think are the most important in fulfilling these goals?
- What do you want customers or potential customers to do as a result of seeing your social media content? Read it, repost it, share it, or buy a product/service after seeing it? Something else?

Step 2: Design a Measurement System

There are five things to consider when establishing the measurement framework: awareness, engagement, traffic, fans/advocates, and share of voice. Each one can and should be measured differently (Davis 2012):

- For **awareness**, you want to determine how far your message has spread. To track this, you use metrics such as reach, exposure, and volume.
- If you are looking at **engagement**, you are trying to see how much your campaign yields interactions with the public. You want to look at the number of comments, reposts, retweets, and replies the campaign receives.
- If you are hoping to drive **traffic** to your website, you will look for the number of times the URL is shared, clicks, and conversions.

Likes, shares, and retweets are essential components of social media measurement

- If you are trying to discover **fans and advocates**, you will look to see who is contributing and the number of followers they have.
- If you want to build your influence and increase your organization's **share of voice**, you will gauge your volume compared to your competitors. This is where you look to determine how much people are talking about your company relative to others in the market.

Step 3: Launch the Program

After establishing the primary metrics, assemble a toolbox to measure them. Some social media channels offer their own metrics system, while others require the use of third-party tools. In some cases, you may decide to create your own APIs specific to your client's goals and objectives. Since most social analytic tools happen in real-time, it is essential to set up the tracking system before launching the program. Otherwise, you are likely to miss capturing some early data.

PR TIP

Using charts and visuals to report campaign results, can bring them to life for a client. Numbers on a page may show success but visuals can showcase the enormity of it (Davis 2012). This will help client appreciate the magnitude of your efforts.

Step 4: Track Your Results

Just like measuring the results of a traditional PR program, you will need to establish some benchmarks. With social media, these come from the figures gathered in the initial days or weeks of a campaign. Usually, you will be looking to measure your campaign's success in two areas:

- *Results versus Expectations:* How did the campaign do versus the original predictions?
- *Results versus Competition:* How did the campaign perform relative to the competition?

Given that social media channels yield an incredible amount of data, it is important to determine a reporting schedule that supports—not overwhelms—the client's objectives. This could be anything from daily to weekly to monthly depending upon the focus of the campaign. When calculating results, be sure to include benchmarks so the client appreciates the enormity of the campaign's success.

Step 5: Tweak and Repeat

The last step is to monitor—and if necessary—adjust your measurement program. The beauty of social media measurement is also the challenge—there are so many things to be examined it can become overwhelming. It is important to stay focused on program objectives and keep three primary things in mind: How are the metrics doing? What are we missing? What has become irrelevant? Think about what you can improve, make the necessary adjustments, and then continue the measurement and monitoring process. In doing this, you'll want to review your initial program goals and make sure the metrics are still supporting your program's objectives.

> "PR can influence (business outcomes) metrics, unquestionably. Getting the right audience is absolutely our job. We see PR's impact on search, social and media. But ultimately, at the end of the day, we do not control those down funnel functions, and I would no more hold PR accountable to a potentially bad sales team than I would hold advertising's performance to customer service metrics."
> —*Christopher Penn, Vice President of Marketing Technology at Shift Communications*

STRATEGIES FOR PROFESSIONAL SUCCESS

In this chapter, we have learned how to create, develop, and implement a framework for measuring and evaluating the success of a communications program. As measurement is becoming increasingly important, knowing the best way to speak with a client and create a framework for their program is paramount. Writer Melissa Hoffman offers a few great ideas for speaking with clients about tricky subjects such as measurement and evaluation programs.

Identify Goals Early: Meet with your client at the start of the relationship and discuss the potential PR program in detail with them. Ask them for their goals and overall program objectives. In her article, Hoffman notes a comment by Annie Scranton, founder and president of Pace Public Relations, "Without clearly defined goals, nothing is possible." As Hoffman explains, "locating the end-posts will allow a strategy to be formed that respects pain points and helps to deliver ROI." For example, suggests Hoffman, if a client refuses to speak to the media but a goal is media coverage then there needs to be "a thoughtful conversation" between the client and the PR team.

Develop Client Relationship Based on Trust: Without a sense of trust between the client and the PR professional, a successful campaign is nearly impossible. Early in the relationship, it is important to ask your client the tough questions and listen carefully to their answers. Be honest in your opinion of a situation—especially a potentially challenging one. Hoffman looks to Patrick Gevas, vice president of GreenRoom for insights in this area, "It may sound cliché, but having symbiotic trust with a client is critical to navigating potentially sensitive issues that come your way," Gevas said. "It may be that trust that allows you to speak more candidly if they botch an interview and provide a teachable moment and change course. It may also be the thing that comes into play when a damaging decision or piece of messaging comes across your desk."

Remember: Patience Is a Virtue: Sometimes there are decisions or opportunities that are time-sensitive, that's probably where the phrase "here today, gone tomorrow" comes from. There will be times when the PR practitioners realize the opportunity of a media interview or event but the client refuses it. "Often, it's been because of a bad experience or a time where the client felt unprepared or lacked confidence in front of the media," said Gevas. "While there are some very bright and innovative thinkers, they may struggle with articulation in front of a camera or even another person who is asking questions they aren't used to." If this is the case, try to understand the client's perspective and gracefully decline. But be sure to take note of the potential rewards the opportunity could have delivered in the event it comes up later with the client.

Republished with permission of Access Intelligence LLC (MD), from "4 Tips for Success with Your Difficult Client," by Melissa Hoffmann, *PR News*, October 18, 2018; permission conveyed through Copyright Clearance Center, Inc.

EXECUTIVE SUMMARY

Now that you have finished reading this chapter, you should:

- Understand the importance of measurement and evaluation in public relations.
- Realize the different stages and facets of the measurement and evaluation process.
- Appreciate the role of measurement and evaluation in supporting a PR campaign.
- Recognize the various terms and techniques of the measurement and evaluation process.
- Acknowledge the difference in measuring social media campaigns versus traditional public relations campaigns.

KEY TERMS

Barcelona Principles: A set of seven guidelines to measure the efficiency of PR campaigns developed by the IAMEC. *p. 153*

Brand Value: Enhancements or degradation in an organization's reputation. *p. 157*

Impacts: The overall effect a campaign had on a client's business. *p. 161*

Inputs: Items such as the target publics of the campaign, as well as the strategic PR plan to support it. *p. 157*

Metrics: The criteria used to measure the success of a program or campaign. *p. 155*

Monetary Value: Cost of a campaign versus revenue generated from it. *p. 157*

Outcomes: The effect of a campaign on the targeted publics. *p. 161*

Outputs: The results of campaign activities. *p. 160*

Outtakes: The response targeted publics have to campaign techniques. *p. 160*

ROI: Return on Investment. *p. 155*

SMART Objectives: Refers to the idea of a specifically defined objective that stands for: Specific, Measurable, Achievable, Realistic and Timely. *p. 157*

Utility Value: Improvements resulting from campaign efforts. *p. 157*

DISCUSSION QUESTIONS

1. Prior to the early 2000s, how was the success of a PR campaign judged?
2. What are the Barcelona Principles? Why are they so important?
3. Why is the measurement and evaluation of a PR program critical to its success?
4. What are the most important elements of a measurement and evaluation campaign?
5. What are the differences between measuring and evaluating traditional PR campaigns versus social media campaigns?

PART 2: THE PRACTICE OF PUBLIC RELATIONS

CHAPTER 8
MEDIA RELATIONS

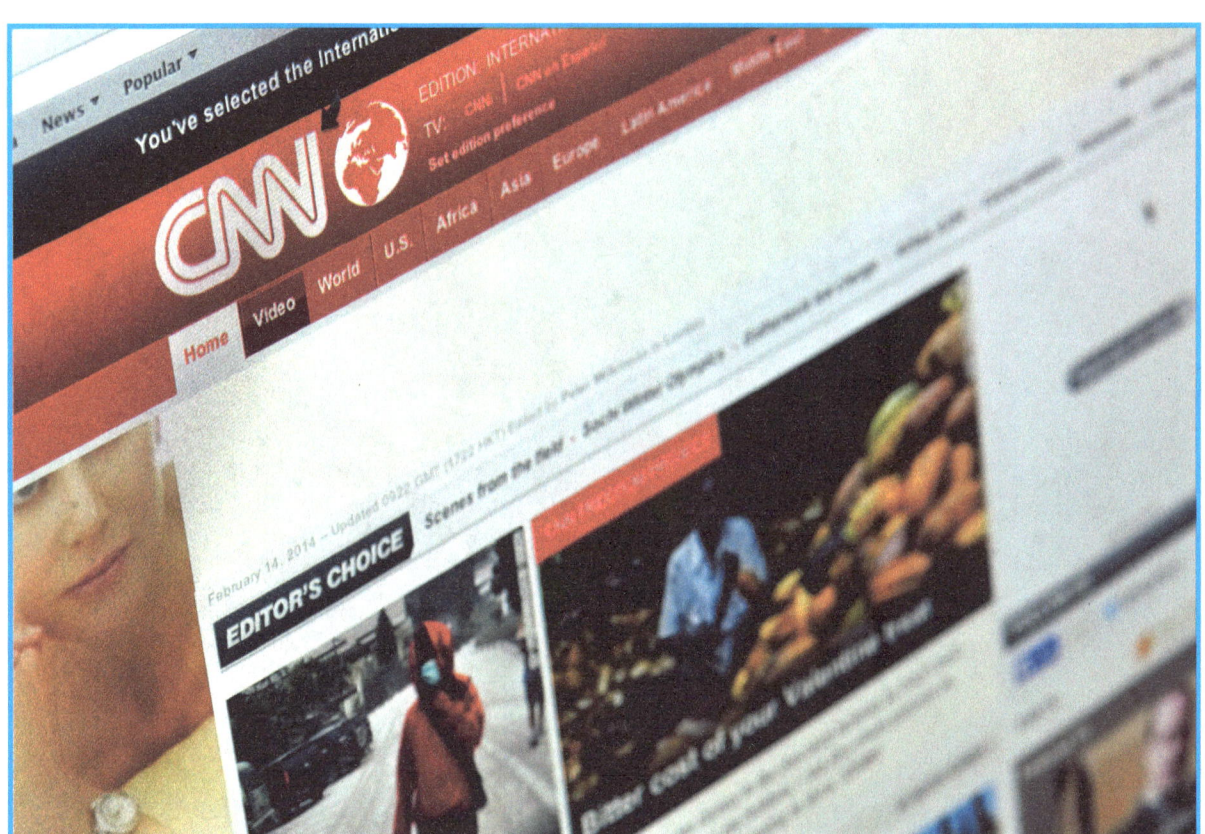

Media visionary Ted Tuner created the concept of the 24-hour news cycle with his founding of CNN in 1980. It was the first TV channel to offer 24-hour news coverage and to feature the all-news format.

CHAPTER OUTLINE

Public Relations versus Media Relations
Definition of Media Relations
Importance of Media Relations
Establishing and Developing Media Relationships
      Establishing the Drumbeat
      Role of the PR Professional
      Approaching the Media
Types of Media
Strategies for Professional Success
Executive Summary
Key Terms
Discussion Questions

CHAPTER OBJECTIVES

After studying this chapter, you should be able to:

1. Understand the difference between public relations and media relations.
2. Define media relations.
3. Appreciate the influential role media relations plays in influencing a consumer's purchase decision.
4. Understand how to establish and curate relationships with members of the media.
5. Identify the different types of media.

Ripped from the Headlines

Pure Sweets is an independent, vegan, organ, kosher and gluten-free bakery headquartered in Philadelphia, Pa. Since opening their doors in 2009, this boutique bakery has experienced the media relations roller coaster. They employed large, global PR firms and small solopreneur operators, each time only enjoying blips of media success. Why? They were employing the wrong media relations strategy, one primarily focused on trying to be all things to all people. The reality is with the specialized nature of their products, Pure Sweets needed to leverage their differences. Eventually, that is what happened. After being approached by a start-up PR agency with direct industry experience, Pure Sweets took a leap a faith and signed with the firm. The agency promised strategic media outreach, consistent placements and innovative approaches. The big question — would it work? Within 30 days of signing the contract, the firm secured a media opportunity for Pure Sweets with the Philadelphia Inquirer. The story focused on the Passover holiday and appeared in both the Inquirer's print and online editions. Less than 24 hours after the story ran in the publication, the bakery's sales soared. Pure Sweets secured new customers, experienced growth in sales and established itself as one of the leading boutique bakeries in the Philadelphia area.

As showcased in the piece above, strategic media relations can make or break a brand. When done effectively, a strong media relations program can be a company's most important asset in times of success or crisis. As we move into the next part of this book, we will explore the relationship between public relations and each of the communication disciplines commonly found in most organizations as noted in the PPR model in Chapter 1, including: Community Relations, Crisis Management, Customer Relations, Employee Relations, Investor Relations, Media Relations and Public Affairs. We will begin by looking at one of the most important areas- media relations.

PUBLIC RELATIONS VERSUS MEDIA RELATIONS

To fully understand the concept of media relations, it is important to define it relative to public relations. Many people think media relations is public relations, but the reality is there is a huge difference between the two terms. As explained in Chapter 1 of this book, **public relations,** is defined by the Public Relations Society of America (PRSA), is "a strategic communication process that builds mutually beneficial relationships between organizations and their publics." Publics are the audiences a company targets in its communication outreach: employees, customers, community members, media, analysts, suppliers, and investors.

Media relations refers to a specific part of the public relations process. It focuses on the way a company interacts with one of its publics: the news media. This includes every type of journalist ranging from editors at daily newspapers such as *The New York Times, The Washington Post,* and *The Wall Street Journal* to on-air reporters with CNN or CBS news online media to the DJs on SiriusXM or local radio stations. It also covers the relationships with citizen journalists—individuals who are not members of the media who report on news events via such avenues as social media or blogging.

The Universal Accreditation Board for the APR , a certification program for PR professionals, explains: "The goal of media relations is to establish and maintain solid and ethical relationships with media for accurate, balanced, timely information release."

A few other distinctions between the two concepts:

- **Channels:** Public relations uses multiple channels to communicate with its many publics while media relations uses one—the press. Most PR professionals leverage a variety of tools including blogs and social media posts, thought-leadership articles and special events to support their efforts. In media relations, PR pros use the media as the platform to disseminate their information to targeted publics. Instead of reaching out directly to targeted publics through social media posts, events, or advertisements, the press is used to provide third-party validation of the concepts. Media coverage is often referred to as earned media, publicity gained through proactive communication campaigns. An example would be coverage of a company's announcement in the *Sunday New York Times* versus a billboard advertisement on the side of the highway. A news story in *The New York Times* is going to be much more powerful and influential than a billboard ad (Roolf 2017).

Media Relations: A specific part of the public relations process. Specifically, it focuses on the way a company communicates with one public: the news media.

Citizen Journalists: Individuals who are not members of the media but report on news events via such avenues as social media or blogging

Earned Media: Third-party coverage of an organization in a media outlet

February 4, 2020, Concord, New Hampshire: Democratic candidate Joe Biden talking to the media after his speech at The International Brotherhood of Electrical Workers Local Union 490.

- **Subsection:** If you have not figured it out by now, public relations and media relations are closely aligned but one is not the other. The best way to think about this is media relations is a subsection of public relations. It is the means by which organizations receive earned media.
- **Create versus Pitch:** Public relations is where key messages are developed, appeals are set, and talking points are written. Media relations is the broadcasting of these thoughts and ideas to press and ultimately the external world.
- **Audience as Platform:** Media relations is unique as not only is the media the delivery mechanism for earned media, it is also the focus of the practitioner's efforts. The audience and platform are one in the same. This cannot be said about the overarching concept of public relations.

Owned Media: Promotional content created by an organization and placed in select media outlets for a fee

Consideration Stage: The initial stages in the consumer decision-making process

IMPORTANCE OF MEDIA RELATIONS

The role of the media in helping to develop a corporate brand is undeniable. A 2014 study conducted by research giant Nielsen reveals earned media is the most effective way of influencing consumers throughout the purchase process. This study of nearly 1,000 consumers, suggests most individuals respond to three types of content: earned media, owned media, and user-generated content. When compared to owned media (branded content), researchers found earned media is 80% more effective at influencing consumers in the early stages of a purchasing decision, commonly referred to as the consideration stage. This holds constant at 80% for the middle stage of the consumer purchasing cycle, called the affinity stage. It drops to 38% in the final stage of the purchase process called the familiarity stage as noted in Figure 8.1.

Affinity Stage: The middle part of the consumer decision-making process where significant thought is given to the purchase decision

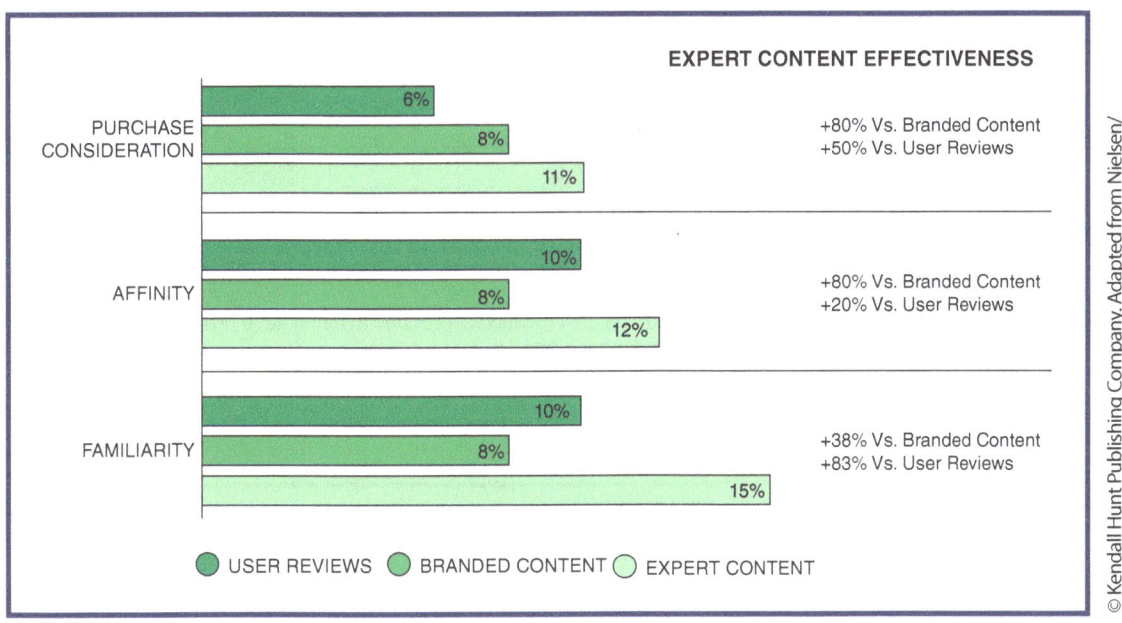

FIGURE 8.1: IMPACT OF CONTENT TYPES ACROSS PURCHASE PROCESS

Another significant finding relates to the concept of objectivity. It turns out 85% of consumers regularly look to third-party sources (news articles and user reviews) when contemplating a purchase. Nearly 70% of consumers read product reviews before making a purchase, and 67% say a positive review from an unbiased source makes them more likely to purchase a product. These facts underscore the importance of earned media to the consumer. It is the single most significant force in influencing a consumer's purchasing decision. In fact, according to the study, earned media increases brand familiarity 88% more than branded marketing content and 50% more than user reviews. These facts showcase the integral role of media relations as part of a comprehensive public relations campaign. In many ways, it is the single most important element of a public relations campaign.

In addition to influencing a consumer's buying decision, media relations impacts the creation and establishment of a company's brand. When a

Familiarity Stage: Final stage of the consumer decision-making process

Objectivity: News stories written without bias

Third-party Sources: Information written about a company that it does not create. This includes news coverage or user reviews.

PRODUCT TYPE	EXPERT CONTENT			USER REVIEWS			BRANDED CONTENT		
	FAMILIARITY	AFFINITY	PURCHASE	FAMILIARITY	AFFINITY	PURCHASE	FAMILIARITY	AFFINITY	PURCHASE
Smartphone	22	13	22	9	6	2	7	10	13
Smart TV	8	6	7	1	9	4	0	7	0
Video Game	30	22	11	25	28	20	17	3	12
Car Seat	28	19	14	11	16	19	19	15	16
Electric Toothbrush	3	12	9	2	16	0	11	10	7
Dryer	18	10	16	21	9	0	10	12	9
New Automobile	6	4	15	4	0	8	6	2	4
Auto Insurance	3	6	5	0	1	2	0	4	1
Camera	19	12	6	11	6	6	16	12	12

Lift presented as difference between pre and post measures, provided in percentage points; darker highlighting indicates relatively strong lift for cateory

pB2. /B2. How familiar are you with the following brands or products?
pB3. /B3. How do you feel about the following brands or products?
pB4a. /B4a. How likely are you to consider purchasing [PRODUCT]?

© Kendall Hunt Publishing Company. Adapted from Nielsen/inPowered MediaLab

FIGURE 8.2: POSITIVE LIFT BY CONTENT AND PRODUCT TYPE (IN PERCENTAGE POINTS)

company receives objective, third-party coverage in a newspaper, magazine, on television or the radio it provides them with a level of credibility and authenticity no amount of advertising can ever achieve. The challenge with media relations is it is not a one-time event. It must be a regular, predictable part of a company's communication program. What does that mean? Developing a plan for regular, proactive media relations efforts encompassing a variety of tactics and techniques selected specifically to engage targeted media. The success of such an effort often comes down to one thing—the drumbeat.

ESTABLISHING AND DEVELOPING MEDIA RELATIONSHIPS

Establishing the Drumbeat

Anyone who has spent any time in the public relations field understands the concept of the drumbeat. Successful media relations is predicated upon the

Drumbeat: The proactive dissemination of a clear, continual flow of information about a company to target media

concept of maintaining a constant and consistent flow of information about a company in the marketplace. That is where the idea of the **drumbeat** comes in. Simply put, it involves the proactive dissemination of a clear, continual flow of information about a company to target media.

Role of the PR Professional

In today's 24 × 7 × 365 news cycle reporters barely have time to think, let alone know everything about every company in their beat. This is where the PR professional and the concept of media relations come into play. In this capacity, it is helpful to think of PR as press relations. The role of the PR professional is to connect the media to the company. In many ways, they represent and help them stay abreast of the organization's developments. This process involves more than simply writing and distributing a press release or calling reporter on a whim with an idea. In order to build successful, long-term relationships, there is a significant amount of work that goes into understanding the publication a journalist writes for, the angles they cover, and their readership. It is this process that is backbone of a successful media relations program.

Securing an interview for an executive involves much more than a simple phone call

Approaching the Media

Step 1: Research

Pitch: The professional approach a media relations will take when proposing a story idea to a reporter

Before developing a *pitch* or contacting a reporter, it is critical to research the angle being considered. You must determine whether it has been used before or if you are offering a fresh perspective. Give thought to what, if any, news outlets have covered the story or a related story in the recent past. Some important things to remember when conducting research for the pitch:

- **Look for the white space:** Identify the media who haven't covered this topic in the past, or a question left unanswered by existing news that only your company can answer.
- **Read the coverage:** Review what the target reporter has written in the past as it provides insight into their writing style and approach. A pitch can then be crafted that specifically addresses a reporter's style and niche, which ultimately ensures a greater likelihood of it being successful (Grossman 2015).
- **Offer a complete package:** Don't just pitch the idea of a story to a reporter but, instead, offer the complete package. Include market statistics, trend insights, customer references, and other third-party ideas when discussing.

Step 2: Craft the Pitch

Think of a pitch as the unique angle you are offering a specific reporter. It usually comes in the form of a brief email or short phone call to a journalist at a newspaper, magazine, radio, or TV station. The goal—generate interest in writing about the company you represent. Usually, a pitch is designed to appeal to the interests and curiosities of one specific reporter. Evergreen pitches don't work; as they are so broad, they appeal to no one. It is important to keep the following things in mind when crafting a pitch—is it:

- Relevant
- Newsworthy
- Brief
- Organized
- Timely

Step 3: Gather Support Materials

In addition to constructing a comprehensive pitch, it is important to anticipate the other elements a reporter many need to complete a news story. Especially if they are operating on a tight deadline, reporters require a significant number of items besides a compelling angle to write a news story including:

- **Executive Spokesperson:** Before going out with a pitch, it is important to decide who from the organization will speak to the media.
- **Talking Points:** Establish the three to five key messages the spokesperson should say in the interview. These thoughts should be supportive of the pitch and reflect the market position of the organization.
- **Supporting Materials:** Finalize the supporting materials for a pitch before making it public. This could include the press release, customer testimonials, corporate fact sheets, executive bios, and supporting visuals.
- **Contributions from Third-Party Experts:** Periodically, a reporter will ask to speak with an industry analyst, financial analyst, or another individual who can provide a third-party perspective on a company. It is important to have these sources lined up in case such a request is made.

- **Q & A:** Develop an in-depth set of questions and answers and review them with the spokesperson prior to the media interview. Such preparation will mitigate the possibility of incorrect responses or an inaccurate story.
- **Pictures or B-Roll:** If you are a publicist or you do product PR, the chances are a reporter is going to request headshots, product shots, and other items. As it can take significant time to receive usage permission, it is best to start the process before pitching the story.

Step 4: Pitch the Story

Regardless of whether the pitch is by email, phone or text, the thought of approaching a reporter can be intimidating, especially to individuals new to the field. Often, there is only one shot to pitch a story and the chance of rejection is high. It is important to be fully prepared before sending the email or picking up the phone. A few things to keep in mind:

- **Don't Skip the Intro:** If it is the first time pitching a specific reporter, be sure to introduce yourself and the company/brand you represent. Avoid jumping right into the pitch as soon as they answer the phone. And, never, ever, make a follow-up to call to confirm a reporter received your pitch or press release. Don't worry—they have it and if interested they will contact you.

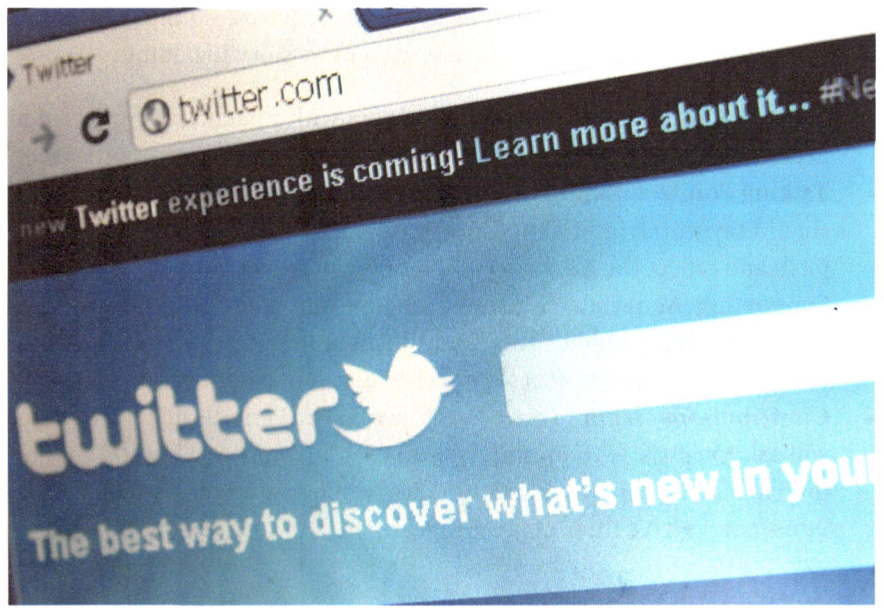

A simple re-tweet of a reporter's story can a long way in building a relationship with them

- **Question the Reporter:** If possible, take time to ask the reporter if they have questions about the company or product you represent. Be sure to inquire as to whether they are open to discussing story ideas and receiving company updates. View the reporter as a partner you are working with to create a positive news piece about the organization you represent.
- **Be Open and Honest:** Trying to work amicably with the reporter from the beginning will make the process much easier and, in all likelihood, more successful. Let the reporter know you will do your best to share relevant and accurate information in accordance with their deadlines.
- **Show Your Human Side:** It is okay to ask a reporter how their weekend was or share a few facts about yourself. Remember, you are trying to build a relationship where you work together to create factual, well-written news stories about the company you represent. As explained in the *AdWeek* article "The PR Pro's Guide to Effective Media Relations," written by Andrew Grossman, "These kinds of genuine relationships extend beyond the beat that reporter is assigned to and can help both of you in your careers down the line."
- **Leverage Social Media:** Most reporters are required to maintain some sort of social media presence in connection to their media outlet. Use the reporter's social media presence to strengthen your relationship with them by reading their stories, commenting on them, and sharing them with others. Such actions will show the reporter you value their work in the industry. As Grossman explains, "Take advantage of the opportunity to connect via platforms like Twitter, where it's expected and even encouraged to interact with the wider public, not just close-knit friends. This can help you stand out in a crowded inbox."

Step 5: Develop the Relationship

Your first conversation with the reporter should not be your last. Try to think about the story from the reporter's perspective and treat the reporter in the manner in which you would like to be treated. It is important to remember:

- **Respect Deadlines:** Do your best to beat not meet a reporter's deadline. Be sure to get them the requested information as soon as you review it; don't procrastinate sending it. Delivering information that is timely and accurate will go a long way in establishing a long-term relationship with a reporter.
- **Pitch an Exclusive:** If coverage by one specific news outlet is vital to the success of a campaign, try offering an exclusive the reporter. This could be in the form of a one-on-one interview with a company's CEO or CFO, preview of a news release, interview with a high-profile customer, or anything else you think the reporter would find compelling. Be sure to only offer what you can deliver.

 **PR TIP**

Be sure to clarify with a reporter their preferred means of contact and the best time to contact them. Most reporters are happy to share their schedules and appreciate being asked.

- **Promote Media Coverage:** Once you receive coverage, share it with the world. Let the reporter know you appreciate their work by sharing the article on social media, including it in a corporate newsletter, and posting it the newsroom on the company's website. Reporters want to know an audience is engaged and actively reading their work. They will appreciate any support in showcasing it to the public (Grossman 2015).
- **Remember: It's Not All About You:** Let the reporter know you are interested in all the things they write, not just those about your company. Follow them on social media and comment or share when it is appropriate. This will help you understand the way the reporter thinks, how they write, and the approach they take. It is also likely to strengthen your relationship with them.
- **Reporter as Expert:** Consider featuring a reporter as a guest speaker or participant at an industry roundtable or webinar. They know your company's field better than anyone else as they are constantly pitched story and trend ideas from competitors. Don't forget—it is their job to know what is going on in the industry.
- **Stay Top of Mind:** Don't just contact a reporter when you want to pitch a story idea to them—contact them when it makes sense. If you come across an article or have insights you think they might find interesting, don't be hesitant to reach out to them. Remember, you are trying to establish and build a relationship with them. That cannot be done with pitch calls every six to eight weeks, it comes by going out of your way to be a credible source of ideas and information to them.

TYPES OF MEDIA

It is important to keep in mind that establishing and building relationships with the media is not limited to traditional type of reporters such as those from local or regional newspapers or a broadcast outlet such as CNN. It should include a mix of traditional and emerging outlets at multiple levels, including local, regional, national, and global levels:

Newspapers: *The New York Times, The Wall Street Journal, The Los Angeles Times, The Philadelphia Inquirer, The Miami Herald, The Times of London (UK), The Sydney Morning Herald (Australia), The Middle East Times (Middle East), El Diario (Bolivia),* and *The News International (Pakistan)*

Wire Services/News Syndicates: *Reuters, Associated Press (AP), Dow Jones, Bloomberg, China News Service, Agence France-Presse, Deutsche Presse-Agentur GmbH,* and *African News Agency*

Magazines: *Bloomberg Business Week, Forbes, Fortune, The Economist, Vogue, Harper's Bazaar, The New Yorker, New York Magazine, Elle, Good House*

Keeping, GQ, House & Garden

Radio: NPR, Sirius XM, CBS-FM, and many local/regional stations

Television: BBC, BBC World, CNN, CNN International, CNBV MSNBC, FOX, SKY News, Reuters, BSKYB, ABC, NBC, CBS, PBS, ESPN, as well as thousands of local, regional, and international affiliates

Blogs/Chat Rooms/Podcasts: Millions of different blogs, podcasts, and chat rooms exist around the world. These vary in specificity and application by industry. It is important to focus on the ones that are most influential on the client's business.

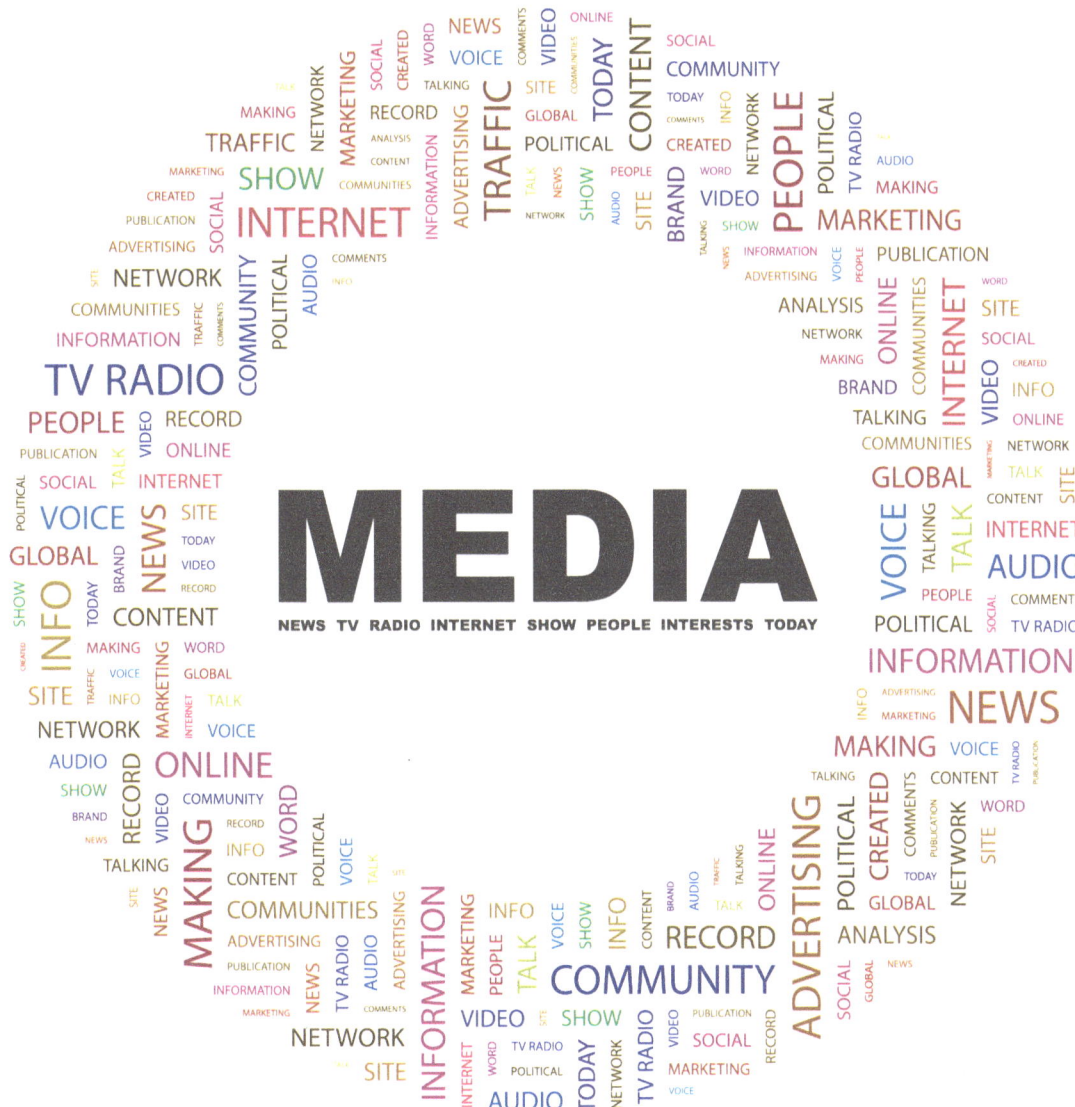

Other Media Relationships

In addition to journalists, there are a few others in the media relations arena that are important for PR professionals to establish and build relationships with to ensure the success of their media relations program (UAB):

- Newspaper and Magazine Editors
- TV and Radio Production Staff
- Social Media Influencers
- Bloggers
- Freelance Writers
- Photographers

STRATEGIES FOR PROFESSIONAL SUCCESS

In a 2015 presentation at Ragan's PR & Media Relations summit in New York City, entitled, "Achieving the Nirvana of Communications: How Bayer hit the 'C-suite spot', boosted budgets and tied media relations to reputation," Raymond Kerins, Jr., SVP and Head Communications and Government Relations at Bayer Corporation offered the following pieces of advice (Sheares 2015):

1. **If the media don't know you, they won't cover you:** Act as a resource to the media and through the process help them understand why they should pay attention to you.
2. **Pitching is secondary. Relationships matter most.** As Kerins explains, "A good media relations campaign is like fine wine, it gets better with time. There's really no substitute for relationships built over time and experience. Senior practitioners need to keep getting their feet wet and not pass all pitching off to junior team members."
3. **Leave the office**—Media relations practitioners should spend at least 50% of their time in the field getting to know their target media.

EXECUTIVE SUMMARY

Now that you have finished this chapter you can:

- Appreciate the difference between public relations and media relations.
- Explain the critical role media relations plays in establishing a company's brand and market position.
- Understand the influence of earned media in the consumer decision-making process.
- Detail the steps of creating a media pitch and disseminating it to target media.
- Explain the different types of media in media relations.

KEY TERMS

Affinity Stage: The middle part of the consumer decision-making process where significant thought is given to the purchase decision. *p. 175*

Citizen Journalists: Individuals who are not members of the media but report on news events via such avenues as social media or blogging. *p. 173*

Consideration Stage: The initial stages in the consumer decision-making process. *p. 174*

Drumbeat: The proactive dissemination of a clear, continual flow of information about a company to target media. *p. 176*

Earned Media: Third-party coverage of an organization in a media outlet. *p. 173*

Familiarity Stage: Final stage of the consumer decision-making process. *p. 175*

Media Relations: A specific part of the public relations process. Specifically, it focuses on the way a company communicates with one public: the news media. *p. 173*

Objectivity: News stories written without bias. *p. 175*

Owned Media: Promotional content created by an organization and placed in select media outlets for a fee. *p. 174*

Pitch: The approach a media relations professional will take when proposing a story idea to a reporter. *p. 178*

Third-party Sources: Information written about a company that it does not create. This includes news coverage or user reviews. *p. 175*

DISCUSSION QUESTIONS

1. How does media relations differ from public relations?
2. How does media relations influence a company's brand?
3. What are some things to keep in mind when crafting a pitch?
4. What role does research play in creating a pitch and developing a relationship with a reporter?
5. What types of media fall under the media relations umbrella?
6. How can you build a relationship with a reporter over the long term?

CHAPTER 9
INVESTOR RELATIONS

A trader on the floor of the New York Stock exchange watching market activity.

CHAPTER OUTLINE

Definition of Investor Relations
Role of the Investor Relations Department
Goals of an Investor Relations Program
Activities of Investor Relations Practitioners
Need for Investor Relations: Sarbanes-Oxley (Sox) Act
Specifics of Sox
    Section 404
    The Public Company Accounting Oversight Board
    External Verification
    Whistleblower Protection
Benefits of Investor Relations
    Educating Senior Executives
    Addressing Valuation Concerns
    Communicating the Strategic Vision
    Managing Unexpected Challenges
    Handling Difficult Investors
Working Together: IR & PR
Strategies for Professional Success
Executive Summary
Key Terms
Discussion Questions

CHAPTER OBJECTIVES

After studying this chapter, you should be able to:

1. Define investor relations.
2. Understand the critical role of investor relations in supporting the financial health and strategic growth of an organization.
3. Explain the difference between investor relations and public relations.
4. Appreciate the role of the investor relations professional.
5. Identify the primary activities of an investor relations professional.
6. Realize the benefits of an investor relations program.

Ripped from the Headlines

Ray Kelvin, the founder of Ted Baker, opened the company's first boutique in March 1988 in Glasgow, Scotland. The company experienced rapid growth, eventually becoming included in the UK's FTSE (Financial Times Stock Exchange) 250. At its high point, the company had over 490 stores around the globe. In August 2018, KPMG, Ted Baker's accounting firm, was fined £2.1 million by the Financial Reporting Council after admitting reporting erroneous numbers on the company's financial statements in 2013 and 2014. A partner with KPMG was also fined £46,800 (Blackburn).

In 2019, it was discovered the company had overestimated the value of the stock it held on January 26, 2019 by £20m to £25m. Later, however, the company reported the error was significantly larger than originally thought totaling nearly £58 million. In January 2020, Ted Baker hired Deloitte to explore the issue. The company's stock dropped 10% after the restatement of the error. As noted by The Guardian, an overstatement of £58 million would be more than the company's annual profits before tax for 2019 (Jolly).

Ted Baker has continued to struggle announcing in June 2020 a 36% drop in revenues for the period of January - May 2020 due primarily to the Corona Virus pandemic.

©mindscanner/Shutterstock.com

To most aspiring PR professionals, the field of investor relations is puzzling. Most colleges and universities do not offer investor relations courses as part of their public relations curriculum or the opportunity to major in investor relations. In this chapter, we are going to explore the field of investor relations and its many intricacies. Hopefully, by the end of this chapter, you will not only understand the practice of investor relations but also its strategic importance in the business arena.

DEFINITION OF INVESTOR RELATIONS

Investor Relations (IR) focuses on the relationship between a company and its investors, particularly its shareholders. IR also covers the company's relationship with many other audiences, including the following: research analysts, financial media, stockbrokers, financial and investment advisors, creditors, contractors, and many others who monitor the financial health of an organization (Gackowski 2017).

The role of the investor relations professional is critical as they play an invaluable role in developing the organization's relationship with the financial community. As noted by Gackowski, "According to the regulatory framework, all participants of the stock market should have equal access to the information regarding the general condition of stock-listed companies. Therefore, IR is not only a matter of corporate image, marketing strategy, or an ability to win over potential investors it is also a matter of compliance with legal regulations and the underlying business principles" (Gackowski 2017, 2).

Investors can also learn more about a company or evaluate it as a possible investment by reading media coverage, reviewing analyst reports, listening to interviews with corporate spokespersons, and comparing it to other organizations in the sector. Despite their focus on a company's financial health, investor relations professionals also play a critical role in shaping an organization's image in the marketplace.

Investor Relations: The relationship between a company and its investors, particularly its shareholders

NIRI: National Investor Relations Institute

In 2003, the National Investor Relations Institute (NIRI) developed a more detailed definition of investor relations that has become commonly accepted by the industry: "Investor Relations is a strategic management responsibility that integrates finance, communication, marketing and securities law compliance to enable the most effective two-way communication between a company, the financial community, and other constituencies, which ultimately contributes to a company's securities achieving fair valuation" (NIRI n.d.).

Similar to PRSA, NIRI is the association for investor relations professionals responsible for communication among corporate management, shareholders, securities analysts, and other financial community constituents. With more than 3,000 members, it is the world's largest professional investor relations association. In total, it members represent over 1,600 publicly held companies and $9 trillion in stock market capitalization (NIRI n.d.).

ROLE OF THE INVESTOR RELATIONS DEPARTMENT

The investor relations department "helps investors make informed decisions in their actions regarding the company's equity" (CFI). This is done through the distribution of accurate and current information about the company's operations, as well as copies of financial statements to potential and current investors and third-party equity research analysts. This includes such items as quarterly releases, annual reports, recordings of conference presentations, and explanations of a company's business model.

The information flow of an investor relations department is two-way—it disseminates information proactively to investors, as well as receives feedback from important shareholders that it reviews with executive management. In times of crisis, the IR department counsels management on issues relating to share price and its relationship with investors (CFI).

CFO: Chief Financial Officer of an organization

The structure of an investor relations department varies among organizations. Sometimes it is a separate entity reporting directly to a company's Chief Financial Officer (CFO), while other times it is located in the same department as public relations. Occasionally, it is located within the finance, legal, or accounting departments.

Most companies with public securities have an individual or a group of people versed in investor relations. It is these individual (s) who carry out the required and proactive activities of the department. These efforts support the three primary roles of the IR function:

1. **Wall Street Liaison:** Investor relations professionals are the link between a company and the financial world. Investor relations teams act as the communication highway between a company's C-suite and its public investors. A company's top executives—its chief executive officer (CEO) and chief financial officer (CFO)—provide the official comments, during financial reporting events such as quarterly earnings calls and financial conferences. Apart from these events, however, most senior executives do not have the flexibility to speak to investors or the financial media at a moment's notice. This is where IR professionals come in. They engage in regular conversations with investors and financial media to monitor the pulse of the company in the marketplace. When they come across something troubling or requiring a higher-level comment, they will enlist someone from the C-suite (CFI).

    > C-Suite: Senior-most executives in an organization with responsibility for managing the company. Examples include: CEO (Chief Executive Officer), CFO (Chief Financial Officer), CMO (Chief Marketing Officer, CSO (Chief Sales Officer), and CTO (Chief Technology Officer)

2. **Information Gate Keeper:** The investor relations team fulfills the majority of the information requests coming from investors, analysts, and others in the financial community. This ranges from the distribution of financial releases and supporting data to the explanation of the company's financial metrics.

3. **Financial Translator:** The senior members of a company's IR team are responsible for monitoring its reputation in the market. A critical part of their job is tracking how the company is perceived by the markets and investors. They are looking to gauge public perception of a company's strengths/weaknesses, market risks, competitive position, value proposition, and a myriad of other issues. Simultaneously, they offer answers to questions and concerns in the marketplace in a language that Wall Street understands. Usually, this is in reference to such items as profit margins, EPS (earnings per share), EBITDA (earnings before interest, taxes, depreciation, and amortization). and dividends (CFI).

    > Wall Street: A term used to describe the U.S. financial markets.

GOALS OF AN INVESTOR RELATIONS PROGRAM

According to the Corporate Finance Institute, the goals of most investor relations programs include (CFI n.d.):

- Share Price: Help an organization reach a share price that supports its overall fundamental value.
- **Information Source:** Provide investors and potential investors with relevant financial information in a timely and accurate way.

> Share Price: The cost of one share of a company's stock

- **Representation:** Serve as a liaison between the company and its investors.
- **Oversight:** Ensure adherence to the regulations of the relevant securities commissions and stock exchanges.
- **Friendly Markets:** Create and maintain positive relationships with capital markets to support future events.

ACTIVITIES OF INVESTOR RELATIONS PRACTITIONERS

In the world of investor relations, there are two main categories of activities—mandatory and elective. Mandatory actions are those required by law, and elective are those that enhance the relationship between a company and its shareholders (Gackowski 2017, 4). The required activities depend on the regulations of the stock exchange the company is associated with and guide a company's shareholder communication policy—detailing everything from date and scope of communications transmissions to the system and tools being used. These actions provide investors or potential investors with up-to-date financial information about the organization (Gackowski 2017, 5).

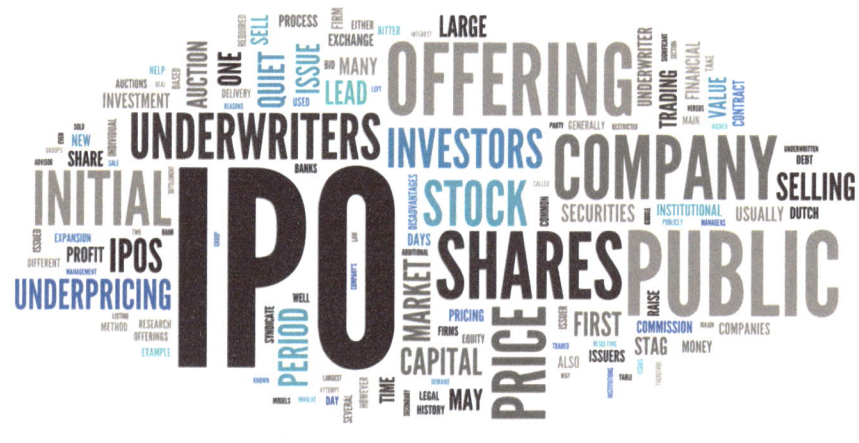

With elective activities, investor relations professionals partake in initiatives that go beyond simply providing information about the company's health. Similar to public relations efforts, the goal is to implement strategies and tactics to deepen the relationship between a company and its investors. These actions are conducted as a means of "gaining capital advantage over the competition" (Gackowski 2017, 5). For many in the C-level suite, a successful investor relations program is perceived as being supportive to those of a company's overall operational goals.

Most of these responsibilities are not carried out exclusively by a company's investor relations group. Many, if not all, require coordination with other parts of an organization, including: finance, accounting, legal, public relations, and the C-suite (CFI).

PR TIP

Be sure to note the overlap between investor relations and media relations. Although the audience is different, the responsibilities and potential image are an organization's image are similar.

IR RESPONSIBILITIES

What are some specific responsibilities of an IR professional? Between the mandatory and elective responsibilities, the tasks for any IR pro are extremely varied, ranging from the mundane to the exhilarating. Here's a broad list of what this could include:

- Scheduling and organizing investor meetings
- Drafting and distributing quarterly earnings releases
- Creating and distributing the company's annual report
- Developing key messages for conversations with analysts and financial media
- Creating investor presentations
- Organizing shareholder meetings
- Writing speeches for CEO, CFO, and other corporate spokespersons
- Representing the company at financial conferences and summits
- Supporting capital markets activities, such as a debt or equity offering
- Acting as a corporate spokesperson to investors, analysts, and financial media
- Counseling senior executives (CEO & CFO) about the company's reputation in the financial markets
- Providing strategic recommendations about the company's market direction
- Developing and executing the company's overall investor relations program
- Ensuring the company's adherence to SEC (Securities & Exchange Commission) regulations

NEED FOR INVESTOR RELATIONS: SARBANES-OXLEY (SOX) ACT

Passed by the U.S. Congress in 2002, the Sarbanes-Oxley Act was enacted to reduce corporate fraud. Creating an entity called The Public Company Accounting Oversight Board, the goal was to create a series of rules and

Sarbanes-Oxley Act: Passed by the U.S. Congress in 2002, the Sarbanes-Oxley Act was enacted to reduce the amount of corporate fraud in the business world

Public Company Accounting Oversight Board: The nonprofit that serves as a watchdog agency over auditors who work with SEC-registered companies

SEC: The Securities and Exchange Commission

regulations to reduce the amount of negligence in corporate accounting departments. Specifically, it eliminates the opportunity for executives to receive loans from employers, as well as provides job protection to whistleblowers. It also enhances the requirements for the independence and financial literacy of a company's board of directors. Adherence to the Act is enforced by the Securities and Exchange Commission (SEC).

When first introduced, many in the business community thought the Act was too strict. Named after its sponsors, Senator Paul Sarbanes and Congressman Michael Oxley, some business executives feared the Act and thought it would make the United States a less appealing place to do business. But to many, it was "on the right track" (Amadeo 2019).

SPECIFICS OF SOX

There are four major outcomes from Sarbanes-Oxley: creation of Section 404 and its associated requirements, formation of The Public Company Accounting Oversight Board, external verification requirement, and protection of whistleblowers:

Section 404

One of the most interesting parts of SOX is Section 404. It mandates a company's executives personally certify the accuracy of its financial statements. If found guilty of fraud, corporate leaders could face up to 20 years in prison. Since 2002, the SEC has filed more than 200 civil cases against corporate executives, but only a handful have faced criminal charges. Additional regulations in Section 404 require managers to create

a comprehensive internal control system for tracking a company's financial reporting. Similar to the requirements placed on senior executives, auditors must explain the rationale for and efficiencies of the system, as well as identify possible weaknesses (Amadeo 2019).

The Public Company Accounting Oversight Board

A second outcome was the creation of The Public Company Accounting Oversight Board. This nonprofit serves as a watchdog agency over auditors who work with SEC-registered companies (Hanna 2014). It enforces a set of requirements for audit reports, mandates registration with the Board for auditors of U.S. public companies. The Board's job is to review, investigate, and maintain adherence to the rules by the auditors.

It also prevents accounting firms from offering anything beyond auditing and tax services to corporate clients and requires an accounting firm's head audit partner to leave the account after five years of advisory work (Amadeo 2019).

External Verification

Under the terms of SOX, public companies must hire an outside auditor to review their accounting procedures and practices. This requirement is deferred for companies with a market capitalization of under $75 million, commonly referred to as small-cap companies. Since the requirement was enacted, eighty-three percent of large corporations report Sarbanes-Oxley has increased investor confidence and thirty-three percent that it reduced fraud according to a study done by the Financial Executives Research Foundation in 2005 (Hanna 2014).

Whistleblower Protection

Any employee or contractor who reports fraud and testifies against their respective company in court, commonly referred to as a whistleblower, is protected. It prevents them from having changes to the terms and conditions of their employment, as well as being fired, punished, or blacklisted by others in the organization. If the company is found to have violated any of the whistleblower's rights, it risks being prosecuted by the SEC (National Whistleblowers Center n.d.).

Whistleblower: Any employee or contractor who reports fraud and testifies against their respective company in court

BENEFITS OF IR

Clearly, investor relations professionals play an important role in an organization. But what are the greatest benefits of an investor relations program? Most IR professionals will highlight five invaluable services they provide to an organization:

- Educating executives
- Addressing valuation concerns
- Communicating the strategic vision
- Managing unexpected challenges
- Handling difficult investors

Educating Senior Executives

Senior executives—CEOs, CFOs, CMOs, CTOs, and CSOs (often referred to as the C-suite)—do not necessarily understand all of the nuances of Wall Street. One of the greatest values an IR professional provides to upper management is explaining the critical aspects of Wall Street in a way they understand. As noted by Charles Triano, SVP of IR at Pfizer, "One of IR's most valuable roles is demystifying Wall Street for our executives. We spend a lot of time internally with different groups talking about what the value drivers are in terms of how shareholders are viewing Pfizer. We explain what the investment community measures, what they are most interested in, their criticisms, and the areas of

the business where we think the company is least understood. It helps our executives in the business understand how their day-to-day work connects to the Street's perception of shareholder value, and what we do in IR to make sure investors really understand our story" (Deloitte 10/14).

The importance of this role is further explained by Rob Binns, CFO and VP of HP Software, "Unless you make a conscious effort to understand the shareholder perspective, it doesn't always align with what you might think. . . . Business finance people tend to focus on the P&L and the balance sheet as they support their business. However, investors can often focus on other things, such as cash flow and capital allocation, and so it is key to address these issues" (Deloitte 7/14).

Addressing Valuation Concerns

Sometimes there is a gap between a company's stock price and its perceived value. Typically, it is the Wall Street analysts who ask corporations to provide a rationale for this disparity, especially if it is higher than anticipated. As explained by Chris Jakubik, vice president of IR at Kraft Foods, "Dialogue

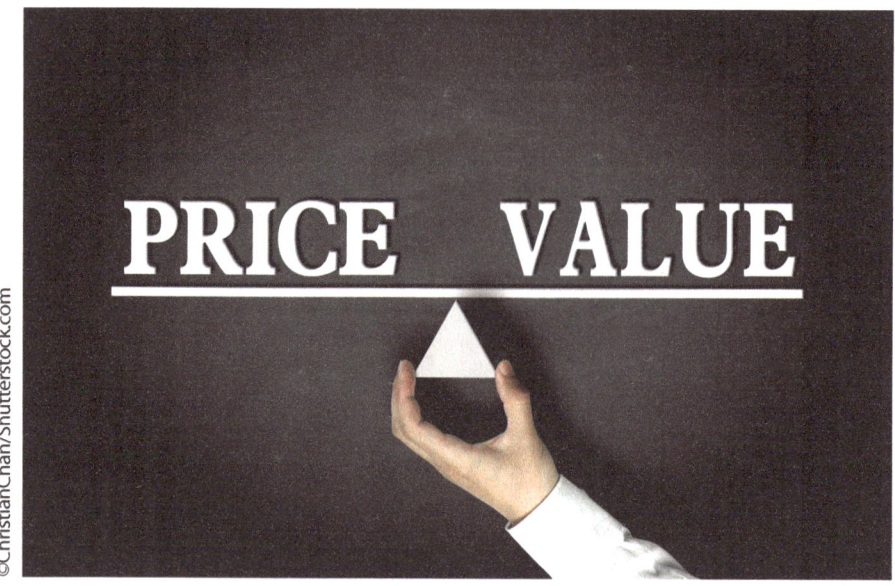

is key, but it's the type of dialogue you have that makes the difference. For example, management arguing valuation with analysts is like analysts telling management how they should change the way they run their business; it generally falls on deaf ears. Instead, a dialogue that focuses on identifying the gaps in perspectives on fundamentals and opportunity sets—the things that drive valuations—and discussing them directly, in a fact-based, well-supported manner, is very effective" (Deloitte 9/23/14).

In addition, Regina Nethery, vice president of IR at Humana adds, "When we don't fully understand what we're hearing back in terms of the view from the Street, we will proactively do outreach to the sell side. If we have a major shareholder that has a question or a concern, again, we will proactively reach out to better understand the view. We may not agree with it, but we're at least trying to see where they're coming from" (Deloitte 9/2/14).

Communicating the Strategic Vision

Every company has a vision and strategic objectives to support it. The challenge comes in communicating it in a manner that resonates with investors. Investor relations professions play a critical role in making a corporate vision become a plausible reality. As Jakubik explains, "Number one: you have to provide context for your audience, whether it's the analysts who generally look within your industry for a benchmark, or for your ultimate audience, the portfolio

managers, who look across industries. It also comes back to doing a lot of listening. We listen to what our broader consumer-staples peers say and how they define themselves. We listen to analysts and investors to understand how they define what they're seeing as good or bad, or value-building or value-destroying. Number two: you've got to provide a thread of logic over time. So you map things out based on what you know or expect to unfold over the coming months and make sure that the construct of your communications and presentations today can accommodate the future" (Deloitte 9/23/14).

Changes to a corporate vision or a shift in strategy can be even more complicated to explain, simply because you have to support the "what" behind the "why." In Binns' opinion, "If you're introducing a change in corporate strategy, think about the company's ability to deliver consistently against that plan and execute on it. Be realistic about nonlinear progress; if it's going to be three steps forward, two steps back, say so. Then help investors understand how you're measuring your progress against your goals. Explain the metrics and signposts investors should use to monitor your progress against the plan. You build credibility first with transparency and then by consistently delivering and executing" (Deloitte 7/14).

Managing Unexpected Challenges

Sometimes organizations unexpectedly encounter situations not factored into their annual financial plan. Such developments pose substantial challenges for corporate executives to explain to investors, especially when it results in a significant drop in share price. In such a circumstance, sometimes it is not what you say but how you say it. Nethery explains, "[at Humana] when

we have had issues in the past, we have tried to be very clear with investors about what happened, why it happened, and how we are addressing the issue, rather than simply saying that we had a problem. We really try to be expansive in terms of ensuring investor understanding and building their confidence that when these things happen, the management team has a plan to get things back on track" (Deloitte 9/2/14).

At HP, the executive team uses a similar technique. As Binns recalls, "One of [HP former CEO Meg Whitman's] leadership principles is 'run to the fire': If you've got a tough message to deliver, don't shrink from it. Address it head on, with a frank assessment of the issue, the reasons behind it, and what's being done to address it. You've got to have a plan and really think through the implications of what you're telling people, and make sure that message is consistent across all the audiences you're trying to address. You need to be aware of prior public commentary from the company to bridge any gaps between what you said before and what you're saying now" (Deloitte 7/14).

Handling Difficult Investors

Periodically, investor relations professionals encounter difficult or activist investors. **Activist Investors** attempt to purchase a significant percentage of a company's stock and then use their position to influence management (Lemke 2020). These individuals aim to force specific actions such as the sale of the company to another organization, or the merger of it with another entity. Periodically, it is done to secure a seat on the organization's board or influence its strategic direction. According to a report by *McKinsey & Company*, in 2015, activist investors demanded some type of action by 637 companies around the globe, and, by October 2017, this number increased to 625 (Beatty 2017, 4). As of the end of 2017, there were approximately 650 activist investors around the globe representing more than $180 billion in "embedded capital—up from $51 billion in 2011" (Beatty 2017, 4).

The influence of activist investors on **capital markets** is increasing at an alarming rate. Over the long term, its popularity stands to greatly impact the way companies communicate with investors. As noted in the *McKinsey &*

Activist Investor: Investors who try to buy a big percentage of a company's stock and then use their position to influence management

Capital Markets: Stocks, bonds, and other types of long-term investment vehicles

Company report, "the growing influence of activists on global capital markets will fundamentally transform how public-company boards interact with investors. This includes the role of the board in investor relations, the importance of outside voices, and more transparent relationships between directors and company managers" (Beatty 2017, 5).

What does this mean for investor relations professionals? Simply put, greater interaction with the company's board. Due to the increase in the number of activist investors, many boards, shareholders, and executives review lists to identify those with the largest percentage of holdings and subsequently decide how to mange the relationship with each of them. Mary Jo White, chair of the U.S. Securities and Exchange Commission, believes shareholder relationships are now a board responsibility: "The board of directors is—or ought to be—a central player in shareholder engagement." An example of this is Andy Bryant, the independent chair of the board at Intel, who meets with the company's biggest shareholders each quarter. Bill McNabb, the CEO of Vanguard Group, recommends boards increase communication with shareholders via such techniques as "shareholder liaison committees," while the board of Tempur Sealy International has created a Stockholder Liaison Committee (Beatty 2017, 5).

There is no one right way to handle activist investors—it all depends on who they are, what they want, and the company's current market position. Jakubik from Kraft Foods explains:

> Just like any other investor, the key is dialogue. If you study the history of the most contentious situations between activists and companies, more often than not, problems arose because management declined to engage in the type of frank, open discussion that they would normally have with a traditional investor. When you look at the people on the investment side, it would be rare to find investors or even activists who truly believe they know your business better than you do. They may come to the table with some very strong views and convictions; that's understandable because if you think about those on the other side of the table who might be investing billions of dollars in one company, they'd

better have conviction. I think the more you embrace and educate activists and others with differing views, the more successful you'll be in pacifying a lot of those views, particularly the ones that are misinformed or off-base. (Deloitte 9/23/14)

Dexter Congbalay, of Mondelez International, suggests:

First, you've got to engage with them at some level, whether through IR or management, depending on prior interaction or relationships. A mistake many companies make is to ignore activist shareholders for as long as possible. Instead, try to have a discussion with them as soon as possible, to understand how they perceive the company, what they are looking to have the company accomplish that the company isn't doing or is not communicating well to shareholders, and why. If you put off engaging with the activists, it gives the impression you're stonewalling, that you're entrenched and not open to new ideas. Perception becomes reality in a lot of cases and that just emboldens the activists. (Deloitte)

WORKING TOGETHER: INVESTOR RELATIONS AND PUBLIC RELATIONS

Now that you have learned about the world of investor relations, the logical question to ask is: How does it work with public relations? The answer is it depends on the organization it serves. This is for a couple of reasons (Phelan 2014):

- **Focus:** Both PR and IR focus on supporting a company's image with a slightly different focus—IR is focused its financial image, while PR is focused on its corporate image.
- **Organizational Structure:** In most organizations the PR and IR teams report to different executives. Often, the IR team reports to the CFO, while the PR team could report to the CEO or the CMO.
- **Audiences:** The PR and IR teams serve different audiences. The PR team has a wide audience including: customers, media, partners, suppliers, and employees. In contrast, the IR team has a narrow audience of just the financial community: analysts, investors, and shareholders.

In most organizations, coordination between the IR and PR departments is at the discretion of upper-level management. With close coordination, the benefits to the organization vastly outweigh the challenges:

- **Common Voice:** In the ideal world, the PR and IR teams would sing from the same song sheet, but this is often not the case. Most PR departments work with the CMO or CEO to set the company's overall vision and messages to support it, while the IR team works with the CFO to develop messages specifically for the financial community. There is a time and a place for different interpretation of messages, but coordination between both areas guarantees they start from the same place.
- **Coverage:** It is the public relations department that is charged with securing and tracking media coverage as well as interacting and speaking with the media on a routine basis, except in rare situations. In most cases, the IR department does not see the coverage unless they search for it. Close coordination ensures the IR team reaps the benefits of the PR team's work, as well as keeps them apprised of negative sentiments about the company in the marketplace (Phelan 2014).
- **Trends:** The PR team searches for trends or identifies emerging developments by monitoring media coverage. In most cases, the IR team is the last to know. This can cause problems with investors or analysts who ask how the company is going to take advantage of the trend or compete in a quickly changing market. In the ideal world, the PR team would update the IR team enabling them to craft appropriate responses or even provide market statistics and facts to support their observations. By keeping each other apprised of industry happenings, the PR and IR teams can respond to each of their respective audiences with a unified voice, instead of two disparate ones. Such coordination makes the company seem unified in the marketplace (Salvo 2018).
- **Coordination:** Both the PR and IR teams have schedules to support upcoming events. For the PR team, this includes the press release distribution schedule,

trade show calendar, social media posts, and conference calendar. For the IR team, this relates to dates of quarterly results announcements, schedule of filings, and a calendar of investor meetings. With one coordinated calendar between both groups, communication professionals capitalize on each other's efforts (Salvo 2018).

By working together, the PR and IR teams can produce optimal results for the organization they support. It ensures the company identifies the greatest opportunities for growth, responds most effectively to the audiences it serves, and mitigates the possibility of encountering unidentified risks. Sadly, for many companies, such coordination is a dream and not a reality.

STRATEGIES FOR PROFESSIONAL SUCCESS

Tips for Managing Investors in Times of Crisis

In this chapter, we have learned about the critical role the investor relations team plays in supporting an organization's relationship with the financial markets and investors. Periodically, there will be times when the organization experiences some type of financial crisis. During such periods, it is important to consider:

1. **Lead:** In times of crisis, leaders must be front and center. If the company's leaders are not present, people and investors will take note. Management teams must go the extra mile to control the the narrative, as it can quickly spin out of their control.
2. **Communicate, communicate, communicate.** In a crisis, you can't over communicate. Most companies make the mistake of communicating only new developments but history shows the more regular, frequent communication you have, the calmer investors will be. This is the time to increase—not decrease participation—in investor conferences, meetings and other related events.
3. **Stick to the schedule.** To the outside world, a canceled meeting is a sign something is wrong. Do whatever it takes to stick to the schedule and meet with investors, analysts and others. You can speak with concerned parties between meetings or after hours.
4. **Avoid predicting or talking about the future.** The worst thing you can do is make a prediction or state an unconfirmed fact during a crisis. Stick to what you know and the facts confirmed to be true.
5. **Discuss the realities not the strategy.** In times of crisis, investors don't want to hear about a CEO's strategic vision or hope for the future. They want to know how the crisis is going to be rectified and understand the associated time line.
6. **Know more than the market:** It is important to understand every possible nuance of a crisis. Go out of your way to track the media's coverage of the crisis, as well as any relevant competitive responses. You need to be prepared to address issues and answer questions covering every angle.
7. **It is a marathon, not a sprint.** Remember, most crises cannot be rectified overnight. Based upon the confirmed facts and direction from management, assemble a realistic plan for handling the crisis and execute against it. Communicate this plan to investors and the financial markets and provide routine updates.

EXECUTIVE SUMMARY

Now that you have finished this chapter you can:

- Define the concept of investor relations and explain its important role in an organization.
- Explain the role of the investor relations department and how it is organized.
- Appreciate the fundamental difference between public relations and investor relations.
- Understand the difference between the obligatory and proactive responsibilities of an IR professional.
- Detail specific activities of investor relations professionals.
- Highlight the benefits of an investor relations program.

KEY TERMS

Activist Investor: Investors who try to buy a big percentage of a company's stock and then use their position to influence management. *p. 200*

CFO: Chief Financial Officer of an organization. *p. 190*

Capital Markets: Stocks, bonds, and other types of long-term investment vehicles. *p. 200*

C-Suite: Senior-most executives in an organization with responsibility for managing the company. Examples include: CEO (Chief Executive Officer), CFO (Chief Financial Officer), CMO (Chief Marketing Officer), CSO (Chief Sales Officer), and CTO (Chief Technology Officer). *p. 191*

Investor Relations: The relationship between a company and its investors, particularly its shareholders. *p. 189*

NIRI: National Investor Relations Institute. *p. 190*

Public Company Accounting Oversight Board: The nonprofit that serves as a watchdog agency over auditors who work with SEC-registered companies. *p. 194*

Sarbanes-Oxley Act: Passed by the U.S. Congress in 2002, the Sarbanes-Oxley Act was enacted to reduce the amount of corporate fraud in the business world. *p. 193*

SEC: The Securities and Exchange Commission. *p. 194*

Share Price: The cost of one share of a company's stock. *p. 191*

Wall Street: A term used to describe the U.S. financial markets. *p. 191*

Whistleblower: Any employee or contractor who reports fraud and testifies against their respective company in court. *p. 195*

DISCUSSION QUESTIONS

1. Why do you think it is important to have an investor relations department in an organization?
2. Do all organizations need to have an IR department?
3. What do you think is the greatest benefit of having an IR department?
4. Do you think there is a significant difference between public relations and investor relations?
5. Do you think the public relations and investor relations teams should work together or separately? Why or why not?

CHAPTER 10
COMMUNITY RELATIONS

Start of race at JP Morgan Chase Corporate Challenge, Buffalo, NY on June 9, 2006. In addition to its sponsorship of this global event, JPMorgan Chase implements a successful, much-admired global community relations program.

CHAPTER OUTLINE

Definition of Community Relations
Assembling a Community Relations Program
    Step 1: Define the Community
    Step 2: Conduct an Audit
    Step 3: Evaluate the Findings
    Step 4: Identify Target Audiences
    Step 5: Create Key Messages
    Step 6: Develop the Program
    Step 7: Evaluate, Revise, and Repeat
Community Relations Program Essentials
Redefining the Community: Community Relations and Social Media
Community Relations and CSR
Problems and Pitfalls of Community Relations and CSR Programs
Company Spotlight: JP Morgan Chase
Company Spotlight: Patagonia
Strategies for Professional Success
Executive Summary
Key Terms
Discussion Questions

CHAPTER OBJECTIVES

After studying this chapter, you should be able to:

1. Define community relations.
2. Understand how to design a community relations program.
3. Explain the relationship between community relations and CSR.
4. Appreciate the role of technology in the community relations arena.
5. Identify some of the challenges in implementing a successful community relations program.

THE PRACTICE OF PUBLIC RELATIONS

Ripped from the Headlines

In 2020, during the height of the COVID-19 pandemic, the NFL faced an unprecedented challenge: How to create a live event in a remote world? The event at hand was the NFL draft which is typically done live with draft prospects and their families, the media and together in one location. Due to the restrictions of COVID-19, this live event had to be re-imagined. Three Proctor & Gamble brands (Gillette, Head & Shoulders and Old Spice) teamed up to create a virtual #NFLDraftRedCarpet experience. Emulating the traditional player fashion show taking place during the draft, each of the NFL's 43 prospects did it live from their living room. The P&G brands offered prospects the chance to show off their style to the world by sending in a video of themselves highlighting their style. Each video was compiled into one large video. P&G then worked with Taylor PR to develop social media copy for each of the prospects which went live on NFL draft night. In addition, a partnership between the NFL and P&G, delivered a 21 retweets of #NFLDraftRedCarpet content on Twitter by @NFL, a 12-tile Instagram story showcasing player videos and a multiplayer video across the biggest social media channels: Instagram, Facebook and Twitter. Proctor & Gamble also worked with Taylor PR to select five players to represent each of the three brands during the two-days of earned media interviews. The result? 638 million earned media impressions and coverage in leading outlets including: ESPN, Fox News, The New York Times and Yahoo! (PR Council)

In the last two chapters, we explored two areas of communication that work heavily with the PR department - media relations and investor relations - and in some cases carried out by members of the PR team. We will now learn about another area that works closely with and is supported by the public relations function - community relations. The structure of the community relations function varies by organization. In some it is included in the human resources department, in others it is housed in public relations while it some it is a stand-alone functional areas. This often depend upon the complexity and depth of the program.

Community Relations: The relationship between an organization and the outside world

DEFINITION OF COMMUNITY RELATIONS

In its simplest form, the idea of community relations refers to the relationship between an organization and the outside world. In today's business arena, the concept of community relations is much more than that. As noted in a recent article in *INC*, "One defines community relations as the corporation's unforced contributions to the community. The other makes community relations a branch of public relations—a form of communications" (Inc. n.d.). Neither of these explanations is wrong. Each underscores the crucial role a community relations program plays in supporting the relationship an organization has with the world around it.

The idea of community relations means different things to different people. To some, it is simply supporting the initiatives and programs in the local community, while to others it encompasses a comprehensive program done proactively by an organization. Regardless of their size or type, most organizations have some type of community relations program, but the depth and structure of these programs vary greatly. It could include everything from simple financial donations to event sponsorship to the creation of community programs.

For decades, corporations, nonprofit organizations and other institutions have implemented community relations techniques with the hope of establishing and developing "positive, cooperative relationships between themselves and the public" (Kane, Fichman, Gallaugher, and Glaser, 1). Prior to the birth of the Internet and the dawn of social media, companies could strategically plan and execute these programs. Often, these programs were specifically designed for the immediate community in which they operated or were based. But in today's fast-paced, social-media-focused society, "that luxury has vanished, leaving a community-management vacuum in dire need of fresh skills, adaptive tactics, and a coherent strategy. In fact, in today's hyperconnected world, a company's community has few geographical barriers; it comprises all customers and interested parties, not just local neighbors" (Kane, Fichman, Gallaugher, and Glaser, 1).

Regardless of the depth or the structure of the program, "community relations is a conscious expression of corporate will and that the motives behind it become visible to the public over time. The more free the activity is, i.e., the less it is necessitated by unfavorable events, the more the community will value it; similarly, the less credit the company seeks, the more credit it will get" (Inc. n.d.).

ASSEMBLING A COMMUNITY RELATIONS PROGRAM

Designing and implementing a program to support positive relationships with community stakeholders is not an easy task. But, if done properly, a successful community relations program will deliver both short- and long-term benefits. Putting together such a program isn't complicated. It simply

entails taking stock of the programs underway (if any) and making appropriate adjustments to address the needs of the community. If there are no existing programs, it is essential to implement initiatives that balance the needs of the community with the mission of the organization.

Here is a suggested roadmap for designing or updating a corporate community relations program (Loscocco 2016):

Step 1: Define the Community

Community: An organization's definition of its world comprised of employees, customers, suppliers, investors, and other stake holders

The first consideration—the organization's definition of its community. Is it the town, city, state, or country where it does business? Is it something else? Before creating or reworking a community relations program, it is essential to have a tangible understanding of the audience. It is important to remember a community doesn't have to only be the actual community in which a company operates. It could also be its virtual community. Very often, it is a combination of both.

Step 2: Conduct an Audit

Impressions Audit: A survey done with an organization's community members to determine its reputation in the market

After defining the audience, the next step is to conduct an impressions audit. In order to construct an effective program, it is critical to determine a company's reputation with local stakeholders. The audit entails speaking with significant leaders in the community, as well as those influencing it. The objective is to determine how these individuals and groups perceive the organization and its impact on the local social and political environment. It is essential to speak with everyone who has an affiliation or relationship with the organization, including:

- Employees
- Owners and managers of neighboring companies
- Local elected officials
- Media

When conducting the audit, ask a series open-ended and short-answer questions to qualify and understand the individual's perspective. Possible questions include:

- What do you think of the organization?
- Would you consider the organization to be a friend or foe of the local community?

- What have you heard others say about the company?
- What concerns do you have about the organization?
- What are the biggest challenges facing the community?
- How can the organization help the community tackle these challenges?
- In your opinion, what is the single greatest service the organization could do for the community?

Step 3: Evaluate the Findings

PR TIP

When talking with community members, look for similarities in respondents answers. Such patterns might be indicative of undetected issues.

After completing the interviews, the next step is to evaluate the results of the audit. It is important to note unexpected attitudes or responses received from interviewees as they might point to undiagnosed flaws. Also, look for trends among respondents, especially those from different parts of the community. For example, if the owner of a local business and a reporter from the regional newspaper have the same observations about the company's strengths, it is likely to be a common perception among the community.

Step 4: Identify Target Audiences

Once analysis of the data is complete, it is time to identify the target audience for the new or updated community relations program. The *target audience* will most likely include representatives from the groups included in the audit, as well as those who comprise the majority of the community.

Target Audience: A company's target market for any external communications campaign

Step 5: Create Key Messages

Using the data from the audit as the springboard, create a series of three to five key messages to convey the fundamentals of the program to the target audience. These messages should be supported by audit findings and emphasize both short- and long-term program objectives.

Step 6: Develop the Program

Leveraging the information gathered from the entire process, put together the platform for the *Community Relations Program*. Similar in structure to a public relations program, it will incorporate the target audience and key messages, as well as strategies, tactics, budget, timeline, and evaluation techniques. It should highlight specific details of the strategies and tactics being

Community Relations Program: The program an organization puts together to support its interaction with its community

used to address any deficiencies identified in the audit. Other things to keep in mind:

- Focus on community priorities.
- Don't over-promise and under-deliver as it relates to tactical execution.
- Engage in activities that can effectively and efficiently address community concerns and logical to the business.
- Develop tactics leveraging both human and financial corporate resources.
- Create a calendar of activities to encourage and demonstrate a 365-day commitment to the work.

Step 7: Evaluate, Revise, and Repeat

The trick to implementing a successful community relations program comes in monitoring its effectiveness. Tactics cannot be executed and then forgotten. They must be monitored and reviewed to see if they are truly addressing the needs of the community. If not, they are a waste of time and resources. Quarterly or six-month reviews of activities are recommended to detect any program faults. These programs are not one-shot efforts; instead, they are systemic initiatives designed to support the development of relationships between a company and the external community, as well as to strengthen the bond with employees.

COMMUNITY RELATIONS PROGRAM ESSENTIALS

A successful community relations program cannot be done by a small functional area within an organization; it needs to be embraced by everyone.

In today's business arena, "No longer an afterthought or corporate window-dressing, community relations, as more chief executives are acknowledging, is now a serious, strategic aspect of business for American companies, a fundamental ingredient for the health of the enterprise" (Googins 1997). A survey of almost 200 community relations professionals suggests support for community relations activities by the C-suite is on the rise. More than 40% of those surveyed report increasing support from both the chief executive and senior vice presidents, as well as enhancements to budgets by 36% and supporting staff by 23%. In addition, 87% of survey respondents report management encourages employees to participate in community relations initiatives with 31% offering bonuses to those demonstrating tangible involvement (Googins 1997).

PR TIP

Community relations programs require the support of other communications functions. A silo mentality will result in failure while a cooperative one will garner success.

In addition to support from senior staff, a successful program must be coordinated with other communication functions: public relations, marketing, employee relations, and investor relations. It should also feature (Diversity Best Practices 2009, 203):

- **Volunteer Opportunities:** An abundance of opportunities for employees to become involved in the local community or the support of independent initiatives are hallmarks of a strong community relations program. For example, AARP gives employees a day off with pay to volunteer with an organization such as Habitat for Humanity or the local pet shelter.
- **Partnerships:** An increasing number of organizations are partnering with local colleges and universities to support CSR (Corporate Social Responsibility) projects and other program elements.
- **Opportunities for Input:** Suggestions from others, both internal and external to the organization, are integral to the growth and development of a community relations program. Employees, stakeholders, investors, customers, and others will be more supportive of a program where their suggestions are incorporated.

Some programs go the extra mile and include out-of-the-box ideas such as (SCORE 2005):

- **Community Relations Advisory Board** with representatives from the company as well as the local and/or regional community.
- **Newsletter** reporting on Community Relations program updates, milestones, and success stories.
- **Value Proposition** detailing the fundamental drivers of the community relations program.

REDEFINING THE COMMUNITY: COMMUNITY RELATIONS AND SOCIAL MEDIA

A challenge many companies face is in defining their community. With the strong role of social media in shaping consumer perception, companies and their respective executives must consider both their real and virtual communities. Today's community is much different than those existing 30 years ago. "IT-enabled collaborative tools such as social networks, wikis, and blogs greatly increase a community's speed of formation and magnify its impact and reach. New communities come together and disperse quickly and are often led by different people at different moments. And mobile interfaces keep groups on the alert, ready to drum up information or break into action" (Kane, Fishman, Gallagher, and Glaser).

The rise of the virtual community poses an inordinate number of challenges for communication professionals. Not only does it mandate companies post accurate and up-to-date information on websites and social media platforms, it also forces companies to continually monitor the status of their virtual relationships. Blog posts, discussion boards, social media posts, and product reviews must be examined and responded to as a failure to do so could result in backlash from the public (Kane, Fishman, Gallagher, and Glaser).

Despite the burden of technology on a community relations program, there are many benefits that come with it, especially with regards to social media. As explained by Kane, Fishman, Gallagher, and Glaser in the article "Community Relations 2.0" in *Harvard Business Review*, social media platforms can deepen a company's community relations program in three ways: strengthen relationships with the community, generate knowledge amidst the community, and allow better targeting of information to the proper audience.

- **Enhance Relationships:** Members of virtual communities use social media to develop relationships with a company in a much different way than what is possible in the bricks-and-mortar world. Not only can consumers engage in conversations directly with company representatives, they can explore the nuances of an organization's policies and corporate culture.

Customers can also share their opinion of a company's products or services directly with others.
- **Build Knowledge:** Within virtual communities, an incredible array of knowledge is amassed based on participants' collective experiences. An example of this is Wikipedia, where content is based upon user contributions. An organization's virtual community operates in a similar fashion through user interaction. Community members contribute content others react to through comments, additional posts, or endorsements often in the form of likes.
- **Information Targeting:** Companies can use activity in virtual communities as a means of disseminating information to a targeted audience. Consider platforms such as Yelp or Google Reviews where participants post their opinion about a company's product or service. By monitoring this activity, companies can receive real-time feedback about a product or service and then adjust messages accordingly if they have missed the mark. In addition, companies can use these and other platforms to quickly and effectively proactively release information about a product. Or, in the case of a crisis or product recall, to inform the public about the situation in a timely manner.

As noted in the HBR article, "To many businesses, online communities look like antagonists, not would-be partners with intersecting interests. It's true that they're often formed, in part, as reactions against mainstream practices, values, and philosophies—but don't let a community's pedigree cloud your thinking about opportunities to create value" (Kane, Fishman, Gallagher and Glaser, p. 3).

To take advantage of these opportunities, corporate social media teams must create and implement policies for managing online communities that encourage positive engagement while simultaneously reducing the possibility of negative actions. Such policies should cover the monitoring of social media platforms and online communities, engagement with community participants and triage steps in the event of a social media or virtual crisis. In the video game industry, where customer engagement and feedback play a critical role in product development, companies often have a full-time communications professional designated to support each major product offering. These individuals are tasked with monitoring the chatter in virtual communities and aggregating their findings. They also serve on product development teams and typically report to both the company's community relations manager and its CMO (Kane, Fishman, Gallagher, and Glaser).

CMO: Chief Marketing Officer of an organization

COMMUNITY RELATIONS AND CSR

In the 21st century, the pressure on companies to be more transparent and have social consciousness is enormous. Organizations must think about everything from how and where they manufacture products to the charities they support to the benefits provided to employees. Gone are the days of corporate secrecy and top-secret manufacturing procedures; today, consumers want to believe in the brands they support forcing organizations to be open and honest with their customers. This is where the worlds of CSR and Community Relations intersect. As discussed in **Chapter 11**, a company's CSR program acts as its pledge to the world of how it will be a good corporate citizen. It is a company's community relations program that supports the dissemination and execution of its CSR program to the outside world.

Due to the nature of this relationship, there is a direct correlation in the execution of these programs. Changes in one area tend to effect another area. Some recent notable trends in CSR and Community Relations include (Diversity Best Practices 2009, 202):

- **Cohesive Alignment:** Companies are delving into community relations, CSR, and other outwardly focused programs to make them more cohesive with common goals and objectives.
- **Expanded Philanthropic Support:** Organizations have expanded the way they support charities and other nonprofits to include not just

financial donations but also cause-related marketing, partnerships with local communities, and sponsorship of employee-volunteer initiatives.
- **Greater Focus:** Companies are more focused in their philanthropic efforts, electing to provide significant support to a few organizations instead of minimal support to many organizations.
- **Partnership with Local/State Government:** With growing importance of the idea of the corporate citizen, many companies are partnering with local and state governments to support the implementation and long-term execution of CSR and community relations programs.
- **Coordination with Corporate Strategy:** Alignment with corporate strategy is becoming increasingly popular as organizations look to engage in programs supportive of their corporate mission and business objectives.
- **Consideration of the Bottom Line:** Organizations are looking more closely at striking a balance between bottom-line expenditures and community impact.
- **Transparency:** Successful community relations program showcase the highlights and failures of CSR programs.
- **Revised Idea of Community:** Idea of a community extends beyond the bricks-and-mortar location of a company. It includes everything from where employees reside to the location of customers to the online world.
- **Expanded Reporting:** Companies are under pressure to report more about their operations than ever before. This includes increased reporting of CSR practices, environmental impact, and sustainability efforts.

PROBLEMS AND PITFALLS: COMMUNITY RELATIONS AND CSR PROGRAMS

As well-designed and thoughtful as many Community Relations and CSR programs are intended to be, many prove to be unsuccessful. A recent study of 30 chief sustainability officers (CSOs) done by a team of professors from Harvard Business School, shows the primary challenge facing most companies is implementation of their programs. "They cited poor integration with the company's core businesses, the difficulty of engaging with the multiple actors in local communities, and the lack of relevant measurements to motivate and evaluate benefits for the company and the target populations" (Kaplan, Serafeim, and Tugendhat 2018). As underscored by the research, the primary challenges do not come from implementation but instead from the "limited scale of projects' ambitions" (Kaplan, Serafeim, and Tugendhat 2018).

Most organizations make a series of small investments in infrastructure, environmental, and waste reduction programs, as well as health care and local/regional training programs under the guidance of the corporation. These programs are not selected based on their potential for impact but instead to demonstrate the company's commitment to improving and contributing to the local community. The challenge is most of these programs do not have the impact the company anticipates and wind up benefiting very few people. In addition, these programs are funded from an organization's sustainability budget and are not part of its community relations program. As a result, they are the first programs to be eliminated during tough economic times. To combat this problem, organizations should engage in activities that result in economic gains for themselves while simultaneously generating socioeconomic opportunities for others in the community. The hope is to create "a new ecosystem that is economically self-sustaining and organically growing" (Kaplan, Serafeim, and Tugendhat 2018).

A second challenge companies face comes with trying to independently implement the CSR program. The Harvard study suggests most companies, regardless of their size, cannot create a long-lasting, "transformational ecosystem" on their own (Kaplan, Serafeim, and Tugendhat 2018). It needs to team up with an outside organization to enlist support from multiple forces within the community. Such a partnership results in the development of strategically relevant relationships and comprehensive programs targeted toward economic and social value creation in the community. These partnerships range from local officials and NGOs to consulting and real estate management companies. Regardless of the partner, it is critical "it has a strong reputation as an independent player that understands and respects the perspectives of all participants in the new ecosystem" (Kaplan, Serafeim, and Tugendhat 2018).

A third challenge relates to the funding of CSR and community relations programs. These programs are expensive and often cost more than originally anticipated. Very few companies are prepared to finance these programs, especially when realizing the risk and opportunity for financial loss. The situation puts organizations in a tough position as they may have the desire to undertake a CSR program but lack the financial foundation to support it. In such circumstances, the solution is not to look for traditional sources of capital such as corporate investment funds; instead seed capital from firms with "a mission to create inclusive growth ecosystems and are under less pressure to generate short-term financial returns" (Kaplan, Serafeim, and Tugendhat 2018). Some examples include private equity groups such as Bain Capital and TPG Capital who in recent years have acknowledged the opportunities in this area. Both firms have raised funds for investing in new physical and information infrastructures in poor communities. In the first half of 2017, Summa Equity raised $500 million in capital for investment in companies working toward one or more of the UN's 17 Sustainable Development Goals. As explained in the Harvard research study, "Although we don't believe a corporation needs to be the primary source of funds, it must be an engaged partner, because a significant corporate presence is critical to funders' decisions to invest. The participation of a lead corporation lowers risk and guarantees that a minimum quantity of products or services will flow through the new ecosystem. The developer of a shopping center starts by signing up an anchor store; similarly, external funders will most likely want a lead corporation to anchor the ecosystem."

COMPANY SPOTLIGHT: JP MORGAN CHASE

Copyright © JPMorgan Chase & Co. Reprinted by permission.

JPMorgan Chase is an example of an organization with a multipronged global community relations program. Known around the world for the *JPMorgan Chase Corporate Challenge*, the global financial services giant offers a myriad of other community programs. As noted on the corporation's website, "We know that when communities do well, our company does well. At JPMorgan Chase, we are investing in our customers, employees and communities around the world to break down barriers to opportunity and create an economy that works for more people" (JPMorgan Chase n.d.).

Over the years, JPMorgan Chase has implemented a series of long-term focused efforts aimed at "driving inclusive growth in communities around the world" (JPMorgan Chase n.d.). The company's approach: "We are investing in people and places to tackle barriers to opportunity and create the conditions for lasting change." As part of this initiative, the company has two focal points: communities and people.

Communities

In supporting communities around the world, JPMorgan Chase tackles it from two angles—

- **Cities:** A half-billion-dollar, five-year program aimed at developing solutions to boost the long-term growth of cities around the globe.
- **Markets:** Supporting programs and ideas in local neighborhoods to enhance community development. The company is focused on communities in: Chicago, Columbus, Dallas, Denver, Detroit, Greater Washington D.C., Houston, London, Miami, Nashville, New Orleans, Paris, San Francisco, and Seattle.

As noted by Jamie Dimon, Chairman and CEO of JPMorgan Chase, "Long-term business success depends on community success. When everyone has a fair shot at participating in the rewards of growth, the economy will be stronger and society more cohesive."

People

When it comes to people, JP Morgan Chase considers not only the needs of its employees but also those of the members of the local community.

- **Employees:** The company invests more than $300 million annually in employee training and development to support employees in offices located in 65 countries around the globe.

(continued)

(continued)

- **Students:** As explained on its website, JPMorgan Chase is "committed to preparing young people for life beyond the classroom. The future of our company, our nation and the world depends on the next generation—and we're proud to continuously support and invest in their success."

Each year the firm employs over 3,000 interns in its offices around the globe and operates 32 unique graduate and undergraduate hiring programs.

In 2017, the firm launched a program to support the needs of high school students. It offers teens the opportunity to access career-focused summer jobs with the hope of getting them on a career path. This is part of the firm's five-year, $17-million commitment to provide young workers with the traits and insights necessary to succeed in the global business arena. To date, over 61,000 students have benefited from the program. The company has pledged $150 million to support these and other programs in over 20 cities around the world.

COMPANY SPOTLIGHT: PATAGONIA

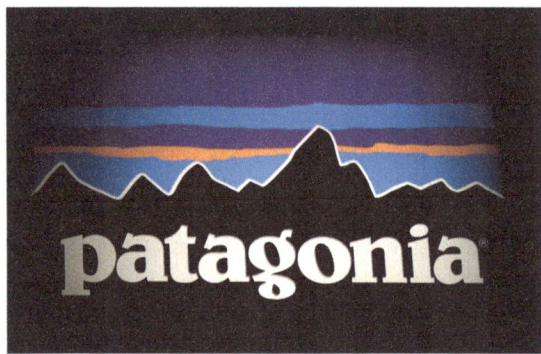

© 360b/Shutterstock.com

Patagonia's community relations program is intertwined with its CSR program. Patagonia is a designer of clothing, apparel, and gear for a range of outdoor sports, including: climbing, surfing, skiing, snowboarding, and trail running. At Patagonia, CSR is positioned as "Corporate Responsibility." As noted on the company's website, "Corporate Responsibility (CR) is a broad-based movement in business that encourages companies to take responsibility for the impact of their activities on customers, employees, communities and the environment. Companies committed to corporate responsibility also agree to abide by international labor and human rights standards" (Patagonia n.d.). Patagonia has a multi-tiered Corporate Responsibility program encompassing everything from its relationships in its supply chain to financial support for environmentally focused nonprofits to a comprehensive activism program. Each of these tenants supports the company's mission: "To create a positive benefit for the lives that we touch through our business." Patagonia's programs are divided into two focus areas: environmental and social.

Environmental Policies

Patagonia looks at the way the manufacturing of its products impacts the environment. In addition to making its products from an array of natural and recycled materials, including wool, cotton, hemp, recycled nylon, traceable down, and recycled polyester, the company supports a vast portfolio of programs in the field to ensure the responsible manufacturing of its product. This includes initiatives focused on:

(continued)

(continued)

- Regenerative Organic Certification
- Responsible Wool Standards
- Traceable Down
- Material Traceability
- Forest Stewardship
- Supply Chain Environmental Responsibility

An interesting facet of this program is the company's Bluesign affiliation. The Bluesign program focuses on elements of a company's supply chain. The goal is to a create supply chain filled with products that are safe for the environment, workers, and customers. In 2007, Patagonia was the first company to join the Bluesign alliance. By taking this step, the company publicly committed to "the highest level of consumer safety and the continuous improvement of environmental performance in [its] . . . textile supply chains by applying the bluesign® system to help conserve resources and minimize impacts on people and the environment" (Patagonia n.d.). Currently, eight of company's top ten material suppliers are Bluesign-certified.

Social Policies

Over the past two decades, Patagonia has developed a social responsibility program that tracks and analyzes the human impact of its business on the workers and communities impacted in any way, shape, or form by its supply chain. It is important to point out Patagonia does not make of its own products; instead, it partners with manufacturers in locations around the world. As the company explains on its website, "We hold our suppliers (and ourselves) to the highest environmental and social standards in the industry. We lean on industry tools and standards to manage this process, and when rigorous enough standards don't exist, we create them." Similar in its approach to the environment, Patagonia has a series of programs in the marketplace to ensure the fair treatment of workers. These include: Fair Trade, Fair Labor Association, Regenerative Organic Certification, and a Migrant Worker program. Patagonia also has a multifaceted activism program through which it looks to actively engage employees, customers, and other members of the Patagonia community.

The company also provides financial assistance to environmental organizations with "bold, direct-action agendas and a commitment to long-term change." It looks to support "innovative work that addresses the root causes of the environmental crisis and seeks to protect both the environment and affected communities" (Patagonia n.d.). These are focused efforts in locations around the globe where it has established connections through sponsorships of outdoor recreation programs and its network of retail stores. It does not discriminate in this support, as it pledges on its website: "From supporting youth fighting against oil drilling to suing the president, we take action on the most pressing environmental issues facing our world. We believe local battles to protect a specific stand of forest, a stretch of river, an indigenous wild species or a community from a polluting refinery build public support and confront larger, more complex issues like climate change, biodiversity loss and environmental justice. We encourage work that brings underrepresented communities to the forefront of the environmental movement and defend communities whose health and livelihoods are threatened by environmental exploitation. We support multi-pronged campaigns that push for greater environmental protections and force the government to abide by its own laws."

To oversee both elements of its Corporate Responsibility Program, Patagonia has a Social/Environmental Responsibility (SER) team. The company has also trained its Sourcing and Supply Planning teams on the components of responsible purchasing practices to mitigate the negative impact on factory workers and their work. It's sourcing and quality control teams work closely with the SER team and have weekly meetings to make supply chain decisions.

STRATEGIES FOR PROFESSIONAL SUCCESS

Now that you have finished reading this chapter you should have a solid understanding of the connection between community relations and CSR. Let's now review some pointers for creating an impactful community relations program.

Remember, your community is not just the physical community outside the doors of corporate headquarters. A company's community includes everyone from its customers and employees to its investors, suppliers and partners to members of its on-line communities. A community relations program should be inclusive all of these groups.

Adopt a realistic, stepped approach. Don't promise to change the world overnight; instead implement a credible, measureable program that supports the needs of community members.

Communicate the goals and objectives of the program across all channels. Be sure to broadcast the details of your program to all members of the community. Provide updates on notably accomplishments and celebrate milestones.

Keep the needs of the community in mind. Think about what will make the greatest impact in the community when creating and implementing CSR and community relations programs. Clearly, you can't be all things to all people so it important to prioritize the needs of greatest significance.

Don't venture into unchartered waters. While keeping your community's needs in mind, implement programs that correlate to your company's strengths. Don't execute programs that are too difficult or expensive to implement.

EXECUTIVE SUMMARY

Now that you have finished this chapter you can:

- Define the concept of community relations and explain the role it plays in an organization.
- Explain the relationship between a company's Community Relations department and its CSR program.
- Design and implement a Community Relations program.
- Detail the challenges of implementing a successful Community Relations program.
- Detail the specific activities of well-respected community relations programs: JP Morgan Chase and Patagonia.

KEY TERMS

CMO: Chief Marketing Officer of an organization. p. 215

Community: An organization's definition of its world comprised of employees, customers, suppliers, investors, and other stake holders. p. 210

Community Relations: The relationship between an organization and the outside world. p. 208

Community Relations Program: The program an organization puts together to support its interaction with its community. *p. 211*

Impressions Audit: A survey done with an organization's community members to determine its reputation in the market. *p. 210*

Target Audience: A company's target market for any external communications campaign. *p. 211*

DISCUSSION QUESTIONS

1. Why do you think it is important to have a community relations program?
2. Why can it be hard for an organization to define its community?
3. What do you think is the greatest benefit of having a strong Community Relations program?
4. How are CSR and Community Relations related?
5. What are some factors that could threaten the success of a Community Relations program?
6. Can a CSR program be successful without a strong Community Relations program?

CHAPTER 11
CORPORATE SOCIAL RESPONSIBILITY

Despite the execution of a thoughtful, comprehensive CSR program, companies often face severe criticism. Read about Coca-Cola India's challenges in the Ripped from the Headlines section in this chapter. Photo taken on December 07 2018 in Hyderabad, Telangana, India.

CHAPTER OUTLINE

What is CSR?
The Triple Bottom Line (TBL)
TBL and CSR
Types of CSR Programs
Designing a CSR Program
Challenges of CSR
CSR Programs That Work
CSR Spotlights: HP and Dell
Benefits of a CSR Program
CSR: Enhancing the Customer Relationship
Strategies for Professional Success
Executive Summary
Key Terms
Discussion Questions

CHAPTER OBJECTIVES

After studying this chapter, you should be able to:

1. Define and explain the term CSR.
2. Explain the framework of Elkington's Triple Bottom Line (TBL) Approach.
3. Explain the importance and role of a well-structured CSR program to an organization.
4. Understand how to create and implement a corporate CSR program.
5. Realize the various communities of a CSR program.
6. Appreciate the challenges of successfully implementing a CSR program.

THE PRACTICE OF PUBLIC RELATIONS

Ripped from the Headlines

Coca-Cola India is one of the largest beverage companies in the country but in early 2002 realized it lacked a comprehensive CSR program. The company knew its operations had a significant influence on the country's environmental landscape and decided it was time to do something about it. As a result, the company created and implemented a mutli-faceted CSR program that would positively contribute to the quality of life of its employees, customers and other members of Indian society.

While Coca-Cola India had the best of intentions with its CSR program, it did encounter several challenges. Environmental experts claimed Coca Cola India was drastically depleting the groundwater supply in the locations of its bottling plants. They also accused the company of dumping hazardous waste materials and waste waters in these areas. These actions greatly impacted local farmers and communities located near the bottling facilities. Despite this criticism, Coca Cola India continued to support many projects it had underway including rainwater harvesting, rebuilding groundwater resources, using sustainable packaging and supporting local communities. The company vowed to be water neutral in India by 2009 as part of a worldwide initiative. Even with the success of and commitment to these programs, Coca Cola India faced continued criticism. Outsiders perceived the company's programs were nothing more than a marketing hoax, aimed at projecting an environmentally-friendly image of the company when the reality was very different. This imbalance between what the company said it was doing and market interpretation caused significantly decline in the company's brand across India and around the world (ICMR).

Corporate Social Responsibility (CSR): A management concept focused on the integration of policies addressing social concerns and environmental needs into an organization's business operations

WHAT IS CSR?

According to the United Nations Industrial Development Organization, **Corporate Social Responsibility (CSR)** is "a management concept whereby companies integrate social and environmental concerns in their business operations and interactions with their stakeholders" (UNIDO n.d.). It is a means by which companies achieve the **Triple Bottom Line Approach**: a balance of economic, environmental, and social objectives.

THE TRIPLE BOTTOM LINE (TBL)

Introduced in 1994 by John Elkington, founder of British consulting group SustainAbility, the Triple Bottom Line (TBL) Approach is grounded in the belief companies should have three different bottom lines for their business: profit, people, and planet (*The Economist*). The first is the traditional bottom line focused on corporate **profit**. A company's **bottom line** refers to its profit after deduction of all expenses; otherwise known as the amount of money the company makes. The second is the relationship between a company and its **people.** The people metric gauges how socially responsible an organization has been in its operations. The third looks at the relationship between a company and the **planet**, specifically, the environmental focus of a company's operations. Elkington's Triple Bottom Line theory is often referred to as the three Ps (**profit, people, and planet**). From Elkington's perspective, "only a company that produces a TBL is taking account of the full cost involved in doing business" (*The Economist*). As noted by *the Economist*, the TBL "aims to measure the financial, social and environmental performance of the corporation over a period of time" (*The Economist*).

At its core, Elkington's TBL provides a framework for companies to examine the social, economic and environmental impacts their operations have on society. The hope is to encourage corporate executives to measure and manage the effects of their corporate initiatives on people and the world around them. Elkington's TBL framework is broken down in the following way (Kraaijenbrink 2019):

- **People:** How an organization's policies affect the people who are part of its daily routine: employees, customers, suppliers, investors, communities, and many others.
- **Planet:** The way an organization's daily operations impact the world around it. Example of this include: use of natural resources, reduction of the carbon footprint, and potential spread of toxic materials.
- **Profit:** The overall effect—either good or bad—an organization has on the economy. This includes everything from the number of people it employs to innovation it develops to the amount of tax revenue it generates.

TBL AND CSR

In 2018, Elkington renounced his Triple Bottom Line Approach. In an article in *Harvard Business Review,* Elkington explains the TBL was designed to promote greater thought about the tenants of capitalism and its

> **Triple Bottom Line:** A management approach introduced in 1994 by John Elkington focused on the balance within an organization on its economic, environmental, and social objectives
>
> **Bottom Line:** A financial term referring to the amount of money a company makes after expenses.
>
> **Three Ps:** Profit, people, and planet part of Elkington's TBL approach

future. Many early subscribers to TBL theory viewed it as as a balancing act between each of the three major focus areas. Instead of inspiring executives to think differently about their company's bottom line, overtime the idea of a TBL became a buzz word in the business community. Many corporations enacted programs appearing to subscribe to the theories of TBL, but in reality were still focusing on their bottom line. The challenge with the TBL approach comes in the analysis of the data. As noted by Elkington, it is unclear whether the resulting analysis helps "decision-takers and policy-makers to track, understand, and manage the systemic effects of human activity (Elkington)." Ironically, according to the creator of the theory, "The Triple Bottom Line has failed to bury the single bottom line paradigm" (Elkington 2018).

Despite the fact Elkington recalled his theory, the effect of TBL on the business arena cannot be over looked. Elkington's goal was to invoke change to cause a "transformation of capitalism" (Elkington, 2018)." In his eyes, it was designed to be much more than an accounting system. He viewed it as "a genetic code, a triple helix of change for tomorrow's capitalism (Elkington, 2018)." Although TBL was not interpreted in the way he desired, Elkington's ideas still greatly influenced modern day corporate CSR policies. Companies around the world ranging from global multinationals, to domestic powerhouses to small local businesses still embrace his ideas in the development of their CSR programs.

TYPES OF CSR PROGRAMS

Over the past two decades, there has been a global movement towards the creation of CSR programs, leaving many to wonder about the nuances and necessary intricacies of a successful program.

 **PR TIP**

Keep in mind the tenants of Elkington's TBL Framework when assembling a CSR program. It provides a solid foundation and effective strategies to follow.

As explained by V. Kasturi Rangan, Lisa Chase, and Sohel Karim in their 2015 article titled "The Truth About CSR" in *Harvard Business Review*, the purpose of a CSR program is to "align a company's social and environmental activities with its business purpose and values. If in doing so CSR activities mitigate risks, enhance reputation, and contribute to business results, that is all to the good. But for many CSR programs, those outcomes should be a spillover, not their reason for being" (Rangan, Chase, and Karim 2015).

Over the course of a decade, Rangan, Chase, and Karim studied the implementation of corporate CSR programs. As part of this work, they interviewed dozens of managers, directors, and CEOs responsible for the execution of their organization's CSR program, as well as 142 managers who attended Harvard Business School's CSR executive education program from 2011 to 2015. Through this research, the team discovered "most companies practice a multifaceted version of CSR that runs the gamut from pure philanthropy to environmental sustainability to the active pursuit of shared value. Moreover, well-managed companies seem less interested in totally integrating CSR with their business strategies and goals than in devising a cogent CSR program aligned with the company's purpose and values" (Rangan, Chase, and Karim 2015).

Rangan, Chase, and Karim determined most corporate CSR programs fall into one of three categories:

1. **Philanthropic:** Focused on giving back to the community, these programs do not generate profits or improve a company's overall business performance. Examples include monetary donations, assistance with community outreach programs, and support for employee volunteer efforts.

2. **Operational Improvement:** Devised with two goals in mind, these campaigns not only support the company's CSR goals but also help drive overall operational efficiencies. Some examples include sustainability programs focusing on waste and emissions reduction, as well as upgrades to the employee experience ranging from upgrades in benefit programs to improvements in working conditions.

3. **Business Transformation:** With these programs, organizations attempt to create new structures to meet environmental challenges. The primary metric is improvement in a company's overall business performance with respect to either its social or environmental agenda.

Each type of program does not operate autonomously, very often there is significant crossover from one part of a business to another. Usually, these effects are not predicted but rather result from the normal course of operations.

Regardless of the focus, most CSR programs: "take responsibility for the impact of their activities on customers, employees, shareholders, communities, and the environment in all aspects of operations. This effort extends beyond simply obeying local laws, as organizations voluntarily take steps to improve the quality of life for employees and their families, as well as society at large" (Tharp and Chadbury 2008).

DESIGNING A CSR PROGRAM

Most companies use a step-by-step approach in the design and implementation of their corporate CSR program with the majority having six distinct phases: introduction, identification, positioning, strategy development, implementation, and monitoring (Tharp and Chadbury 2008). The framework is based on the model proposed by Michael Porter and Mark Kramer in the December 2006 article in the *Harvard Business Review* entitled "Strategy & Society: The Link Between Competitive Advantage and Corporate Social Responsibility." In the piece, Porter and Kramer challenge companies to reexamine their relationship with the world around them that "does not treat corporate success and social welfare as a zero-sum game" (Porter and Kramer 2007, 2).

In the eyes of Porter and Kramer, the development of an effective and genuine CSR programs mandates a company take the following steps:

1. **Determine the logical touch points between the organization and its environment.** In this first step, the goal is to examine the ways the organization interacts with the world around it and identify the nuances its relationships with its various constituencies: employees, investors, customers, suppliers, and community members. It is important to consider (Porter and Kramer 2007, 1) the following criteria:

   - Effect of the organization on its community
   - Quality of the work environment
   - Environmental impact of the company's operations
   - Societal effect on the company's ability to compete
   - Access to a qualified workforce
   - Ability to solicit outside investors

2. **Identify the social issues to be the focus of the CSR program:** After examining the impact of an organization in each of these areas, it is critical to solidify its focus. As explained by Porter and Kennedy, an organization must consider "how might you address social needs in ways that create shared value—a meaningful benefit for society that also adds to your company's bottom line?" (Porter and Kramer 2007, 1).

3. **Launch a few initiatives that produce significant and unique benefits for the company and society:** This is where the specific elements of a CSR program are identified. Assemble a series of efforts the company can reasonably and realistically accomplish that will result in a significant impact while not destroying the bottom line.

PR TIP

It is better to launch a few programs that will work based upon the company's core competencies, instead of a large portfolio of experimental ones.

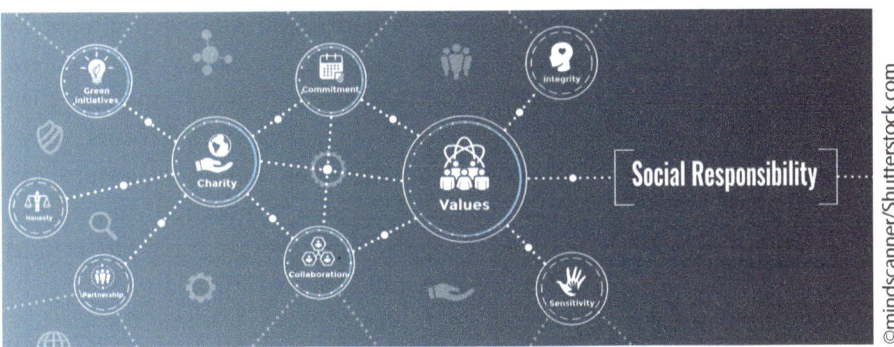

4. **Develop and implement a measurement and evaluation system for the CSR program:** As is the case with a public relations or social media campaign, it is important to specify certain points and define specific metrics by which the CSR program can be judged. Again, similar to deciding the focus of a CSR campaign, the organization must develop its own definition and metric for judging success.

The question you may be asking is: *Are companies required to have a CSR program?* The answer is no; but that being said, most do have CSR policies for four primary reasons (Porter and Kramer 2007):

- **Moral Obligation:** Be a good member of society and execute sound judgment.
- **Sustainability:** Conduct business in a way that "secures long-term economic performance by avoiding short-term behavior that is socially detrimental or environmentally wasteful" (Porter and Kramer 2007, 4).
- **Freedom to Operate:** Carry out business in a way that adheres to rules and regulations of local governments and communities.
- **Market Reputation:** Enhance the image of a company in the marketplace and the value of its brand.

CHALLENGES OF CSR

Despite the fact many companies appreciate the need for a strong, multifaceted CSR program, most fail to successfully implement it. Most corporations depend too heavily on the outside world to decide their CSR agenda, instead of capitalizing on their inherent strengths ultimately resulting in failure. As explained by Porter and Kramer, many companies "rely on the forbearance of their neighbors, such as those, like chemical manufacturing,

whose operations are noxious or environmentally hazardous. By seeking to satisfy stakeholders, however, companies cede primary control of their CSR agendas to outsiders. Stakeholders' views are obviously important, but these groups can never fully understand a corporation's capabilities, competitive positioning, or the trade-offs it must make" (Porter and Kramer 2007, 6).

Instead of looking externally to decide CSR agendas and in many ways, dictate the rollout of the program, companies should focus internally. This starts with an internal examination of any efforts that could be considered CSR related. Companies should capitalize on initiatives already underway and streamline their execution with the hope of yielding maximum results.

As part of this process, they should "eliminate initiatives that do not address an important social or environmental problem in keeping with the company's purpose, identity, and values" (Rangan, Chase, and Karim 2015).

As easy as it sounds, few companies take the time to do this. And, if they do it, they often fail. However, one company that has done it well is PNC.

PNC Financial Services Group, Inc. is an American bank holding company and financial services group based in Pittsburgh, Pennsylvania. The company's banking unit, PNC Bank, has over 2,400 locations in 19 states (PNC). Between 2010 and 2015, PNC Bank's Grow Up Great program provided $100 million in school-preparedness resources to underserved populations across the United States. Prior to the launch of the program, each PNC market had its own CSR budget allocated by regional management to causes they thought deserving of funds. This resulted in approximately 30% of funds going to the arts, 25% to sports, 20% to civic activities, 5% to education, and 3% to health (Rangan, Chase, and Karim 2015).

At the request of the company's CEO, the regions joined forces and formed the Grow Up Great initiative. The focus of Grow Up Great was based on three factors: the CEO's commitment to education, the desire of employees to support a local cause, and the bank's community-focused orientation. By streamlining and focusing its financial and human CSR efforts, PNC was able to build "a well-funded initiative that correlates better with its employees' motivations and is likely to yield significant benefits to the communities the bank serves and relies on" (Rangan, Chase, and Karim 2015).

As explained earlier, an important element of a CSR program is an evaluation component. In the case of PNC's Grow Up Great program, several metrics were used, including: number of hours employees spent reading to children and the subsequent increase in reading comprehension, amount of money awarded to support the creation of educational materials, number of students who received educational materials, and improvement in students' academic performance. In addition, PNC tracked the amount of additional money contributed to its Grow Up Great from external sources (Rangan, Chase, and Karim 2015).

As demonstrated through the program at PNC, participation by individuals from all levels of an organization-the C-suite to the assembly line and everything in between is essential in ensuring the long-term success of its CSR program. There are a couple ways to do this:

- Appoint someone to manage the program and secure implementation across departments.
- Position the CSR director as an authority figure with management responsibility across all facets of the organization.
- If the company is global or has several divisions, have a CSR representative in each area or territory who reports to the program head.

CSR PROGRAMS THAT WORK

In 2020, *Newsweek* teamed up with Statista Inc., a global data research firm to publish it inaugural list of America's Most Responsible Companies. After reviewing the CSR offering of over 2,000 companies, Newsweek and Statista compiled a list of the 300 strongest programs (*Newsweek* n.d.). Incorporating date from two sources: a web-based independent survey of 6,500 U.S. citizens and research of "publicly available key performance indicators derived from Corporate Annual Reports, CSR Reports, Sustainability Reports, and Corporate Citizenship Reports" (*Newsweek* n.d.). The study ranks companies on a scale of one to 100 in three categories—environmental, social, and corporate governance. They were then given a composite score based on the average of the three (*Newsweek* n.d.):

1. HP
2. Cisco
3. Dell
4. Intel
5. Microsoft
6. NVDIA

7. Citigroup
8. General Mills
9. Comerica
10. Jones Lang LaSalle

What was ranked 300? Amazon with an overall rating of 60.1.

CSR SPOTLIGHTS: HP AND DELL

Let's take a look at two of these programs: Hewlett Packard and Dell Technologies.

BENEFITS OF A CSR PROGRAM

In a 2015 article in *Financier Worldwide*, Fraser Tenant wrote, "Corporate social responsibility (CSR) has become one of the standard business practices of our time. For companies committed to CSR it means kudos and an enhanced overall reputation—a powerful statement of what they stand for in an often cynical business world." Flash-forward to 2020—CSR has become even more important in the global business arena.

Companies large and small ranging from HP, Dell, Microsoft, and Whole Foods to Patagonia, LL Bean to the local corner store, all have some element of CSR in their business plan. The growth in CSR programs has been rapid, but it is not unexpected. As explained in 1999, years before the idea of CSR became a cornerstone of business, Rosabeth Moss Kanter in an article in the *Harvard Business Review* titled, "From Spare Change to Real Change: The Social Sector as Beta Site for Business Innovation," explained, "Companies that are breaking the mold are moving beyond corporate social responsibility to social innovation. These companies are the vanguard of the new paradigm. They view community needs as opportunities to develop ideas and demonstrate business technologies, to find and serve new markets, and to solve longstanding business problems."

Many organizations have found a strong CSR policy helps a community and the environment, while simultaneously providing unexpected benefits to its employees, as well as other areas of its business. A 2016 article published in *Frontiers in Psychology* entitled, "Corporate Social Responsibility and Employee Engagement: Enabling Employees to Employ More of Their Whole Selves at Work" details the results of a study that tracks the advantages a strong

HEWLETT PACKARD

Managed by the HP Foundation, Hewlett Packard leverages its global presence to support a multi-tiered CSR program. As explained on the company's website,

"We aim to connect our communities to greater economic and social opportunity through technology and protect our shared environment. We create positive local impact in the communities where we live, work, and do business, through corporate contributions, the work of the HP Foundation,[1] and employee giving and volunteerism. By deploying our technology to help solve global challenges, we create shared value for HP, our customers, and society at large. Since 2015, we have been committed to enabling better learning outcomes for 100 million people by 2025, through application of our technology, training, R&D, and financial contributions. We invest in programs and provide technology solutions that meet learners where they are and take them where they want to go" (HP n.d.).

HP's CSR program has three main components (HP n.d.):

- **HP LIFE (Learning Initiative for Entrepreneurs):** This program provides free training to start-ups and small business owners in IT and business development. Offered globally, the program includes dozens of free web-based courses in multiple languages. Between 2012 and 2018, HP had over 750,000 students take its courses from countries around the world, including Morocco, Saudi Arabia, India, Brazil, and Egypt.
- **HP Matter to a Million:** A five-year campaign done in conjunction with Kiva provided financial support to over one million people. The program ended in 2018.
- **HP Connection Spot—Mobile Disaster Relief:** This program provides emergency services to people in the United States who lose Internet connectivity as the result of a natural disaster. Staffed by volunteers, this mobile technology hub contains HP laptops, printers, and an Internet hotspot. It is also used by first responders and nonprofits supporting disaster relief efforts.

The results of these programs are impressive. In 2018, 6,400 employees donated approximately 140,000 hours to support local volunteer equaling a value of approximately $4.3 million. In addition, HP's employees gave $2.07 million in cash to qualifying organizations through the company's HP Inspires Giving program. The HP Foundation provided $1.89 million in matching funds.

---

[1] www8.hp.com

DELL TECHNOLOGIES

Dell Technologies has a global CSR program focusing on advancements in two areas: technology and human capital. The company's CSR program *Progress Made Real* explores how the company can create a positive social impact around the globe with four main priorities:

- **Advancing Sustainability:** Dell strives to improve its relationship with the planet. Looking at its relationships with customers, suppliers and communities, Dell works to incorporate ethical and sustainability policies into all aspects of its operations. By 2030, the company pledges for every product purchased, it will recycle a similar item. In addition, it will make 100% of its product packaging and half of its product content from recycled or renewable materials.
- **Cultivating Inclusion:** Dell focuses on closing the diversity gap as it believes there is too much untapped talent in the world. By 2030, the company aspires to have women comprise 50% of its global workforce.
- **Transforming Lives:** Dell looks at the applications of its technologies in societies around the globe. By 2030, the company hopes to improve the economic, health and educational opportunities for up to one billion people.
- **Upholding Ethics and Policies:** Dell underscores its commitment to maintaining sound ethical standards and practices. By 2030, Dell has committed to having complete automation of its data control processes.

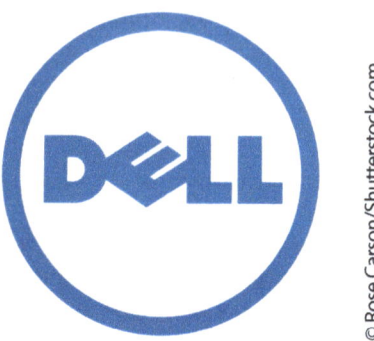

© Rose Carson/Shutterstock.com

corporate CSR program brings to the employees of an organization. In the study, 15,184 individuals working for large professional service firms across the United States were interviewed. The results of the study reveal a strong CSR program, where employees have the opportunity to work together and truly be authentic, positively impacts their feelings about their employer and position, ultimately resulting in better engagement at work. Another study done by the Charlotte-based nonprofit Apparo in 2017 finds "organizations who encourage employees to volunteer through pro bono work during paid business hours create motivated employees who feel that their company respects their development. These employees also feel energized by the opportunity to be creative with their skillset for a good cause" (Lanphear 2019).

CSR: ENHANCING THE CUSTOMER RELATIONSHIP

A CSR program can also enhance the relationship an organization has with its customers. In October 2015, Nielsen published the results of a study, "The

Sustainability Imperative," which examines the correlation between a CSR program and the customer relationship. It found 66% of consumers are willing to pay more for products from a company with a well-respected CSR program. More than 50% of individuals are influenced by factors such as natural and organic ingredients (69%), environmental focus (58%), and dedication to positive social values (56%; Nielsen 2015). Another study also conducted in 2015 by Cone Communications reveals (Cone Communications 2015, 3):

- **Ninety-one percent** of consumers expect companies to do more than make a profit, but also operate responsibly to address social and environmental issues.
- **Eighty-four percent** seek out responsible products whenever possible.
- **Ninety percent** would boycott a company if they learned of irresponsible or deceptive business practices.

Through the Cone Communications study, researchers discovered "global consumers have officially embraced corporate social responsibility—not only as a universal expectation for companies but as a personal responsibility in their own lives. Consumers see their own power to make an impact in so many ways: the products they buy, the places they work, and the sacrifices they are willing to make to address social and environmental issues" (Cone Communications 2015, 2). Done is conjunction with Ebiquity, Cone Communications conducted an online survey of 9,709 individuals from nine of the largest countries in the world by GDP: the United States, Canada, Brazil, the United Kingdom, Germany, France, China, India, and Japan. Researchers described the concept of CSR

to participants as "companies changing their business practices and giving their support to help address the social and environmental issues the world faces today" (Cone Communications 2015, 4).

The global study underscores several important beliefs regarding consumer perception of corporate CSR programs:

1. **Act Responsibly:** Consumers expect companies to act responsibly but more than 50% need to see proof of it.
2. **Say vs. Do:** People remember companies that deliver on their promises, as well as those that fail in their attempt to implement their CSR programs.
3. **Keep It Simple:** CSR messages should be simple and specific, as opposed to lengthy and complex.
4. **Remember, the World Matters:** Consumers are willing to pay more, buy less, and give up some features if it is better for the world around them.
5. **Highlight Responsibly Made Products:** Responsibly made products matter to consumers, but they don't always purchase them.
6. **Make More of a Difference:** Only a little more than 25% of people feel companies are helping the environment.
7. **Increase Communication:** Individuals are getting their information about corporate CSR programs from multiple platforms and sources. The more companies communicate about what they are doing, the better off they will be.
8. **Leverage Social Media:** Social media platforms are playing an increasingly important role in supporting corporate CSR programs. Companies need to make sure it is integrated into the nuances of their CSR offerings.
9. **Highlight the Data:** Much of the data companies publish about their CSR programs gets lost in corporate reports. Organizations should look for opportunities to highlight CSR accomplishments.
10. **Engage Customers:** Consumers want to do more than shop, but they don't know how. Companies should look for ways to engage customers in their CSR efforts.

In a 2017 study by Cone Communications, the increasing importance of CSR to the consumer is highlighted even further. In this study, Cone focuses on consumer beliefs, perceptions, and behaviors toward corporate social responsibility and the position companies should take relative to issues regarding social justice. As noted in figure 11.1, Cone found 87% of individuals would buy a product if a company advocates for an issue they personally believe in. Over 75% of consumers would not buy a product if they discover a company support an issue contradicting their personal beliefs.

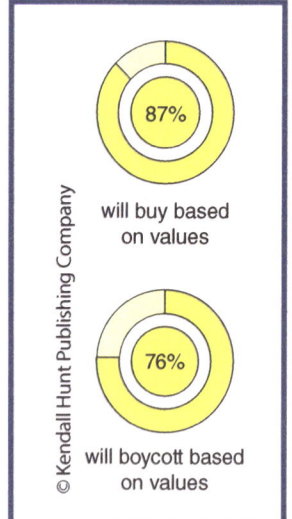

FIGURE 11.1:

In the mind of the consumer, the most important step an organization can take is to do the right thing. Consumers believe if an organization treats its employees well, the chances are likely it will be a good corporate citizen.

The study also reveals more than 50% of individuals boycotted products of companies conducting irresponsible business practices or supporting issues contrary to their own beliefs, as noted in Figure 11.2. Consumers understand organizations are not perfect and periodically take measures that may contradict their own belief. Consumers want organizations to be honest and report success, as well as failures. Nearly 80% of individuals are more likely to believe a company's CSR commitment if they communicate their experience in executing the program. Consumers want to know the realities of these programs and reality is the key to credibility in the mind of the consumer.

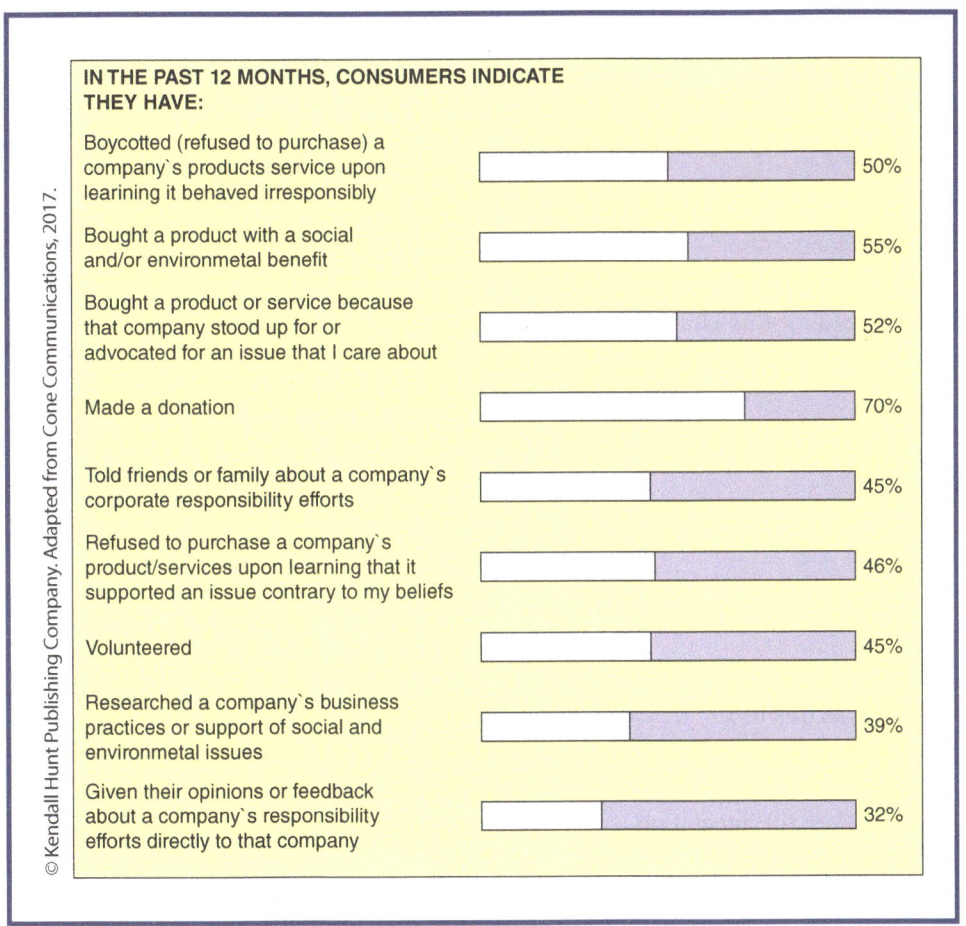

FIGURE 11.2:

STRATEGIES FOR PROFESSIONAL SUCCESS

In this chapter, we have learned the importance of developing and implementing a thoughtful, impactful CSR program. CSR programs are vital in developing, preserving and supporting a company's relationship to its local, national and global communities. But, for many companies, the challenges in designing and executing a realistic and effective CSR campaign can be daunting.

The reality is it is impossible for all companies to design the same type of CSR program or execute an identical strategy. The key to a successful CSR program is assembling one that supports the overall objectives of the organization. In constructing a CSR program, organizations need to consider the issues that are most relative to their community and how they can most effectively address them. In the most impactful CSR programs, as explained by Rangan, Chase, and Karim, "Some of their initiatives indeed create shared value; some, though intended to do so, create more value for society than for the firm; and some are intended to create value primarily for society. Yet all have one thing in common: They are aligned with the companies' business purpose, the values of the companies' important stakeholders, and the needs of the communities in which the companies operate" (Rangan, Chase, and Karim 2015, 15). As Philip Kotler said in his book *Corporate Social Responsibility: Doing the Most Good for Your Company and Your Cause*, "A good company offers excellent products and services. A great company also offers excellent products and services but also strives to make the world a better place."

EXECUTIVE SUMMARY

Now that you have finished reading this chapter, you can:

- Define CSR.
- Explain the concept of the TBL.
- Describe the relationship between TBL and CSR.
- Discuss the three types of CSR programs.
- Explain the challenges of implementing CSR programs.
- Discuss the benefits of a CSR program.

KEY TERMS

Bottom Line: A financial term referring to a corporation's balance of its profit and loss. *p. 227*

Corporate Social Responsibility (CSR): A management concept focused on the integration of policies addressing social concerns and environmental needs into an organization's business operations. *p. 226*

Triple Bottom Line: A management approach introduced in 1994 by John Elkington focused on the balance within an organization on its economic, environmental, and social objectives. *p. 227*

Three Ps: Profit, people, and planet part of Elkington's TBL approach. *p. 227*

DISCUSSION QUESTIONS

1. What is the difference between CSR and TBL? How do they relate?
2. What are the steps an organization should take in designing a CSR program?
3. What are the benefits of having a CSR program? What can an effective program do for an organization?
4. What are some examples of companies with strong CSR programs? What makes these programs more effective than others?
5. What are some companies that you admire? Why do you admire them? What sets them apart from their competition?

CHAPTER 12
CRISIS MANAGEMENT

In March 2019, the Boeing 737 MAX passenger airliner was grounded worldwide after 346 people died in two crashes, Lion Air Flight 610 on October 29, 2018 and Ethiopian Airlines Flight 302 on March 10, 2019.

From *Public Relations Principles: Strategies for Professional Success,* by Shawn T. Wahl and Michelle M. Maresh Fuehrer. Copyright © by Kendall Hunt Publishing Company. Reprinted by permission.

CHAPTER OUTLINE

Definition of a Crisis
    Situational Crisis Communication Theory
The SCCT Framework
Crisis Communication Planning
    Pre-Crisis
    The Crisis Event
    Post Crisis
The Crisis Response
    Part One: Initial Crisis Response: Speed, Accuracy, Consistency and Sympathy
Platforms for Crisis Communication Response
    Part Two: Reputation Repair
    Attribution Theory and Reputation Repair
Strategies for Professional Success
Executive Summary
Key Terms
Discussion Questions

CHAPTER OBJECTIVES

After studying this chapter, you should be able to:

1. Understand the concept of crisis management.
2. Identify the concepts and framework associated with Coombs' Situational Crisis Communication Theory.
3. Appreciate the Crisis Communication Planning Process.
4. Develop a crisis communication plan and assemble an appropriate response framework.

Ripped from the Headlines

Between October 2018 and March 2019, 346 people died in two air plane crashes—one Lion Air Flight 610 and the other Ethiopian Airlines Flight 302. Both planes were a Boeing 737 MAX jet. These tragedies rocked the aviation industry, sparked many investigations, and resulted in the grounding of hundreds of Boeing 737 Max jets worldwide.

Lion Air Flight 610 took off from Jakarta, Indonesia on Monday, October 29, 2018, at 6:20 am local time. Its destination was Pangkal Pinang, the largest city of Indonesia's Bangka Belitung Islands. Twelve minutes after takeoff, the plane crashed into the Java Sea, killing all 189 passengers and crew.

Nearly five months later, Ethiopian Airlines Flight 302 took off from Addis Ababa, Ethiopia on Sunday, March 10, 2019, at 8:38 am local time. Its destination was Nairobi, Kenya. Six minutes after takeoff, the plane crashed near the town of Bishoftu, Ethiopia, killing all 157 people aboard. Both crashed jets were Boeing 737 Max 8s, a variant of the best-selling aircraft in history. When Airbus announced in 2010 it would make a new fuel-efficient and cost-effective plane, Boeing rushed to get out its own version. That version was the 737 Max airplanes.

As you learn about Crisis Management, think about the circumstances surrounding each of these tragedies. What could Boeing have done to support the victims and their families? What did these crises do to the company's reputation.

Crisis Management: The process of preventing or lessening the harm a crisis has on an organization and its stakeholders.

Crisis management is an important function in any organization. According to the Institute for Public Relations, the term **crisis management** refers to the process of preventing or lessening the harm a crisis can have on an organization and its stakeholders. Failing to successfully address a crisis can result in serious harm to an organization, as well as its stakeholders. Public relations professionals play a vital role in the development and execution of any crisis plan.

In this chapter, we will explore the overall process of crisis management and dive deeply into each of the three phases of crisis planning. We will discover the most effective way to design a Crisis Communication Plan (CCP) and implement it in the marketplace.

Crisis: An unexpected, non-routine event or series of events that creates uncertainty and potential challenges for an organization.

DEFINITION OF A CRISIS

As discussed briefly in Chapter 1, a **crisis** is "a specific, unexpected, and non-routine event or series of events that create(s) high levels of uncertainty and

simultaneously present(s) an organization with both opportunities for and threats to its high-priority goals." (Ulmer, Sellnow, and Seeger 2011, 7). As noted by David Sturges in his article "Communicating Through Crisis," for organizations, "any unusual or out-of-the-ordinary event may be considered a crisis if it is perceived by organizational members to have high values on one or more of three dimensions: importance, immediacy and uncertainty" (Sturges 1994, 298).

A crisis has the potential impact in an organization in three areas - consumer safety, organizational reputation and the bottom line. Some crises, such as those involving industrial accidents or consumer products, can result in serious injury or even death to members of the public. Those involving financial loss can result in a significant drop in a company's stock price, disruptions to its operations, and even bankruptcy. Almost any type of crisis, if not handled effectively, can harm a company's reputation. Unfortunately, there is not one organization that is immune to crises or the damage they cause. As a result, crisis planning is an essential skill for anyone pursuing a career in public relations. To be able to engage effectively in crisis planning, public relations professionals should be familiar with Situational Crisis Communication Theory (SCCT) and CCP.

Situational Crisis Communication Theory

Created by W. Timothy Coombs, Situational Crisis Communication Theory (SCCT) provides an "evidence-based framework for understanding how to maximize the repetitional protection afforded by post-crisis communication" (Coombs 2007a, 163). At its base level, SCCT "identifies how key facets of

Situational Crisis Communication Theory (SCCT): A theory focused specifically on maintaining a favorable reputation during crisis response.

the crisis situation influence attributions about the crisis and the reputations held by stakeholders. In turn, understanding how stakeholders respond to the crisis informs the post-crisis communication. The empirical research from SCCT provides a set of guidelines for how crisis managers can use crisis response strategies to protect a reputation from the ravages of a crisis" (Coombs 2007a, 163).

Reputation and Reputational Threat

To fully understand SCCT, it is important to begin by exploring the idea of the reputational threat as many organizations experience damage to their reputation following a crisis. An organization's **reputation** is the opinion of its stakeholders as to how well it is meeting expectations. In this sense, a stakeholder is defined as "any group that can affect or be affected by the behavior of an organization." (Coombs 2007a, 164) An organization's reputation is considered an intangible asset and critical to its long-term survival. A strong reputation positively supports all facets of a company, ranging from sales and employee retention to financial performance and market position.

An organization's reputation develops over time as stakeholders learn more about it. Often, "stakeholders compare what they know about an organization to some standard to determine whether or not an organization meets their expectations for how an organization should behave. A failure to meet

Reputation: The opinion of an organization's stakeholders as to how well it is meeting expectations.

expectations is problematic for an organization." (Coombs 2007a, 164) As a crisis is by definition an unexpected event, it has the potential to impact an organization or its stakeholders in a variety of ways. These stakeholders include investors, employees, customers, suppliers and community members. For any organization, one of the most significant ramifications of a crisis can be a potential decline in its reputation, commonly referred to as a **reputational threat**.

Reputational Threat: The potential for a decline in an organization's reputation.

Reputational Capital

Another significant concept for the basis of Coombs' SCCT is reputational capital. **Reputational capital** refers to an organization's "stock of perceptual and social assets—the quality of the relationship it has established with stakeholders and the regard in which the company and brand is held" (Formbrun and van Riel 2004, 32). Any time an organization experiences a crisis, it stands to lose some amount of reputational capital. A strong reputation prior to the onset of a crisis helps an organization safeguard against a significant drop in its reputational capital if and when a crisis occurs. In general, "a favorable prior reputation means an organization suffers less and rebounds more quickly" (Coombs 2007a, 165).

Reputational Capital: The perceived assets and intellectual capital of an organization.

While an organization's reputation and reputation capital are important, the biggest priority in a crisis is to "protect stakeholders from harm, not to protect the reputation" (Coombs 2007a, 165). As echoed by Sturges, in managing a crisis, "the intent is to prevent drastic negative changes in relationships with environmental components" (Sturges 1994, 307). But, as Sturges notes, "planning only for damage control results in activities that may be too late to secure positive relationships important to the organization. The real work of influencing relationships should be done long before a crisis arises when issues, although salient to the public, are still latent" (Sturges 1994, 307).

Part of the secret to ensuring strong reputational capital, comes in maintaining a positive relationship with stakeholders. Sturges explains, "The foundation that may prevent an organization from suffering a severe negative is the foundation of positive opinion about the organization held by groups of people whose behavior may affect the organization's operation" (Sturges 1994, 307).

CAPTIVATING VISUAL DEMONSTRATIONS

The most important rule of public presentations focuses on presentation aids: If a visual presentation can stand alone, it is wrong. The problems with PowerPoint and Prezi are common, so consider these simple tips: 1. Do not simply use bullet points. Show what you have to offer. 2. Do not read off the screen. Know the value proposition. 3. Do not be overly technical or overly simplistic. 4. Attend a respectable workshop or seminar to learn the best practices of presentation aids.

SOURCE: http://www.10bestpr.com/tips/11-15/

THE SCCT FRAMEWORK

The Syrian crisis challenged many nations of the world to respond in a positive and helpful way.

Denial: A posture in Situational Crisis Communication Theory that seeks to remove any connection between the crisis and the organization.

Diminishment: A posture in Situational Crisis Communication Theory that seeks to reduce attributions of organizational control over the crisis.

Rebuilding: A posture in Situational Crisis Communication Theory that seeks to improve the organization's reputation in the wake of a crisis.

The framework for Situational Crisis Communication Theory (SCCT) focuses on maintaining a favorable reputation during a crisis response. This theory includes a set of specific strategies based on four postures: denial, diminishment, rebuilding, and bolstering. When implementing these postures, organizations must communicate three types of information: instructing information that tells "stakeholders what to do to protect themselves physically in the crisis" (Coombs, 2012, p. 146), adjusting information which explains the "what, when, where, why, and how of the crisis" (Coombs, 2012, p. 148), and a reputational strategy.

Coombs defines the four postures as *denial*, which seeks to "remove any connection between the crisis and the organization" (p. 156); *diminishment*, which seeks to "reduce attributions of organizational control over the crisis" (p. 156); *rebuilding*, which seeks to "improve the organization's reputation" in the wake of the crisis (p. 156); and *bolstering*, which is combined with one or more of the other strategies to "build a positive connection between the organization and the stakeholders" (p. 157). To identify the appropriate strategy to use within these postures, the organization must identify the type of crisis, their history with crises, their reputation prior to the crisis, and the amount of responsibility the organization has for this crisis. Once this information has been considered, SCCT provides 13 strategic recommendations (Coombs, 2012, p.159):

1. "Provide instructing information to all victims or potential victims in the form of warnings and directions for protecting themselves from harm."
2. "Provide adjusting information to victims by expressing concern for them and providing corrective action when possible. (Note: Providing instructing and adjusting information is enough of a response for victim crises in an organization with no crisis history or unfavorable prior reputation)."
3. "Use diminishment strategies for accidental crises when there is no crisis history or unfavorable prior reputation."

From *Public Relatins Principles: Strategies for Professional Success,* by Shawn T. Wahl and Michelle M. Maresh Fuehrer. Copyright © 2016 Kendall Hunt Publishing Company. Reprinted by Permission.

4. "Use diminishment strategies for victim crises when there is a crisis history or unfavorable prior reputation."
5. "Use rebuilding strategies for accident crises when there is a crisis history or unfavorable prior reputation."
6. "Use rebuilding strategies for any preventable crisis."
7. "Use denial strategies in rumor crises."
8. "Use denial strategies in challenges when the challenge is unwarranted."
9. "Use corrective action (adjusting information) in challenges when other stakeholders are likely to support the challenge."
10. "Use reinforcing strategies as supplements to other response strategies."
11. "The victimage response [when the organization is clearly the victim in the crisis] strategy should only be used with the victim cluster."
12. "To be consistent, do not mix denial strategies with either diminishment or rebuilding strategies."
13. "Diminishment and rebuilding strategies can be used in combination with one another."

Bolstering: A posture in Situational Crisis Communication Theory that is combined with one or more strategies to build a positive connection between the organization and stakeholders.

CRISIS COMMUNICATION PLANNING

In addition to the SCCT framework, another facet of Coombs approach relates to the three stages of crisis communication planning outlined in **Chapter 1.** According to Coombs (2007a), the life cycle of a crisis consists of three stages: pre-crisis, the crisis event, and post crisis. Planning is required in each stage of the crisis life cycle. The pre-crisis focuses on prevention and preparation, the crisis response is the handling of the crisis, while the post crisis explores ways to prepare more effectively for the next crisis (Institute for Public Relations, 2007).

Crisis Life Cycle: A model that argues a crisis consists of three stages: pre-crisis, the crisis event, and post-crisis.

Pre-Crisis

In the pre-crisis stage, an organization proactively takes the necessary action to prevent the occurrence of a crisis. The pre-crisis efforts are largely unseen to the public unless a crisis occurs. In the event of a crisis, "it becomes explicitly obvious when an organization did not have effective pre-crisis planning" (Maresh-Fuehrer, 2013, p. 12). In this stage, crisis planning begins with the creation of a crisis communication plan (CCP). According to Maresh-Fuehrer (2013), the CCP is a document consisting of four phases—Organizational History, Risk Assessment, Strategic Communication Action

Crisis Communication Plan (CCP): A document consisting of four phases—Organizational History, Risk Assessment, Strategic Communication Action Plan, and Evaluation Plan.

Plan, and Evaluation Plan—with the purpose of helping an organization proactively prepare for, respond to, and evaluate their performance during a crisis. As a public relations practitioner, one of your duties may be to create a CCP for your organization. If your organization has an existing CCP, pre-crisis planning should consist of regularly updating, rehearsing, and revising the plan. For a sample CCP table of contents page, see Figure 12.1.

The first phase of the CCP consists of researching the history of your organization. According to Maresh-Fuehrer (2013), the Organizational History includes a discussion of:

- When/where/why/how and by whom the organization was founded.
- The location of each individual branch of the organization.
- The services provided by the organization
- The organization's community involvement.
- The organization's Internet and media presence.
- The organization's public reputation (via stakeholders, media, social media).
- The titles and responsibilities of organizational members/employees.
- An identification of stakeholder groups and their needs and expectations.
- Goals and objectives for the crisis plan.

While the content may appear to be common knowledge for an organization, it plays an important role in crisis planning. Revisiting the services provided by the organization helps you remember the promises the organization has made to the public. Reviewing the organization's community service record helps identify deficiencies that may exist in the community relations program. As Maresh-Fuehrer (2013) emphasizes, "an attractive record of community service demonstrates a commitment to your community, which is often the main source of stakeholder trust" (p. 36). When a crisis befalls

TABLE OF CONTENTS

Organizational History
- Name and Responsibility of Organization
- Employees and Hierarchy
- Stakeholder Expectations
- Crisis Philosophy, Goals, and Objectives

Risk Assessment
- Past Crises at [Organization's Name]
- Crises at Other [Organization's Name] Locations
- Crises at Similar Organizations
- Vulnerability Assessment

Strategic Communication Action Plan
- Crisis Team
- Media Center Location
- Contact List
- Crisis Communication Log
- Tabletop Exercises
- [List Each Crisis Identified in Risk Assessment]

Evaluation Plan
- Post-Crisis Evaluation Overview
- Data Collection
- Damage Assessment
- Performance Assessment
- Post-Crisis Improvement Plan

FIGURE 12.1: SAMPLE TABLE OF CONTENTS PAGE FOR A CRISIS COMMUNICATION PLAN

your organization, having the trust of your stakeholders is crucial in crisis recovery. Furthermore, researching your organization's media presence can help you discover a deficiency in positive coverage. A public gets to know you both directly, through interaction and experience, and indirectly, through word of mouth and media coverage. Media coverage helps paint a picture of your organization to those who have not directly done business with you. Researching the organization's Internet/social media presence is also important to the planning process as it may help identify unresolved and/or recurring issues that could potentially become a crisis in the future. Creating a list of employees and their respective job duties will help you select members for the crisis team based on knowledge of varying departments of the organization. Finally outlining each stakeholder groups' expectations for the organization will provide you with an idea of some of the crises that could occur, as most crises begin as a violation of stakeholders' expectations.

In addition to this research, the Organizational History section of the crisis communication plan should include establishing goals and objectives for the organization in times of crisis. In this case, a goal is the desired result the organization envisions during a crisis, such as keeping stakeholders informed of important information. An objective is a specific, measurable means by which to achieve your goal(s). For example, publishing at least two updates in the organization's online newsroom daily.

The second phase of the CCP is the Risk Assessment. The contents of this portion of the CCP are important in the planning process, as they allow us to

Having a crisis plan in place before any issues arise is essential in any public relations department.

Risk: A factor that has the potential to cause harm, loss, or danger to an organization.

identify **risks**—factors that have the potential to cause harm, loss, or danger to an organization—and prevent them from becoming crises. Each organization faces risks caused by various factors, such as: the industry, location of the organization, size of the organization, day-to-day operations, personnel, and nearby facilities. Take a moment to reflect on the university that you attend or the place that you work. What facilities are located nearby? Are there any characteristics of those facilities that could potentially cause a crisis for your organization?

Issues Management: The identification of trends that could become crises if left unsolved.

In addition to risk identification, another component of the risk assessment should be **issues management**, or the identification of trends that could become crises if left unsolved. Issues can be easily found when you analyze your research on the organization's public image and Internet/media presence. Consider any issues that have been raised by stakeholders—such as complaints on an app such as Yelp! or on your organization's Facebook page. Look specifically for patterns of complaints and consider the ways that you can communicate with your stakeholders to address these issues before they spiral out of control. This is closely related to another aspect of risk assessment: **reputation management**. To monitor the reputation of your organization, consider the results of your research on your Internet/media presence and supplement this research by communicating with stakeholders.

Reputation Management: Monitoring the reputation of your organization.

Finally, try to identify crises that have occurred at the organization in the past, crises that have occurred at other branches of the organization (if your organization has multiple locations), and crises that have affected similar organizations (Maresh-Fuehrer, 2013). The results of this research will culminate in a lengthy list of risks to the organization that can subsequently be used to conduct a **vulnerability assessment** of each risk. A simple mathematical equation may be used to assess an organization's vulnerability to each risk: V (vulnerability) = L (likelihood of the risk becoming a crisis) x I (impact on the organization if the risk becomes a crisis). Likelihood should be measured on a scale from 1 (unlikely) to 10 (very likely), and impact should be measured on a scale from 1 (weak) to 10 (strong). Each risk will have a vulnerability rating that ranges from 1 to 100. This score should be used to help prioritize crisis planning, allowing you to first prepare for the risks with the highest vulnerability.

Vulnerability Assessment: A simple mathematical equation (V = L x I) used to assess your organization's vulnerability to each risk.

The next phase of pre-crisis planning should be developing a Strategic Communication Action Plan for crisis prevention and response. According to Maresh-Fuehrer (2013), this plan should include:

Crisis Team: A group of employees representing all levels of the organizational hierarchy that will lead crisis efforts in the organization.

- Establishing a **crisis team**, or group of employees representing all levels of the organizational hierarchy that will lead crisis efforts in the organization.

- Training **spokesperson(s)**, or individuals on the crisis team who serve as the face of an organization during a crisis by releasing statements to the public and interacting with the media.
- Establishing a **media center**, or a safe location away from the organization's office where the crisis team and media can assemble during a crisis.
- Practicing responding to crises by regularly conducting **crisis drills**.
- Preparing necessary documents, such as a contact list.
- Identifying precautions that may be taken to prevent risks from becoming crises.
- Creating templates of crisis response statements and documents that may be rehearsed and quickly revised for use during a crisis.

The Strategic Communication Action Plan serves as an insurance policy for an organization, ensuring everyone is prepared to respond effectively to a crisis.

The final phase of the CCP is the Evaluation Plan. No crisis communication plan is complete without devising a method for recognizing strengths and weaknesses with the purpose of improving future crisis prevention and response efforts. The evaluation should consist of collecting data with the purpose of assessing the damages caused by the crisis and the effectiveness of the organization's performance in each stage of the crisis life cycle. This data should be collected from Internet and social media comments, media coverage, internal documents (such as e-mails and voicemails), and interviews with or a survey of stakeholders. The results of evaluation research should be condensed into an executive summary that outlines what was done effectively along with a list of improvements that need to be made to the CCP (Coombs, 2012). This summary should be dated and placed in the crisis communication plan for reference.

Spokesperson(s): Individuals on the crisis team who serve as the face of an organization during a crisis by releasing statements to the public and interacting with the media.

Media Center: A safe location away from the organization's office where the crisis team and media can assemble during a crisis.

Crisis Drills: Exercises used to practice crisis response.

The Crisis Event

The second stage of the crisis life cycle, the crisis event, begins with a **triggering event**, or an issue that results in stakeholders believing that a crisis exists. In this stage, effective communication with **stakeholders**—anyone who has an interest in the organization and would be impacted emotionally, physically, or financially by a crisis—is critical. If you spent time developing the Strategic Communication Action Plan section of your CCP, you should be adequately prepared for this stage of the crisis life cycle. If you were able to proactively identify your organization's vulnerability to the crisis, you should be equipped with crisis response templates for this particular situation. However, planning

Triggering Event: An issue that results in stakeholders believing that a crisis exists.

Stakeholders: Anyone who has an interest in the organization and would be impacted emotionally, physically, or financially by a crisis.

does not stop here! You should never simply fill out a pre-designed crisis response template and expect automatic success. A template is simply a guide for your crisis response. An organization's crisis team will need to take time to collect information about the crisis and consult with each other regarding the appropriate crisis response strategy for use in this situation before modifying the template to communicate a strategic message to the public. Organizations that spend time planning thoughtful response messages typically experience swift crisis containment, minimal damages, and a quick return to business continuity.

Post-Crisis

The final stage of the crisis life cycle consists of the post-crisis actions taken by the organization. It is important to note that a crisis exists until its stakeholders agree the organization has met their needs and adequately responded to the crisis event. As a result, this stage of the life cycle requires an evaluation of the organization's crisis response efforts. If you have included an evaluation plan in your CCP, this plan should be enacted at the end of a crisis. If stakeholders are satisfied and you have experienced minimal damages, it is safe to say the organization has effectively overcome the crisis. However, even the best crisis response examples contain important lessons for future preparation. The fact that a crisis occurred may signal a need to devise a better prevention plan

Crisis management is much more effective with an entire team dedicated to the problem.

for the future. Thus, as we discussed at the beginning of this chapter, your CCP should be constantly evolving. The post-crisis evaluation is one way of ensuring that your organization learns from each crisis.

The role of planning in crisis communication should not be taken lightly. Having a crisis communication plan can literally be the difference between life and death. Organizations are quickly learning that a crisis does not have to be a negative event; rather, a crisis should be viewed as an opportunity for improving their business practices and relationships with stakeholders. Public relations centers on building and maintaining positive relationships between an organization and its stakeholders, and crisis planning is an important responsibility of the members of this profession.

Now that we have explored each of the phases of the Crisis Communication Plan, let's look specifically at the crisis response.

THE CRISIS RESPONSE

In most organizations, a crisis response is carried out by the public relations team in partnership with senior management.

As noted earlier, most crisis events can be divided into three stages:

- Stage One: Pre-crisis
- Stage Two: The crisis event
- Stage Three: Post crisis

We will now explore response strategies to be used in stages two and three of a crisis—the initial response and reputation repair and behavioral communication in the post crisis.

Part One: Initial Crisis Response: Speed, Accuracy, Consistency And Sympathy

In the initial phases of a crisis response, the focus should be on speed, accuracy, and consistency. Research studies show the importance of providing a fast response, typically within the first hour of a crisis occurring. Companies must share their perspective in a quick, controlled manner before the finger pointing begins. Usually, these are the key messages an organization's management team wants to share with its stakeholders. "Crisis experts often talk of an information vacuum being created by a crisis. The news media will lead the charge to fill the information vacuum and be a key source of initial crisis information. If the organization having the crisis does not speak to the news media, other people will be happy to talk to the media. These people may have inaccurate information or may try to use the crisis as an opportunity to attack the organization" (Institute for Public Relations, 2007).

In the initial response, there may not be a lot of information to report, but at least the organization starts to frame the story, mitigating the likelihood of rumors or falsities.

In their article, "Prepare for Business-Related Crises," A. Carney and Amy Jorden explain a timely response shows an organization is in control of the situation (Carney and Jordan 1993). It gives the impression the company is organized and addressing the issues at hand instead of avoiding them. A study done by Arpan and Rosko-Ewoldsen in 2005 underscores the importance of timely, early response in securing greater credibility from the public and stakeholders than a slow response.

Accuracy

The value of accuracy in managing a crisis cannot be emphasized enough. PR professionals and executives must remember to only use the facts they can prove. Executives should never comment or make a statement about something unless it is confirmed. The use of erroneous facts and figures can sabotage an organization's crisis response efforts and pose a significant threat to its reputational capital.

As noted above, in addition to ensuring accuracy, organizations must strive to provide a timely response especially in situations concerning the public's safety. If a crisis poses a threat to the public, the organization responsible for the crisis must provide clear direction on how to proceed. Sturges calls this type of information as "instructing information." An example would be that people must know as soon as possible not to eat contaminated chicken or to shelter-in-place during a pandemic. Over the long term, quick responses and actions by an organization will not only reduce the severity of damage, but also save an organization money by lessening the possibility of further harm and safeguard its reputation.

Consistency

Regardless of the type of crisis, one of the most significant factors is the consistency of the response. As part of his SCCT framework, Coombs stresses the important role the public relations department plays in *supporting a crisis response instead of leading it* (Coombs 2007a). The role of the PR professional is to ensure the designated spokespersons deliver consistent messages and fully understand the nuances of the crisis. Whatever a spokesperson says to *The New York Times* or *The Wall Street Journal* should be in accordance with what is being posted to an organization's social media platforms or its corporate website. The PR professional also needs to support the efforts of the designated spokespersons by providing updates, pointing out inaccuracies of facts and tracking media coverage. As noted by the Institute for Public Relations, "Ideally, potential spokespersons are trained and practice media relations skills prior to any crisis. The focus during a crisis then should be on the key information to be delivered rather than how to handle the media" (Institute for Public Relations 2007).

Sympathy and Concern

It is important to express sympathy for the victims effected by a crisis. Research shows when an organization expresses concern for victims, it rebounds faster, often experiencing less financial and reputational loss. In a 2004, Dwane Hal Dean conducted a study looking at "the effects of company reputation for social responsibility prior to a crisis event, response to a crisis event, and responsibility for the event on overall consumer regard for the firm" (Dean 2004, 1). It turns out the impact of a crisis on an organization's brand varies depending upon its pre-crisis reputation. Specifically, "an inappropriate response by a 'bad' company resulted in an increase in regard toward the firm, whereas the same response by a 'good' company resulted in a decrease in regard for the firm" (Dean 2004, 1). This same observation was expressed by Coombs in his research as noted earlier in this chapter.

PLATFORMS FOR CRISIS COMMUNICATION RESPONSE

It is inarguable that traditional news media offers an effective platform for communicating the details of a crisis as it enables an organization to quickly reach a wide array of stakeholders. There are other tools organizations can also use to disseminate critical news such as social media, corporate websites, public service announcements (PSAs), and emergency response systems.

In a seven-year study of over 100 organizations, Michael Kent and Maureen Taylor discovered organizations were increasing their use of websites and mass notification systems to alert the public. Taylor and Kent propose several ways to use the Internet to support a crisis communication response (Taylor and Kent 2007):

1. Upload traditional crisis response materials to the corporate website, including press releases, media statements, transcripts/video of news conference, and fact sheets in a specifically designated area.
2. Leverage interactive communication technology—social media platforms, chat bots, help section. Enabling such features as real-time monitoring of the event and video/audio feeds where it makes sense.
3. Offer the organization's perspective on the crisis at hand directly on the corporate website or on a page specifically devoted to the crisis.
4. Create distinct webpages for each group of stakeholders with details relevant to them.
5. Work directly with government agencies such as The Centers for Disease Control (CDC), Federal Drug Administration (FDA), and the Consumer Product Safety Commission (CPSC) during a crisis.

BEST PRACTICES FOR CRISIS COMMUNICATION (INSTITUTE FOR PUBLIC RELATIONS 2007)

1. Speed is of the essence—initial response within the first hour of the crisis.
2. Only use accurate, verifiable facts.
3. Ensure consistency with spokespersons and messaging.
4. Remember public safety is the top priority.
5. Leverage all possible communication channels.
6. Offer expressions of concern/sympathy for victims.
7. Include employees in the initial response.

Part 2: Reputation Repair

The second part of an organization's crisis response focuses on repairing the potential damage to its reputation and corporate brand. In 2007, Coombs, architect of Situational Crisis Communication Theory, incorporated findings from Benoit's Image Repair Theory into his own resulting in the "Master List of Reputation Repair Strategies" (Coombs 2007b)

1. *Confront the accuser:* Approach the organization or individual claiming something is wrong.
2. *Denial:* Simply respond there is no crisis.
3. *Shift the Blame:* Position another organization or group as being responsible for the crisis.
4. *Make an Excuse:* Claim the situation was out of the organization's control.
5. *Result of Provocation:* Crisis resulted from another individual's actions.
6. *By Accident:* Situation resulted from series of uncontrollable events.
7. *Positive Intent:* Goal was to do well.
8. *Justification:* Damage from the crisis is not as bad as anticipated.
9. *Reminder*: Leverage the organization's positive reputation.
10. *Ingratiation*: Organization's stakeholders are applauded for response.
11. *Compensation*: Victims are compensated for their losses.
12. *Apology*: Organization accepts responsibility for the crisis.

These strategies can be used at any time during a crisis response and are often used in combination with each other. An extensive amount of research has been conducted under the framework of attribution theory to determine the most appropriate and effective ways to implement them.

Attribution Theory And Reputation Repair

The principles of attribution theory are based on the belief individuals try to understand why things happen, particularly those that are negative and unanticipated. Usually, responsibility for an event is associated with the organization or person involved in it. Typically, the organization associated with the crisis is the focus of the blame, especially initially. These attributions can affect all aspects of a crisis, particularly the relationship of the people involved in it. Organizations face three potential repercussions when blamed for a crisis: (1) damage to its reputation, (2) negative word-of-mouth publicity, (3) drop in sales (Coombs 2007a).

Researchers such as Timothy Coombs and Sherry Holladay have done extensive work exploring the connection between a crisis and an organization's brand. Coombs was the first to explore this relationship, ultimately leading to the debut of his Situation Crisis Communication Theory (SCCT) in 1995. Coombs' SCCT approach, which has been discussed extensively in this chapter, is "premised on matching the crisis response to the level of crisis responsibility" (Coombs 2002). Coombs discovered crisis managers typically implement a crisis response plan based on the level of threat to the organization's reputation. He recommends organizations implement progressively supportive communication response tactics as the intensity of the crisis increases. To assess the growing level of risk, Coombs suggests crisis managers implement a two-part approach—define the crisis and then pinpoint the strength of the organization's brand prior to its occurrence (Coombs 2002).

Research by Coombs, Holladay and others has determined if an organization has a history of related or similar crises, its reputation is likely to be significantly affected (Coombs and Holladay 2001). The public assumes organizations learn from a crisis experience and enact the necessary precautions to eliminate

TYPES OF CRISES AND ASSOCIATED LEVELS OF RESPONSIBILITY

Minimal Responsibility:

- **Natural Disasters:** Natural disasters such as hurricanes or earthquakes
- **Rumors:** Incorrect, maligning information being spread about an organization
- **Violence in the Workplace:** Crime committed by currewnt or former employee towards others on company property.
- **Product Tampering:** An individual or group not associated with an organization causes damage to its product/service line.

Low Responsibility:

- **Challenges:** An organization's stakeholder claims it is operating erroneously.
- **Technical accidents:** A technical or equipment error that causes a product malfunction.

Strong Responsibility:

- **Human-error accidents:** Industry or product-related accidents caused by human error.
- **Corporate wrongdoing:** Actions taken by an organization's management team that breaks the law or puts stakeholders at harm.

the likelihood for re-occurrence. As a result, even if a crisis is not due to the organization's error, it could still harm its brand and reputation if it resembles one from the past (Coombs 2004).

Below is a series of best practices in crisis communication based on the concepts of Attribution Theory and SSCT (Coombs 2007a, Coombs and Holladay 1996, 2001, 2006):

- Clear instructions should be communicated to everyone affected or potentially affected by the crisis.
- Organizations should be sympathetic to victims of the crisis and provide necessary support services (counseling, help-line).
- In crisis situations with **little** attribution of responsibility and little to no threat from outside factors, organizations should provide instructing information and a care response program.
- In crisis situations with **minimal** attribution of responsibility but the potential for additional problems, organizations should incorporate a justification or explanation for the potential challenges into the instructing information.
- In crisis situations with **low** attribution of responsibility and no potential for additional threats, organizations should incorporate a justification or explanation of the situation into the instructing information.
- In crisis situations with **low** attribution of responsibility but with the potential for additional problems, organizations should incorporate an apology and some form of compensation into the instructing information.
- In crisis situations with **high** attribution of responsibility, an apology and some form of compensation should be incorporated into the response strategy.
- Any time a victim of a crisis experiences significant harm, he/she should receive compensation.
- Confronting the accuser or completely denying allegations should be only used in combatting misinformation or a challenge crises.

STRATEGIES FOR PROFESSIONAL SUCCESS

Adapted from "What To Do When Crisis Strikes: Five Tips On Crisis Management," written by Beth Doane and published in Forbes on October 17, 2018.

These days a communication crisis can be anything from a data breach to a maligning tweet to a chemical explosion to a product failure. Regardless of the type or nature of the problem, every crisis needs to be addressed quickly. What is often shocking is how poorly some of the smartest brands and public figures mishandle them.

(continued)

Here are some tips to keep in mind when navigating a crisis:

Move quickly. In today's digital world, news travels fast. When something goes wrong, we don't have the opportunity to wait to respond. Even if you do not have all of the facts, or even half of them, it is important to acknowledge the crisis, even if it means putting out a simple statement or tweet saying the organization is aware of the situation and has launched an investigation.

It is important to be careful about the information included in a preliminary response. In the 2013 data breach of Target's IT system, the personal data of nearly 110 million customers was leaked. Target botched its response by issuing a number of statements prematurely. Some of the responses were factually wrong, forcing Target to issue retractions, which confused and angered customers. It positioned the company as incapable of handling the breach and its customers personal information.

Take responsibility: It's simple: Even if the issue is not your fault, it is best to apologize. While you may legally be correct, it is important to take the high road, especially when it comes to the public.

Remember *Cosmopolitan Magazine,* in 2017 when it posted an article with the headline "How This Woman Lost 44 Pounds without *ANY* Exercise." The weight loss was not a miracle but the result of a rare cancer. Readers were upset when learning the truth but Cosmo refused to issue an apology, only changing its headline online.

Then there was Adidas, who successfully avoided its own PR disaster. In 2017, four years after Boston Marathon bombing, the company sent out an email to race participants with the subject line "Congrats, you survived the Boston Marathon!" Realizing its grave error, the company immediately issued an apology.

Be human.

When something goes wrong, it is best to be human. Organizations facing a crisis should resist the desire to be reactive or defensive and try to be empathetic. Make sure your spokesperson can communicate a sense of calm and a sense of sympathy.

Remember the BP's Deepwater Horizon oil spill in 2010? It is considered the worst marine oil spill to date. In total, it killed 11 people and spilled nearly five million barrels of oil into the ocean. Instead of projecting a sense of sympathy and humility to the public about the crisis, its CEO at the time Tony Hayward was insincere and cold hearted. Over a decade later, BP is still recovering from the crisis.

Establish channels of communication.

Set up channels of communication using a combination of new and traditional technologies where the public can access

(continued)

information, ask questions or voice their complaints. The greater the transparency and truth that is expressed by an organization, the less of a reputational crisis the brand will face after the crisis subsides.

Plan for next time.

Regardless of how careful you are, disasters can still occur. Hold vulnerability audits to determine where problems could occur, ask questions about social media, security and rapid response capabilities. Have an action plan developed in the event a crisis strikes and a designated team of professionals to support it.

EXECUTIVE SUMMARY

Now that you have finished reading this chapter, you should be able to

- Understand the decision and purpose of Situational Crisis Communication Theory.
- Appreciate the stages of the Crisis Communication Planning Process.
- Realize the impact of a crisis on an organization's brand and reputational capital.
- Comprehend the connection between the type of crisis and the expected level of response.
- Understand the critical factors integral in any crisis response plan.

KEY TERMS

Bolstering: A posture in Situational Crisis Communication Theory that is combined with one or more strategies to build a positive connection between the organization and stakeholders. p. 249

Crisis: A specific, unexpected, and nonroutine event or series of events that creates high levels of uncertainty and simultaneously presents an organization with both opportunities for and threats to its high-priority goals. p. 244

Crisis Communication Plan (CCP): A document consisting of four phases—Organizational History, Risk Assessment, Strategic Communication Action Plan, and Evaluation Plan. p. 249

Crisis Drills: Exercises used to practice crisis response. p. 253

Crisis Life Cycle: A model that argues that a crisis consists of three stages: pre-crisis, the crisis event, and post-crisis. p. 249

Crisis Management: The process of preventing or lessening the harm a crisis has on an organization and its stakeholders. p. 244

Crisis Team: A group of employees representing all levels of the organizational hierarchy that will lead crisis efforts in the organization. p. 252

Denial: A posture in Situational Crisis Communication Theory that seeks to remove any connection between the crisis and the organization. p. 248

Diminishment: A posture in Situational Crisis Communication Theory that seeks to reduce attributions of organizational control over the crisis. *p. 248*

Issues Management: The identification of trends that could become crises if left unsolved. *p. 252*

Media Center: A safe location away from the organization's office where the crisis team and media can assemble during a crisis. *p. 253*

Rebuilding: A posture in Situational Crisis Communication Theory that seeks to improve the organization's reputation in the wake of a crisis. *p. 248*

Reputation: The opinion of an organization's stakeholders as to how well it is meeting expectations. *p. 246*

Reputational Capital: The perceived assets and intellectual capital of an organization. *p. 247*

Reputational Threat: The potential for a decline in an organization's reputation. *p. 247*

Reputation Management: Monitoring the reputation of your organization. *p. 252*

Risk: A factor that has the potential to cause harm, loss, or danger to an organization. *p. 252*

Situational Crisis Communication Theory (SCCT): A theory focused specifically on maintaining a favorable reputation during crisis response. *p. 245*

Spokesperson(s): Individuals on the crisis team who serve as the face of an organization during a crisis by releasing statements to the public and interacting with the media. *p. 253*

Stakeholders: Anyone who has an interest in the organization and would be impacted emotionally, physically, or financially by a crisis. *p. 253*

Triggering Event: An issue that results in stakeholders believing that a crisis exists. *p. 253*

Vulnerability Assessment: A simple mathematical equation ($V = L \times I$) used to assess your organization's vulnerability to each risk. *p. 252*

DISCUSSION QUESTIONS

1. What are the tenants of Coombs Situational Crisis Communication Plan?
2. What is the prescribed framework for an effective crisis response? What are the three phases of CCP?
3. According to Coombs, what is the role of the PR practitioner is supporting a crisis?
4. What are critical elements of an effective and successful crisis communication response?
5. What are some things to avoid?

CHAPTER 13
PUBLIC AFFAIRS

London, UK. 15 October 2016. EDITORIAL—Hundreds marched to Downing Street, London, calling on the British government to enact Lord Dubs' amendment now, to relocate 3,000 child refugees into the UK.

CHAPTER OUTLINE

Introduction to Public Affairs
    Evolution of the Public Affairs Industry
    Importance of the Public Affairs Department
    Influence of the Public Affairs Department
    Responsibilities of a Public Affairs Practitioner
    Lobbyist vs. lobbying: Big L vs. Little l
    Organization of a Public Affairs Department
    Public Affairs Campaigns
    Planning A Public Affairs Campaign
    Positions in Public Affairs
    Public Affairs vs. Public Relations
Strategies For Professional Success
Executive Summary
Key Terms
Discussion Questions

CHAPTER OBJECTIVES

After studying this chapter, you should be able to:

1. Define the concept of public affairs.
2. Track the development of the public affairs industry.
3. Describe the relationship between public affairs and other areas of an organization.
4. Discuss the essential elements of a public affairs campaign.
5. Explain the difference between Lobbying and lobbyist.
6. Identify the differences between public affairs and public relations.

THE PRACTICE OF PUBLIC RELATIONS

Ripped from the Headlines

In 2018, Facebook faced the biggest scandal since its inception. Known as the Facebook-Cambridge Anlaytica Data scandal, the world's largest social media platform was accused of gathering the personal information of over 50 million users without their consent and then using it to target voters in the 2016 US presidential election. The data was collected via the app "This is Your Digital Life" de veloped by scientist Alexsandr Kogan from the company Global Science Research. The ap p used a series of questions to create psychological profiles of users with the data being collected through Facebook's Open Graph platform. Cambridge Analytica then used the data to provide insights to the presidential campaigns of Donald Trump and Ted Cruz.

Facebook users around the globe were shocked by the allegations ultimately creating the #QuitFacebook hashtag. The company's value dropped over night and investors fled the platform in droves. Later that year in November 2018, *The New York Times* reported that Facebook hired public affairs agency Definers to conduct a smear campaign against its critics.

(PR Week, December 18, 2018, "The eight biggest PR stories of 2018?" By Ian Griggs & Rob McKinlay. https://www.prweek.com/article/1521459/eight-biggest-pr-stories-2018)

INTRODUCTION TO PUBLIC AFFAIRS

As explained in Chapter 1, public affairs is one of the critical professions in the communications field. Similar to media relations and investor relations, it is one of functional areas that directly impacts the relationship between an organization and its publics.

According to the Public Affairs Council, the leading nonpartisan, nonpolitical association for public affairs professionals worldwide, public affairs "is an organization's efforts to monitor and manage its business environment. It combines government relations, communications, issues management and corporate citizenship strategies to influence public policy, build a strong reputation and find common ground with stakeholders" (Public Affairs Council n.d.). In his book *How to Manage Your Local Reputation*, Michael Morley describes public affairs as any communications activity directed towards government representatives at local, national, and supranational level. As noted by Morley, "these representatives may be elected legislators or the civil servants whose translation of laws into a host of regulations can often have more impact than the laws themselves" (Morley, 125). Building on Morley's definition, PubAffairs, one of the world's leading public affairs networks, defines public affairs as "an organization's relationship with its stakeholders. These are individuals or groups with an interest in the organization's affairs such as politicians, civil servants, customers and local communities, clients, shareholders, trade associations, think tanks, business groups, charities, unions and the media" (Pub Affairs).

Stakeholders: An owner of shares in a private or public corporation.

As noted in Chapter 1, the PR council views public affairs as, "issues arising from the relationships of the public to an organization such as a government body or a financial institution" (PR Council n.d.).

Public Affairs: Efforts by organizations to engage and track their business processes.

Evolution Of The Public Affairs Industry

Public affairs is a relatively recent entrant in the communications industry. Its roots can be traced to the late 1970s, becoming a functional area within most Fortune 1000 companies by the mid-1980s.

Prior to the creation of the industry, lobbying campaigns were conducted by associations and often ineffective. In a study published by three political scientists in 1963, it was written "When we look at the typical lobby we find its opportunities to maneuver are sharply limited, its staff mediocre, and its typical problem not the influencing of Congressional votes but finding the clients and contributors to enable it to survive at all" (Drutman 2015, 51).

As explained in the 1983 article, "Managing Public Affairs: The Public Affairs Function," by James E. Post, Robert B. Dickie, Edwin A. Murray, Jr. and John F. Mahon, "The 1980s signal an important change in the way companies participate in political decision-making. The era of high-profile chief executives, such as Irving Shapiro at Dupont, Reginald Jones at General Electric, and Thomas Murphy at General Motors, has begun to pass, and new organizational mechanisms are evolving to meet the need for a more systematic means of managing corporate involvement in politics and external

Republished with permission of Sage Publications Inc. Journals, from "Managing Public Affairs: The Public Affairs Function," by James Post, et. al., in *California Management Review*, Vol. XXVI, No. 1, Fall 1983; permission conveyed through Copyright Clearance Center, Inc.

affairs. In many companies, the prominent managerial innovation has been the establishment of a public affairs department to coordinate government relations, community relations, and other external relations activities" (Post, Dickie, Murray, and Mahon 1983, 135).

A 1981 study of more than 1,000 large and medium-sized businesses conducted by the Public Affairs Council, Foundation for Public Affairs, and Conference Board, shows more than 50% of public affairs departments were created during the latter part of the 1970s. The budgets and staff to support these departments grew at the same rate, signifying public affairs was becoming an essential part of many organizations (Post, Dickie, Murray, and Mahon 1983, 136). The addition of the public affairs department represented a new cost center for businesses, but it was one most were willing to take accept. The creation of the public affairs function, was "one of the more significant changes in professional management since the 1970s when strategic planning flowered" (Post, Dickie, Murray, and Mahon 1983, 136).

Fast forward to today and public affairs is booming. In fact, it is one of the fastest growing areas of the communications industry. "The evolution of business lobbying from a sparse reactive force into a ubiquitous and increasingly proactive one is among the most important transformations in American politics over the last 40 years" (Drutman 2015).

Importance of the Public Affairs Department

The importance and strategic role of the public affairs practitioner has been clear since the industry began. In over 60% of the companies surveyed in 1981, the public affairs department reported directly to the president, CEO, or chairman, providing unbridled access to top management on a regular and continual basis. In addition, data from the same survey suggests it has always been a top priority for management. This is particularly important in public affairs as it is often necessary to include senior management in elements of a campaign. The challenge, however, is to strike a delicate balance ensuring an organization's executive team is not overly involved. As noted in the article by Post, Dickie, Murray, and Mahon, "The resulting problem is not with management commitment, but rather with administrative interference in what must become a legitimate staff function. In some companies, the preoccupation of CEOs with public affairs has left the public affairs department bypassed, frustrated, undercut, and administratively underdeveloped" (Post, Dickie, Murray, and Mahon 1983, 138).

Influence of The Public Affairs Department

In most organizations, the public affairs function impacts several areas including community relations, media relations, investor relations, customer relations, and even employee relations. For each of these groups, the public affairs department provides three services:

- **Social and Political Intelligence:** The tracking of social and political intelligence helps an organization identify trends or issues that may pose challenges in the future. It primarily can prove instrumental in supporting actions such as lobbying, contributing to political action committees (PACs), or other creating programs to advance the corporate interest.
- **External Action Programs:** As part of gathering intelligence, public affairs practitioners report industry developments to senior management and business unit managers. They are often tasked with designing and/or recommending strategies and tactics to combat developments that could negatively impact the organization.
- **Internal Communications:** Public affairs professionals often serve as the bridge between an organization and the external world. Practitioners brief management on issues of concern and then work with other communication functions to translate the impact of these developments on the organization's stake holders (Post, Dickie, Murray, and Mahon 1983, 139).

As noted by one public affairs professional, "I am precisely at the point of intersection between the company and the community. I spend ninety percent of my life trying to help them to understand each other. The trouble takes place when someone reacts on the basis of a mere supposition about the other side or on the basis of a misleading quote in the media," (Post, Dickie, Murray, and Mahon 1983, 139).

Responsibilities of a Public Affairs Practitioner

Public affairs managers look to "advance the interests of their employers with decision-making bodies, such as the UK government and Parliament, the EU, industry regulators, local governments and non-departmental public bodies"(PR Week, 1/14/2017). Similar to PR professionals, their overall objective is to create and support a positive image of their institution with other stakeholders such non-governmental organizations and the media.

At the heart of the profession, is the continual monitoring of changes in public policy with the hope of ascertaining and evaluating their potential ramifications. Public affairs professionals can be found in any type of organization, including non-profits, corporations, think-tanks, and trade unions.

As part of this process, public affairs practitioners engage in a variety of activities including:

- **Establishing and maintaining frequent contact** with political advisors, politicians, and government regulators to keep them abreast of an organization's work and policy concerns (Hayley-Jones 2017).

- **Organizing and attending meetings** with relevant stakeholders in order to support their organization's position and develop contact with key decision-makers (Hayley-Jones 2017).
- **Lobbying for specific legislation** and other concerns of the organization (US Chamber of Commerce 2020).
- **Monitoring government proceedings** and providing an analysis for senior management (US Chamber of Commerce 2020).
- **Providing predictive analysis** of the possibility and ramifications of public policy changes (Hayley-Jones 2017).
- **Disseminating information** to and maintaining relationships with stakeholders (Hayley-Jones 2017).
- **Fostering relationships** with relevant media outlets.

> **PR TIP**
> Public affairs practitioners partake in an array of proactive and reactive communication tactics in a similar fashion as their public relations counterparts.

Companies engage the services of public affairs practitioners when there is existing or pending legislation that could affect its operations or when there are ideas or policies it is looking to implement.

Lobbyist Vs. Lobbying: Big L vs. Little l

While it is clear, public affairs focuses more on public policy and legislation than brand building, it still misunderstood by many. Public Affairs is loosely referred to as lobbying, but it important to clarify what this means. While activities conducted by public affairs practitioners in the US can be informally described as lobbying with a small l, it is far from the accepted definition of what entails. As explained by Michael Morley in his book *How to Manage Your Global Reputation*, "A

Lobbying: The act of influencing on an issue.

Lobbyist: A person who takes part in an organized attempt to influence.

Lobbyist deals directly with lawmakers, regulators and their various committees. The very word 'lobbyist' arises because the practitioner hangs around the lobbies of Congress and the Senate, or the Houses of Parliament in Britain, hoping to waylay lawmakers as they move to and from their chambers" (Morley, 125).

The distinction between the little l and the big L is a way of differentiating between the activities of individuals and firms practicing the different kinds of public affairs. As noted by Morley, a "Lobbyist is any individual who is paid by a third party to make more than one lobbying contact. A lobbying contact is an oral or written communication to a vast range of specific individuals (or specific job titles) in the Executive and Legislative branches of the Federal Government" (Morley, 126). In the context of this book, we are focused on the activities of a lobbyist with a capital L.

The market opportunities for Lobbyists are enormous. In a 2015 article in *The Atlantic*, "How Corporate Lobbyists Conquered American Democracy" it is estimated United States corporations spent $2.6 million a year on lobbying expenditures. This is more than the $2 billion the U.S. government spends on funding for the House ($1.18 billion) and Senate ($860 million). As noted in the article, "It's a gap that has been widening since corporate lobbying began to regularly exceed the combined House-Senate budget in the early 2000s." Some of the biggest companies have close to 100 lobbyists representing them, allowing them to be ubiquitous in advancing their public policy efforts. For every dollar spent on lobbying by labor unions and public-interest groups together, large corporations and their associations now spend $34 (Drutman 2015).

Even during economic downturns, such as the 2008 financial crisis, lobbying is practiced by most organizations. Data from a study done in 2012

highlights the differences in the total amount of money spent on lobbying by organizations over a 14 year period:

- **Small budgets**—those spending under $50,000—grew from 553 in 1998 to a high of 1,424 in 2008 and dropped to 660 in 2012.
- **Medium budgets**—those investing between $50,000 and $250,000—grew from 1,010 in 1998 to 2,375 in 2008 and dipped to 1,804 in 2012.
- **Large budgets**—those allocating between $250,000 and $1 million—increased from 334 in 1998 to a high of 736 in 2010 before sliding to 630 in 2012.
- **Major budgets**—those spending over $1 million grew from 216 in 1998 to 392 in 2010 and slipping only slightly to 379 in 2012 (Drutman 2015, 84).

In total, the number of companies with registered lobbyists increased from 2,163 in 1998 to a high of 4,083 in 2008 and dipping to 3,473 in 2012. Although these numbers are nearly a decade old, they capture some interesting trends in the industry. As Drutman explains, "the companies bowing out of lobbying are the companies who did the least lobbying, and thus has the most tenuous connections to politics. They didn't institutionalize lobbying. So it makes sense that these small and medium sized lobbying companies would drop out when the economy went downhill. . . . But notice: the population of the 'big' and 'major' lobbying stays stable during this period. These are the companies that have committed most thoroughly to political engagement, and they are thus least likely to be deterred by the short-term changes" (Drutman 2015, 85).

It is interesting to note lobbying expenditures follow a "power-law distribution" according to Drutman. Bigger companies account for the majority of money

spent annually on lobbying. In fact, in 2007, the 297 companies that spent over $1million accounted for 62.6% of total lobbying expenditures and those investing more than $2.5 million represent another 45.7%. The little amount left was spent by small and medium efforts (Drutman 2015, 86).

Organization of a Public Affairs Department

With such a diverse set of responsibilities, the question often posed concerns the organization of the public affairs function. The structure of public affairs departments range from being highly centralized with most work being done at corporate headquarters to heavily decentralized with the majority of the work being done at the business or operating unit level.

There are several factors to consider in designing the function:

- **Coordination:** The mechanisms necessary to coordinate the organization's interaction with government, media, and its stakeholders varies greatly between organizations. In many ways, this comes down to the complexity of the organization and its industry. Global multinational corporations are likely to need a method of public affairs management that is drastically different from that of a single business operating in a stable, regional environment.
- **Constraints:** An additional factor relates to constraints imposed upon or encountered by management. An effective public affairs program must be designed to operate within the environment and resources in which it will be based. This involves everything from corporate culture and financial resources to human resources and organizational values.
- **Senior Management:** As noted earlier in this chapter, in most organizations the public affairs function reports directly into senior management, making it important to incorporate their views into the design of the program. As explained by Post, Dickie, Murray, and Mahon, "Although there are instances in which the sheer force of outside pressures led to the creation of a public affairs unit, there are few stories of thriving public affairs units that did not in some manner come to 'fit' with the personality of the senior management" (Post, Dickie, Murray, and Mahon 1983, 139).

According to research from McKinsey, the business value of a well-structured and smartly-executed program public affairs program is enormous. Researchers at McKinsey estimate a successful public affairs program translates into "about 30 percent of earnings for companies in most industries . . . and higher still in the banking sector, where the figure tops 50 percent. Translating those percentages into euros, dollars, or yen can yield eye-popping results: one European utility found that the ongoing value at stake from regulation was €1.5 billion, or about €30 million for every employee involved in handling the company's regulatory affairs" (Musters, Parekh, and Ramkumar 2013).

Despite the proven value of the public affairs function, many organizations do not have well-organized departments. In a 2013 study conducted by McKinsey, "fewer than 30 percent of the executives responding said that their external-affairs groups had the organizational setup and talent necessary to succeed. Only about 20 percent of executives reported frequent success at influencing government policy and regulatory decisions" (Musters, Parekh, and Ramkumar 2013).

> **PR TIP**
>
> A well organized and strategically structured public affairs department can prove to be invaluable to an organization, especially in conjunction with a public relations program.

One of the biggest challenges for organizations as noted by an executive in the McKinsey study is "We have separate government-affairs and external-communications functions. They operate independently and don't report to the same executive. We don't always communicate on key regulatory issues as much as we should."

It is interesting to note there is "no "normal" level of business lobbying in American democracy" (Drutman 2015). Rather, the public affairs industry and the concept of business lobbying has steadily increased over time. Today, the public affairs industry has "fundamentally changed how corporations interact with government—rather than trying to keep government out of its business (as they did for a long time), companies are now increasingly bringing government in as a partner, looking to see what the country can do for them" (Drutman 2015).

Public Affairs Campaigns

The ultimate goal of a public affairs campaign is to "shape public opinion and in the process influence government actions or decisions in way that aid client interests" (Public Affairs Council n.d.). Public affairs professionals work with an organization's stakeholders to "explain organizational policies and views on public policy issues, assisting policy makers and legislators in amending or laying down better policy legislation. They provide statistical and factual information and lobby on issues which could impact upon the organization's ability to operate successfully" (Public Affairs Council n.d.).

The implementation of public affairs campaigns has increased in popularity over the past several decades; as more and more businesses realize their potential for impact. With digital disruption overtaking the global marketplace, such campaigns can achieve incredible results in a short amount of time.

Similar to public relations programs, public affairs campaigns can be executed using either a targeted approached or mass outreach. While several large public affairs campaigns have been implemented over the years, most tend to be specialized in nature focusing on issues related to the local social, economic, or political landscape. If a public affairs campaign has been designed for a mass audience, it still tends to get interpreted to fit the needs of local market where it will be conducted. Often, it has to be adjusted to address the legal and regulatory complexities of the political environment.

Planning a Public Affairs Campaign

While most public relations campaigns are carried out for commercial reasons, public affairs programs are done in response to social or political issues impacting a local community. As a result, most public affairs programs "tend to be more emotional and delicate due to local culture, politics or religious sensitivities" (See 2020).

It is important to take the following factors into account when planning a public affairs campaign:

1. **Reality of the Situation:** It is necessary to try to understand the true reality of the situation instead of relying on media reports or heresy. In-depth research should be the first step in the development of any public affairs campaign and serve its foundation. "Without understanding the reality on the ground . . . economic and socio-cultural aspects of the market, it is almost impossible to roll out any form of effective public affairs campaign. . . ." (See 2020). Not taking cultural or religious sensitivities into consideration can be risky.

2. **End Goal:** There cannot be a successful campaign without an end goal. Without a clear vision, the campaign will not support the business or its organizational objectives. Regardless of the aspirations, it is important it is credible and supported by the entire organization. Support from the top–down as well as the bottom–up is required

Thousands gather at Portland Place, London for the March Against Racism national demonstration, in protest of increase in race related attacks.

for the campaign to be successful. This goal needs to be carefully written so as to align with the culture of the organization, as well as proactively communicated so it is understood.

2. **Campaign Design:** Once there is a strong understanding of the issues and the goals for the campaign are established, the strategy and approach must be determined. Be sure to keep in mind such factors as resource availability, distribution channels, target publics, and organizational nuances as each of these elements could impact the success of the campaign.

3. **Campaign Execution:** It is one thing to develop a campaign but it is another to execute it. A well-developed tactical plan helps to ensure the success of a public affairs campaign. These tactics should be based on the organization's resources and strengths and take into consideration the sensitivities of the local environment—cultural, political, and socio-economic factors.

4. **Campaign Evaluation:** Similar to public relations and investor relations programs, public affairs campaigns also need to be evaluated. Again, it is important to think about the local climate when determining the most effective way to judge the success of a program.

Positions in Public Affairs

In public affairs, there are no unique job titles as many are identical to their PR counterparts including associate, director, vice president or managing director. The industry itself can be described in a variety of ways ranging from public affairs and government affairs to government relations and external affairs (Public Affairs Networking n.d.):

- Public Affairs
- Government Affairs
- Government Relations
- Parliamentary Affairs
- Parliamentary Relations
- European Affairs
- Regulatory Affairs
- External Affairs
- Political Advisory
- International Affairs
- Corporate Affairs
- Stakeholder Management or Relations

Public Affairs vs. Public Relations

The big question for many people is what is the difference between public relations and public affairs? This can be difficult to answer as there is a significant amount of overlap between the two areas, as well as a common skill set. The fundamental difference between public relations and public affairs comes in the goal of the campaign. Public relations practitioners seek to "build awareness and/or bolster the reputations of products, services, organizations . . . . Most PR campaigns seek to generate true, organic, third-party support for a client's goals and objectives" (Sitton 2018).

Public affairs has "more to do with matters that affect the public directly and is usually more political in nature than public relations" (Public Strategies Impact, 9/2019). Its focus tends to be lawmaking and public policy. When state and federal legislators pass new laws, it can affect an organization's business interests. Organizations also use public affairs practitioners to build goodwill with their stakeholders as well as "bridge the gap between business interests and public policy" (US Chamber of Commerce 2020).

PR and PA professionals work in many of the same industries including nonprofits, corporations, government agencies, and private companies. Both industries involve interfacing with the public and influencing opinion, as well as designing and managing outreach campaigns focused on generating a response and building relationships with stakeholders. Essentially, it comes down to the simple difference that public relations professionals look generate awareness and build third-party support for an organization, while public affairs practitioners look to "create support or opposition regarding maters of public policy" (Sitton 2018).

According to the US Chamber of Commerce, "A public relations campaign will focus on generating goodwill for a company and gaining awareness about its product or service. . . . Public affairs is a more political industry and focuses on influencing policy" (US Chamber of Commerce 2020).

Danielle Blumenthal in her article "The Difference Between Public Affairs and Public Relations," writes, "…the key difference between private sector PR and government public affairs is who is paying the bill and what expectations they're bound by." The PR expert (private sector) helps their client restore and/or improve their name/likeness. The public affairs expert (government) tries to help the taxpayer get pertinent information and help the government run smooth and effectively.

STRATEGIES FOR PROFESSIONAL SUCCESS: TIPS FOR STRUCTURING AN EFFECTIVE PUBLIC AFFAIRS DEPARTMENT

Adopted from McKinsey Quarterly Article "Organizing the Government Affairs Impact Function for Impact"

1. **Clarify Scope and Structure:** In leading public affairs programs, most practitioners are skilled in stakeholder engagement and economic analysis, as well lobbying. Employing individuals devoted to "handling tasks such as identifying issues, developing positions, and gathering compelling international benchmarks, leading government-affairs units can anticipate a much broader range of possible regulatory outcomes." With such an approach, companies see an improvement in the quality of their public affairs efforts and, in some cases, can even have success breaking through complex, difficult situations.

2. **Identify Stakeholders:** The most effective public affairs programs determine critical stakeholders at a program's onset and then assign executives to them. "Designating senior executives as "owners" for important relationships, including those in social media, allows for smoother scheduling and coordination of day-to-day activities. More important, this approach makes it easier for a regulatory-affairs group to provide consistent, coherent, and proactive communication supporting a company's regulatory strategy."

3. **Determine Effective Structure:** Establishing the exact structure of PA function is easier said than done. It is important to consider such variables include: size and location of the team and the reporting relationship. Below is a chart of the most common organizational structures of public affairs department as reported in the McKinsey study:

(continued)

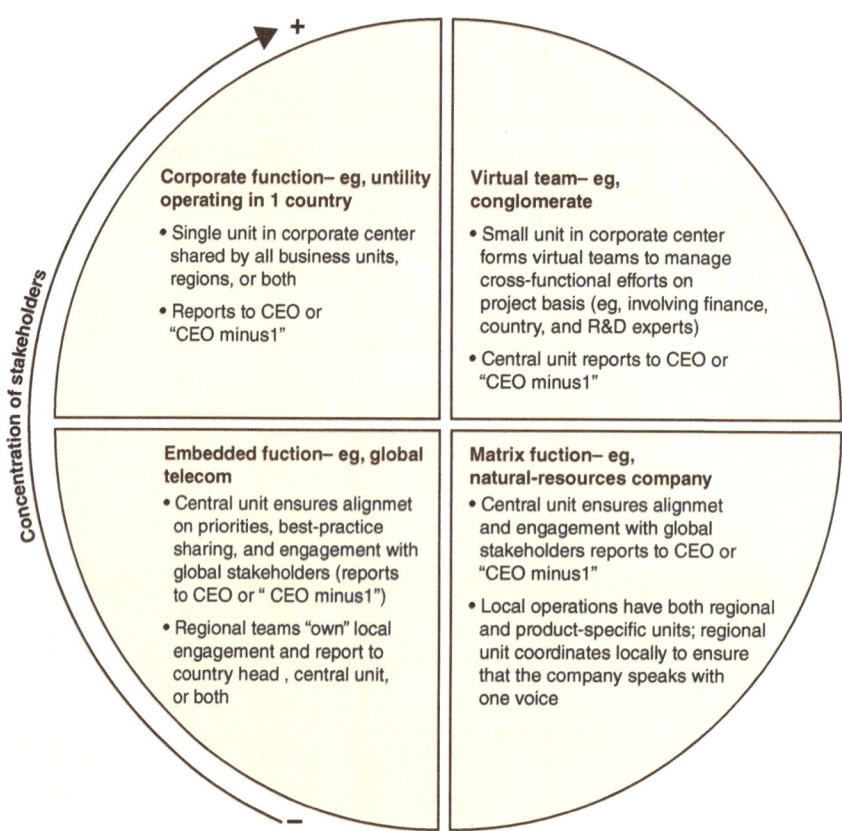

4. **Coordinate Activities Across the Business:** In large global organizations or public affairs departments with a decentralized structure, it is essential to have tight coordination of PA activities. Similar to community relations and public relations, public affairs program should be considered strategic to the overall growth of the organization, being coordinated and managed across business units, as well as functional areas. As explained in the McKinsey article, "When regulatory-affairs units aren't viewed as good partners, they can't help the businesses to engage with regulators, coordinate the development of positions proactively, monitor social media, or profile stakeholders, among other activities."

5. **Employ Experienced and Relevant Talent:** In its research, McKinsey discovered there are "three types of leaders: industry veterans, with deep legal or economic training (the role's classic profile); high-profile lobbyists or former politicians, who bring credibility and clout (useful when companies face pressure on a particular issue); or internally promoted business insiders (useful in strengthening cross-functional connections and gaining buy in)" running public affairs departments. Regardless of the type of individual selected, whoever heads the department needs to have the respect of senior management, understand the company vision, and coordinate efforts across the organization.

EXECUTIVE SUMMARY

Now that you have finished reading this chapter, you should be able to.

- Define the term public affairs.
- Understand the difference between public affairs and public relations.
- Explain the evolution of the public affairs industry.
- Describe the work done by public affairs practitioners.
- Appreciate the significant role public affairs plays in the business landscape.

KEY TERMS

Stakeholders: An owner of shares in a private or public corporation. *p. 269*

Public Affairs: Efforts by organizations to engage and track their business processes. *p. 269*

Lobbying: The act of influencing on an issue. *p. 273*

Lobbyist: A person who takes part in an organized attempt to influence. *p. 274*

DISCUSSION QUESTIONS

1. What is public affairs? Why is it important to an organization?
2. What is the difference between public affairs and public relations? Where is the overlap?
3. What are the important factors to keep in mind when developing a public affairs campaign?
4. What is a lobbyist? What is the difference between Lobbying and being a lobbyist?

CHAPTER 14
EMPLOYEE RELATIONS

May 2016 - Honda Automobile Thailand assembly line of car body parts at Prachinburi plant in Rojana Industrial Park in China.

CHAPTER OUTLINE

Introduction to Employee Relations
Employee Experience
Workforce of the Twenty-First Century
Developing the Employee Experience
    Define and Communicate the Corporate Culture
    Promote Open Communication Between Employees And Management
    Focus on the Organization's Mission and Values
    Showcase Employee Value
    Motivate, Inspire, and Reward
PR versus Employee Relations
Strategies for Professional Success
    The Importance of Being A Mission-Driven Company
    A Mission Statement Drives and Improves Engagement
    Mission-Driven Leaders Matter
    Creating the Right Mission Statement
Executive Summary
Key Terms
Discussion Questions

CHAPTER OBJECTIVES

After studying this chapter, you should be able to:

1. Define the term employee relations.
2. Understand the meaning of the employee experience.
3. Describe the workforce of the twenty-first century.
4. Discuss strategies for implementing a successful employee relations program.
5. Realize the similarities between employee relations and public relations.
6. Detail how employee relations differs from other groups in the PPR model.

THE PRACTICE OF PUBLIC RELATIONS

Ripped from the Headlines

In November 2019, Steve Easterbrook, was fired from his position as CEO of McDonald's after it was determined he was having a consensual relationship with an employee. Easterbrook's conduct violated a longstanding corporate policy against the existence of such relationships. Mason Smoot, the former head of the company HR's department and a 23-year veteran of the firm, was named interim replacement. This is not the first time a McDonald's employee was charged with sexual misconduct. Between January and November 2019, more than 20 women filed complaints with the U.S. Equal Employment Commission alleging inappropriate treatment while working at the golden arches. These complaints include allegations of inappropriate touching, indecent exposure, requests for sex and rude comments. These EEOC filings were the largest and third round of such complaints filed against McDonald's since 2016. In aggregate, these complaints significantly impacted the company's brand and possibly played a role in the board's decision to replace the CEO after his misconduct. (HR Executive, "Here's shy McDonald's turmoil may also be an HR opportunity," Andrew R. McIlvaine, November 6, 2019. https://hrexecutive.com/heres-why-mcdonalds-turmoil-may-also-be-an-opportunity/)

In the last two chapters of the book, we will explore the remaining parts of the PPR model—employee relations and customer relations. In most organizations, these two disciplines are carried out by separate units. This is in stark contrast to media relations, investor relations, community relations, public affairs, and crisis management, which are often executed by members of the public relations team or heavily supported by them. The hope is to provide insight into these areas of communication and explain the relationship of each to the public relations function. In this chapter, we will provide an overview of employee relations, discuss its role in an organization, and the parallels to public relations.

INTRODUCTION TO EMPLOYEE RELATIONS

As explained in Chapter 1, employee relations refers to the relationships between an employer and its employees. Unlike media relations, investor relations, public affairs, community relations, or customer relations, which are external audiences, employees are a company's internal audience. Regardless of this difference, an organization's relationship to its employees is one of its most critical. In most organizations, employee relations is located within the human resources department. There are individuals within the HR department dedicated to supporting the employee relations program.

Let's begin with a definition of the term employee relations. **Employee relations** focuses on the emotional, physical, contractual, and practical relationships between employee and employer. At its core, "it alludes to the relationship between manager and employee and it can either be one that is founded in mutual respect, appreciation, and trust, or fear and lack of transparency" (Officevibe). The term is also used in reference to the effort a company makes to build, manage, and sustain relationships between its employees and managers.

Employee Relations (ER): The relationship between employers and employees

EMPLOYEE EXPERIENCE

Successful employee relations programs involve more than just a competitive salary and benefits package; it includes every element of an employee's relationship with its employer. According to The 2019 Organizational Wellbeing & Talent Insights Report from Arthur J. Gallagher & Co., a global insurance brokerage, risk management, and consulting services firm, "The bottom line is that today's talent-management landscape means U.S. employers must be innovative in the compensation and benefits area, while delivering effective leadership and communication. Success in integrating these efforts, driven by a focus on the employee experience, includes an improved workplace culture that strengthens workforce engagement and reduces turnover" (Starner 2019).

Employee Experience: The experience an individual has while working with an organization

Writer Sophia Lee defines employee experience as "what people encounter and observe over the course of their tenure at an organization" (Lee n.d.). This experience begins the moment an employee makes the decision to work for an organization until they decide to leave. For companies, this means employee relations does not include just the offer letter and the benefits package, but instead a focus on the overall relationship.

According to Deloitte's 2019 Global Human Capital Trends Study, "Eighty-four percent of … survey respondents rated [employee experience] important, and

28% identified it as one of the three most urgent issues facing their organization in 2019" (Deloitte 2019, 6). This annual study included more than 10,000 respondents located in 119 countries around the globe. Deloitte's research argues there is an opportunity for organizations to "refresh and expand the concept of 'employee experience' to address the 'human experience' at work—building on an understanding of worker aspirations to connect work back to the impact it has on not only the organization, but society as a whole" (Deloitte 2019, 6).

A similar study done by Gartner Group in late 2019 suggests "Enhancing the employee experience is a key talent concern for HR leaders and organizations are investing significant resources, yet 46% of employees remain largely dissatisfied." Today, the challenge for many employers is determining how to satisfy the needs of its employees, many of whom are from vastly divergent generations, which makes the situation even more complex.

WORKFORCE OF THE TWENTY-FIRST CENTURY

According to data recently published by Purdue University, there are five age groups currently in the workforce with vastly different motivations and influences. As noted in the chart below, the biggest population in the today's business world are Millennials making up approximately 35%, followed by Generation X comprising 33% of it. The smallest group is known as Traditionalists representing only about 2%.

This stark variance in age and experience can pose significant challenges for employers. As explained in the infographics listed above by Dr. Bea Bourne, DM, faculty member in the School of Business and Information Technology at Purdue University Global, each generation has distinctly different influences, motivations, communication styles, and perspectives. For employers, the big question is how to keep these generations motivated and satisfied. Clearly, this can cause significant complexities for employee relations departments in organizations of any size or industry.

RJ Cheremond from Gartner notes, "Organizations need to focus on not just investing in the employee experience but also shaping how employees feel about it. Organizations should manage the overall employee experience by reminding employees of positive experiences and reframing their

• Traditionalists: Born from 1925 to 1945	2%
• Baby Boomers: Born from 1946 to 1964	25%
• Generation X: Born from 1965 to 1980	33%
• Millennials: Born from 1981 to 2000	35%
• Generation Z: Born from 2001 to 2020	5%

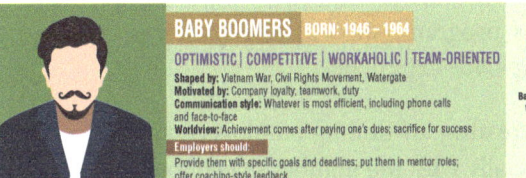

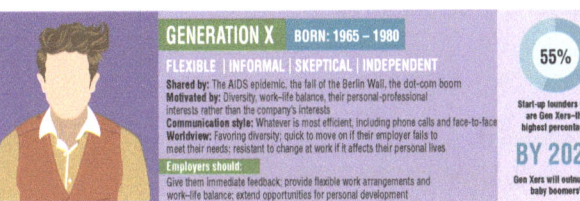

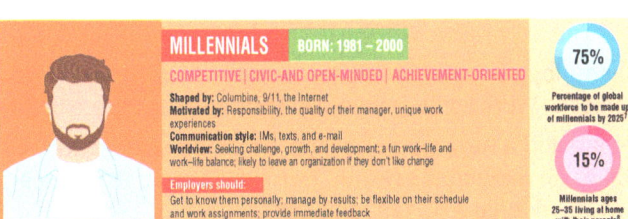

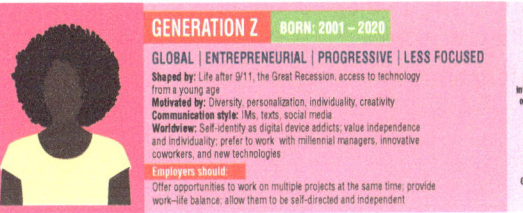

As highlighted in the Purdue University report, each of these generations grew up in dramatically different times and contrasting political environments, resulting in a variety of disparate tendencies:

Shaping Approach: When aspects of the work environment are manipulated with the integration of new technology or the implementation of new programs.

memories of negative experiences" (Cheremond 2019). Gartner's research also suggests the use of a shaping approach in structuring employee experience. In employee relations, a *shaping approach* occurs when aspects of the work environment are manipulated with the integration of new technology or the implementation of new programs or directives that create an ongoing dialogue and alignment between the organization and its employees. Adoption of a shaping approach can significantly improve employee satisfaction, decrease employee turnover, and increase performance.

DEVELOPING THE EMPLOYEE EXPERIENCE

While we won't detail the nuances of structuring and implementing a successful employee relations program, we will briefly discuss some suggestions for developing the employee experience.

The challenge of creating a fulfilling employee experience can be a difficult one to tackle, especially with the number of generations currently in the work force. For human resources and employee relations professionals, it entails focusing on several different areas.

SNAPSHOT OF EMPLOYEE RELATIONS ENVIRONMENT

1. Less than 50% of U.S. (42 percent) employees look forward to coming to work, compared to 84% of those working for "The Best Companies to Work For" as ranked by *Fortune* (Great Place to Work 2019).
2. The World Health Organization has labeled a new type of health condition specific to the workplace and says it could prove detrimental to an individual's health. Termed "Chronic Workplace Stress," the condition is a growing problem in the workforce (O.C. Tanner 2020).
3. More than 50% of employees say they feel stressed all or most of their time at work (Sams 2020).
4. Nearly 90% of millennials (86%) say they would stay in their current position if the company offered career development and training opportunities (Watkins).
5. Workers who rate their managers poorly are four times more likely to look for a new job than those who don't (Bolden-Barrett 2018).

Define and Communicate the Corporate Culture

As explained by John Childress, author of eleven books on corporate culture, "corporate culture is one of the most talked about topics by business leaders today, and for good reason. The business impact of a weak or misaligned culture has become more pronounced over the last 10 years as company after company, from banking, insurance, airlines, auto manufacturers and energy utilities have experienced billions of dollars in fines and share price declines as a result of issues ultimately stemming from a misaligned or even toxic corporate culture. Culture has a powerful positive or negative impact on business performance, company reputation and brand value" (Childress 2019).

What is *corporate culture*? Similar to the idea of employee experience, the term is often misunderstood. When most business professionals hear the phrase corporate culture, they think of corporate mindset and the overall values of an organization. In reality, it is much more than that. As Childress explains, "Corporate culture reflects the complex interactions between business strategy, processes, structures, technology, policies and people. These interrelated culture drivers form an end-to-end system, the corporate culture system" (Childress 2019). In many organizations, the true corporate culture may not be understood or even acknowledged by employees. This is one of the many reasons it is critical an organization's corporate culture be incorporated into the employee experience from the start.

Corporate Culture: The complex interactions between business strategy, processes, structures, technology, policies and people.

Promote Open Communication Between Employees and Management

Ensuring an open, clear path for communication in an organization helps avoid confusion, inaccuracies, and stress. It also mitigates tension between employees and management as well as helps employees, regardless of their role in the organization, understand its overarching mission, goals, and policies. "When millions of employees were abruptly sent home to work in March 2020, communication

THE PRACTICE OF PUBLIC RELATIONS

PR TIP

Consider any and all ways to showcase the organization's programs and procedures. Posting it in the employee section of the corporate website is a good start but think about other places to highlight it. The greater the awareness of corporate policy, the less likelihood for questions or surprises along the way.

became one of the biggest challenges for managers," explains Annemaria Duran in her article, "7 Strategies to Improve Employee Relations." The key to successful employee communication is creating and establishing a simple, effective framework to support open, dynamic conversation across all levels of the organization. As Duran suggests, "Provide a way for employees to express grievances and to resolve conflicts. They need to have a way to express themselves openly and without fear of retaliation. There should be an internal communications process where an employee can gripe" (Duran 2020). Any policies or procedures should be communicated frequently to employees, as well as made easily accessible on such places as the corporate website.

Focus on the Organization's Mission and Values

Most people want to be part of something, whether they realize it or not. When seeking employment, many individuals are drawn to an organization because of its reputation and institutional goals. A significant part of this is a firm's mission and corporate values. "When you promote your mission to your employees, it results in a higher level of employee engagement and positive work culture, keeping them invested in the good work your company does when they go about their day-to-day tasks," explains William Craig in his article "The Importance of Having A Mission Driven Company." Research shows people who believe in their organization are more productive. As Craig writes, "Employees who fall in love with

their work, experience higher productivity levels and engagement, and they express loyalty to the company as they remain longer, costing the organization less over time" (Craig 2018). Recent studies show "purpose-oriented employees are 54% more likely to stay at a company for more than five years and 30% more likely to be high performers than those who work for a pay cheque" (Ross 2015). It comes down to the basic fact individuals who love their jobs and believe in the mission of the organization are more productive and loyal, costing the company less over the long term.

The results speak for themselves. Companies with a high sense of trust between employee and employer are two-and-a-half times more likely to function as a high-performance organization with revenue growth than lower-performance organizations (Solow n.d.). More than 80% of individuals working for companies with a strong, well-communicated mission trust their leadership team, while that number drops to 54% for organizations without a strong mission statement (Craig 2018).

Showcase Employee Value

Employees like to know their work is appreciated and valued. Few individuals intend to do a mediocre job; most put forth their best effort. As a result, it is important to acknowledge an employee's work and celebrate even the smallest of successes. It is suggested managers "focus on the nine things done right, instead of the one thing done wrong. Experts suggest providing two to three positive points of feedback for every one item of criticism" (Duran 2020).

Some easy ways to show employees their efforts are valued:

- **Say thank-you:** It is a simple gesture but it can go a long way. Just saying thank-you in a sincere way shows an employee you appreciate their work. It is important to do it for the little efforts, as well as the big projects. You can thank an employee in person, by e-mail, over the phone, or on a video chat. If you really want to leave a long-lasting positive impression, send them a handwritten note.
- **Use the word value:** Don't be afraid to openly use the word value in a conversation with an employee. The more they are told of the value they provide to the organization, the more they will believe it. In such conversations, be as specific as possible so employees understand which actions were important to the organization.
- **Recognize high achievers:** Certain personalities aim high and need to be recognized for it. For those employees that greatly surpass expectations, be sure to openly commend them. It will go a long way in ensuring their commitment to excellence, as well as provide an incentive to other employees.

Motivate, Inspire, and Reward

Most employees want to establish their performance objectives in conjunction with management. Managers should work one-on-one with employees to set annual goals and performance incentives instead of simply handing them down. Research shows when an employee's performance management is collaborative instead of one-sided, they are more motivated. Google has a very successful dynamic, interactive performance management process. As Duran explains, Google allows employees to set quarterly goals that are difficult and can be measured. This idea was developed by employees and has proven successful across the organization.

PR VERSUS EMPLOYEE RELATIONS

Although public relations and employee relations appear to be vastly different, they share many commonalities.

- **Function:** Both public relations and employee relations focus on communicating information to a target audience. In the case of public relations, it involves talking to an array of people including media, investors,

customers, and suppliers. In employee relations, the communication is focused exclusively on one audience, an organization's employees.
- **Responsibilities:** Employee relations and PR are both communication-based functions with different responsibilities. Employee relations focuses on hiring, responding to employee questions, enforcing organizational policies, and supporting an organization's mission and values. Public relations involves developing/implementing media relations strategies, executing thought leadership programs, event planning, and executing social media programs.
- **Relationship:** Both PR and employee relations focus on building, developing, and sustaining relationships. The difference is the nature of the relationship between the organization and the target audience. Employees are an *internal audience*, while media, investors, and suppliers are an *external audience*.

PR and employee relations frequently work together to support programs and projects within an organization. PR professionals are asked to provide updates on media coverage, competitor announcements, and industry developments to the employee relations department. In addition, they develop content to support internal communications initiatives to keep employees apprised of an organization's activities. It is important to note that PR and employee relations can have a direct effect on each other. The success of an employee relations department in attracting and recruiting qualified talent can influence public perception of an organization, while the maintenance of a positive public image by the PR team can make an organization more attractive to potential employees.

STRATEGIES FOR PROFESSIONAL SUCCESS

THE IMPORTANCE OF BEING A MISSION-DRIVEN COMPANY

Most companies have a mission statement, and possibly even a corporate vision, but how much does it guide their behavior? A mission defines and upholds what an organization represents. It should denote what the organizations stands for, what is its purpose, what is its reason for being, and how does it serve the community.

When a company promotes its mission to its employees, it generates a strong level of employee engagement, promotes a positive work culture, and helps keep top of mind the good work the organization does as part of its daily operations.

(continued)

A MISSION STATEMENT DRIVES AND IMPROVES ENGAGEMENT

Employees who fall in love with their employer demonstrate a higher level of productivity, stay with the company longer, and express a high level of engagement. Mission-driven workers are feel a sense of commitment to an organization, with more than 50% staying in their position for over five years. These same individuals are also more likely to become high performers as opposed to those just looking to collect a paycheck.

Organizations that are highly trusted by their employees are operate more efficiently and achieve higher revenue growth than those who are not. More than 80% of individuals working for companies with a strong mission statement say their stakeholders trust their management team as compared to only 54% for those organizations with an unclear focus.

MISSION-DRIVEN LEADERS MATTER

Mission-driven leaders instill the how and why of an organization beyond that of a simple product explanation. They help to align team and individual employee to-dos in support of the mission. This is invaluable as having a connection to the corporate mission is commonly linked to why employees decide to work for an organization.

CREATING THE RIGHT MISSION STATEMENT

In order to create the right mission and successfully enforce it, it is important to consider the strategic alignment, as it relates to the organization as a whole. Begin with an accessible and clear mission—the rational pails in comparison to the importance of the of how, when and what. A clearly structured mission statement offers "clarity, awareness, engagement, innovation, improvement and achievement."

Think about the "world-class services" the organization offers to its targeted consumer. Keep in mind knowing the mission drives leaders to prioritize what matters most to customers and employees. It also helps to improve the company's product/service offerings to better the company and direct the business toward longevity and success. "When all the elements come together, a mission-driven company steers itself toward success and a brighter future for all" *(Adapted from Craig, William. 2018. "The Importance Of Having A Mission-Driven Company." Forbes)*.

EXECUTIVE SUMMARY

Now that you have finished reading this chapter, you should have an understanding of the field of employee relations and be able to:

- Describe the field of employee relations.
- Realize the importance of such concepts as employee experience and corporate culture.
- Explain the relationship between PR and employee relations.
- Understand the challenges and tips for success in creation and execution of an employee relations program.
- Explain the difference between employee relations and other areas of the PPR model.

KEY TERMS

Corporate Culture: The complex interactions between business strategy, processes, structures, technology, policies and people. *p. 291*

Employee Experience: The experience an individual has while working with an organization. *p. 287*

Employee Relations (ER): The relationship between employers and employees. *p. 287*

Shaping Approach: When aspects of the work environment are manipulated with the integration of new technology or the implementation of new programs. *p. 290*

DISCUSSION QUESTIONS

1. What is the difference between employee relations and other areas of the PPR model?
2. What are the similarities and differences between PR and employee relations?
3. What types of support functions do PR pros provide to employee relations department?
4. Why is a successful employee relations program critical to the long-term success of the organization?
5. What do you think are some of the challenges posed to employee relations professionals with the current multi-generation workforce?

CHAPTER 15
CUSTOMER RELATIONS

December 2018: A Trader Joe's in Columbus, OH. Recognized for its exemplary customer relations, Trader Joe's is an American privately held chain of specialty grocery stores headquartered in Monrovia, CA.

December 2017: The Ritz Carlton in Budapest, Hungary. Ritz Carlton is one world's leading names in luxury hotels offering top-notch customer service.

CHAPTER OUTLINE

Introduction to Customer Relations
Customer Relations versus Customer Service
Functions of the Customer Relations Department
    Proactive Customer Relations Tactics
    Reactive Customer Relations Tactics
Benefits of Successful Customer Relations
Tips for Successful Customer Relations
Working Together: Public Relations, Employee Relations, and Customer Relations
    Customer Relations
Strategies for Professional Success
Executive Summary
Key Terms
Discussion Questions

CHAPTER OBJECTIVES

After studying this chapter, you should be able to:

1. Define the term customer relations.
2. Explain the difference between customer relations and customer service.
3. Understand the parallels between employee relations, customer relations, and PR.
4. Detail how customer relations differs from other groups in the PPR model.

Ripped from the Headlines

In 2016, Samsung faced a unprecedented crisis when its Galaxy Note 7 phone started to experience technical difficulties soon after its highly-anticipated market release. Samsung halted sales of the phone and announced a voluntary recall of September 2, 2016 after it discovered a manufacturing defect in the phones' batteries which made the phone overheat. In some cases, the phones caught on fire. On September 15, 2016, a formal recall of the phones in the U.S. was issued. Samsung offered to exchange faulty phones for those with a new battery source, thinking that action would solve the problem. It was soon discovered, however, the replacement phones had the same problem. As a result, Samsung issued a worldwide recall of the phone on October 10, 2016 and stopped production it the next day. The recall had a significant impact on Samsung's business at the end of 2016 leading to a drop in its operating profits and sales. In July 2017, the company released a new version of the Note 7. Samsung received a significant amount of criticism in its handling of the crisis, especially in regard to its unclear messaging over the safety of the device. (The Verge, September 2, 2016, "Samsung recalls Galaxy Note 7 worldwide due to exploding battery fears," Vox Media).

Customer relations is the last part of the PPR model. Similar to employee relations, it is not typically carried out by members of the public relations team. It is important, however, to understand, as it is one of the many groups that looks to the public relations department for communications guidance, messaging support, and industry intelligence.

INTRODUCTION TO CUSTOMER RELATIONS

Customer Relations: The way an organization interacts with its customers and clientele.

Customer relations is the way an organization "relates to its customers, clientele and patrons" (LaMarco 2019). The importance of a comprehensive, well-structured customer relations program cannot be underestimated. If done well, not only will a customer relations program strengthen relationships with

existing customers, but it will also lead to the development of new ones. For most organizations, "the goal is to retain existing customers and to gain new ones by providing the best customer relations they can, and—hopefully, to find better customer services than those their competitors provide."

As mentioned in Chapter 1, customer relations cuts across all parts of an organization, but the majority of the focus is in the customer service department. Before diving into the details, it is important to briefly examine the difference between customer relations and customer service, as they are two very similar yet contrasting functions. Customer relations is the overarching term given to the development of relationships between an organization and its customers. Customer service, by contrast, is an aspect of customer relations, yet a separate function—similar to the relationship between media relations and public relations.

CUSTOMER RELATIONS VERSUS CUSTOMER SERVICE

Customer service is what an organization does to ensure happy, satisfied customers. It is primarily a reactive effort, although today many organizations launch their customer service protocol the moment a product or service is purchased. By contrast, customer relations includes both proactive and reactive actions taken by a company. It focuses on the forward-thinking steps an organization takes to attract customers and deliver a positive customer experience. It includes the

Customer Service: the actions an organization takes to ensure happy, satisfied customers.

functions customer service carries out, but also the strategies implemented prior to and after the interaction with the customer (Fontanella 2020). In many ways, customer service is a subsection of customer relations.

FUNCTIONS OF THE CUSTOMER RELATIONS DEPARTMENT

Similar to public relations practitioners, customer relations professionals must be skilled in a variety of areas to support the establishment, development, and long-term success of an organization's relationships with its customers. As previously noted, this includes a combination of proactive techniques focused on establishing relationships, and reactive tactics aimed at mitigating unexpected issues between the organization and its customers.

 **PR TIP**

> Successful customer relations programs involve a series of proactive and reactive techniques supported but customer relations and customer service professionals.

Proactive Customer Relations Tactics

Any proactive strategy or task employed by the member of an organization's customer relations team is focused on securing long-term relationships with customers. This includes such activities as:

- Distributing product updates.

- Offering product discounts and special offers.
- Creating and administering customer loyalty programs.
- Acknowledging customer milestones.
- Engaging in proactive conversations with customers.

Such activities help organizations cultivate and foster meaningful, symbiotic, long-lasting relationships with customers (Fontanella 2020).

Reactive Customer Relations Tactics

Reactive tactics are employed to solve issues reported to an organization by its customers. Carried out but the customer service department, this work includes responding to customer complaints, supporting product recalls, and solving unforeseen problems. Most companies use a combination of technologies to support these efforts including 800-numbers, surveys, e-mail responses, text exchanges, chatbots, and social media platforms. Most corporate websites feature a customer service section, a contact-us link as well as customer service click-throughs. All of these activities are aimed at resolving customer problems and preserving the customer relationship.

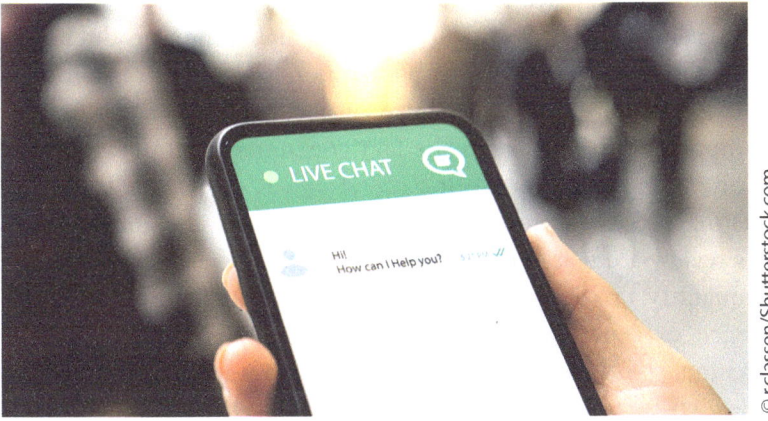

The customer service team will work with crisis management in the event of a significant, unforeseen problem. This was the case with Samsung when it issued the global product recall on its Galaxy Note 7, as detailed in the "Ripped from the Headlines," section earlier in the chapter. In such cases, the crisis management team will design the response strategy and the customer service department will execute it.

BENEFITS OF SUCCESSFUL CUSTOMER RELATIONS

A well-executed customer relations program not only results in satisfied customers but in an improvement to the organization's bottom line. The other areas that benefit are those directly connected to the customer relations program: customer retention, customer loyalty, and customer satisfaction.

Customer Retention:
The percentage of customers an organization retains after the purchase experience.

Customer Loyalty:
the result of customer retention. The more customers an organization retains, the greater the likelihood it will develop a loyal customer base.

Customer Satisfaction:
a measurement to determine the degree to which a customer is happy and satisfied with a product.

- **Customer Retention:** Organizations with successful customer relations programs have a greater likelihood of experiencing a higher level of customer retention than those that do not. According to a 2019 report released by Microsoft, 61% of individuals stop buying from a company if they have a had poor customer service experience (Microsoft 2019). Over the long-term, a high customer retention rate can prove extremely helpful to an organization as a retention rate of only 5% can boost profits by 25 to 95%.
- **Customer Loyalty:** Customer loyalty is the result of customer retention. The greater the rate of customer retention, the higher the customer loyalty. Offered by most major retailers, customer rewards programs showcase the importance of customer loyalty. These programs focus on developing a bond between an organization and its customers. Typically, the more you shop, the more reward points you receive, which, over time, are redeemable for a product or service from the organization. As a consumer, you are incented to return to the merchant with the allure of accumulating additional points. Companies are betting on the fact consumers will develop increased loyalty after each interaction.
- **Customer Satisfaction:** Before we talk about the importance of it, let's review a quick definition of *customer satisfaction*, "a metric used to quantify the degree to which a customer is happy with a product, service, or experience. This metric is usually calculated by deploying a customer satisfaction survey that asks on a five or seven-point scale how a customer feels about a support interaction, purchase, or overall

customer experience, with answers between 'highly unsatisfied' and 'highly satisfied' to choose from" (Bernazzani 2020). Customer satisfaction comes from positive customer experiences, which stems directly from an organization's customer relations department and its customer service tactics.

TIPS FOR SUCCESSFUL CUSTOMER RELATIONS

To conclude our discussion of customer relations, let's examine some prescribed strategies for success.

- Offer consistent service.
- Respond quickly to customer queries.
- Use a variety of technologies in supporting the customer relations effort.
- Promote company offerings, including sales, loyalty programs, and customer service policies.
- Be honest.
- Acknowledge customer loyalty.
- Be thankful.

As noted by Anthony Smith in the *Forbes* article, "How To Build Lasting Customer Relationships," in "today's digital age, the impact of developing stronger customer relationships spreads further than ever. Customers are eager to share their opinions, whether positive or negative and have a great many channels to do so. The work your company puts into maintaining and strengthening relationships will make or break you. Just like any relationship, strong customer relationships require work but the payoff to your businesses' bottom line is worth the efforts" (Smith 2018).

WORKING TOGETHER: PUBLIC RELATIONS, EMPLOYEE RELATIONS AND CUSTOMER RELATIONS

Customer Relations

We have completed the study of the PPR model with the exploration into the worlds of employee relations and customer relations. In most organizations, employee relations and customer relations are distinctly separate functions. While most public relations professionals will not work in either of these areas, they will support them. Each of these departments looks to the PR team for guidance in such areas as the following.

- Corporate Messaging
- Competitive intelligence
- Company announcements
- Product/service updates
- Media coverage
- Analyst insights

Public relations specialists also provide media training, spokesperson training, and presentation training to company executives and designated representatives.

Without clear direction from the public relations department, other communications units within an organization struggle to determine what strategies and tactics to adopt and ultimately implement. After a review of the PPR model and an exploration of each of the functional areas, the hope is that you now have a deep understanding of and appreciation for the critical role public relations plays in supporting an organization. Public relations truly is the communications command center of an organization.

CHAPTER 15: CUSTOMER RELATIONS

STRATEGIES FOR PROFESSIONAL SUCCESS

In the August 24, 2019 edition of *The Economist*, an article entitled "How to keep your customers happy" detailed the connection between happy employees and satisfied customers. Although these areas of communication may appear seemingly unconnected to many, the relationship is quite logical after further thought, as illustrated in the data and points here.

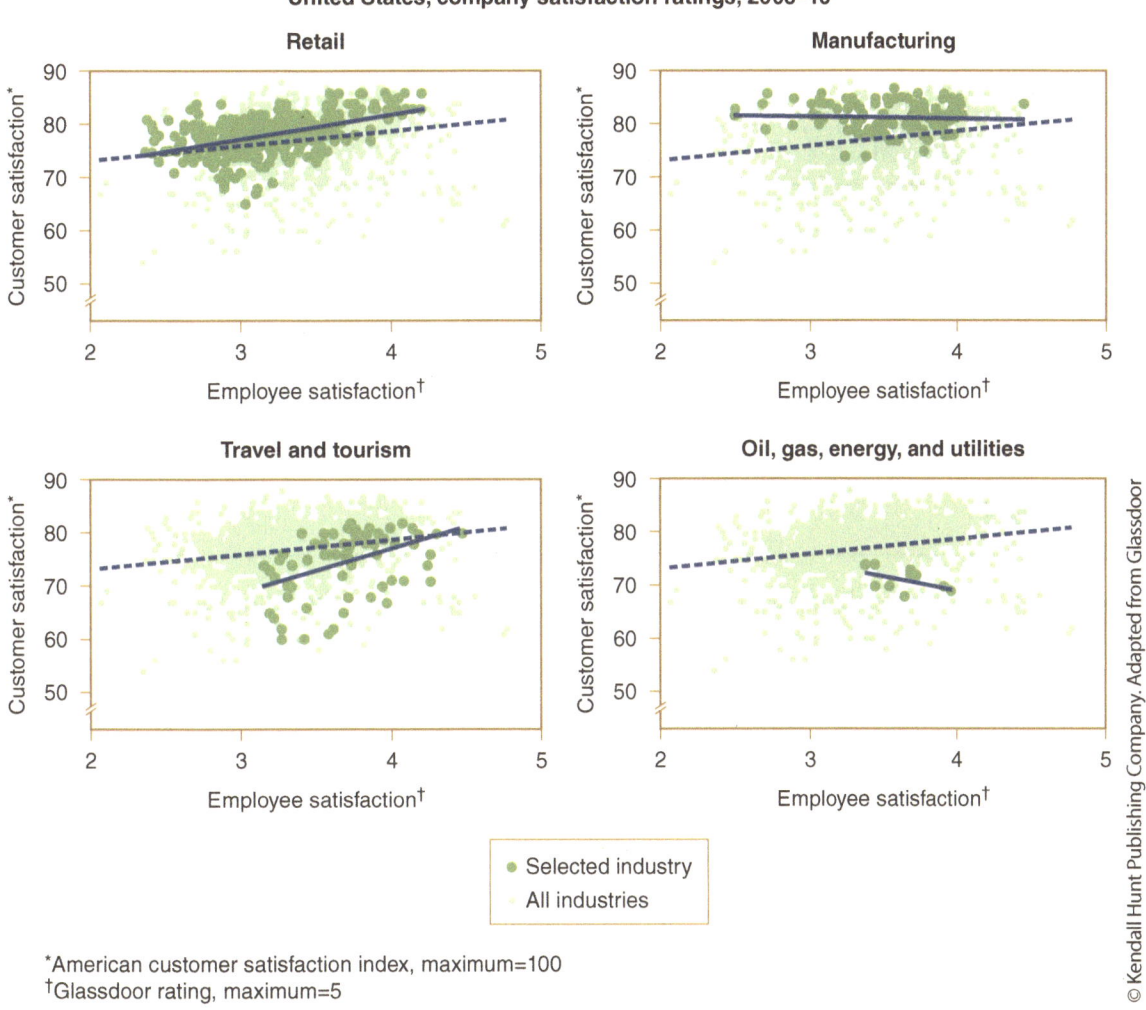

*American customer satisfaction index, maximum=100
†Glassdoor rating, maximum=5

As explained earlier in this chapter, a happy customer typically becomes a repeat customer. Research shows the more positive the purchase or service experience, the greater the likelihood the consumer will come back for more. The question often posed is how can a business keep customers continually satisfied? The answer is not as complicated as one would think. The simple answer—be nice to your employees. Glassdoor, a website that empowers workers to evaluate their employers, reviewed records of 293 companies representing 13 industries between 2008 and 2018. It then looked at the correlation between employee

(continued)

satisfaction, based on its data and the American Customer Satisfaction Index, a methodology for judging shoppers' opinions of an organization.

An improvement of one-point on Glassdoor's five-point rating resulted in a 1.3-point increase in customer satisfaction on a scale of 0 to 100. The link was strongest in industries where employees directly interface with customers such as hospitality, travel, and retail. In such areas, a one-point gain in employee happiness led to an increase in customer satisfaction of 3.2 points as detailed in the charts earlier. Companies with high scores in both employee and customer satisfaction include Trader Joe's, Southwest Airlines, and Hilton Hotels. In industries such as manufacturing and energy, where employees have significantly less contact with customers, the connection was not strong. However, it seems the secret is that happy employees = happy customers.

EXECUTIVE SUMMARY

Now that you have finished reading this chapter, you should understand the area of customer relations and be able to:

- Explain the role of the customer relations department.
- Understand the difference between customer relations and customer service.
- Appreciate the required elements of a successful customer relations program.
- Realize the connection between customer loyalty and customer satisfaction.

KEY TERMS

Customer Loyalty: the result of customer retention. The more customers an organization retains, the greater the likelihood it will develop a loyal customer base. p. 304

Customer Retention: the percentage of customers an organization retains after the purchase experience. p. 304

Customer Service: the actions an organization takes to ensure happy, satisfied customers. p. 301

Customer Satisfaction: a measurement to determine the degree to which a customer is happy and satisfied with a product. p. 304

Customer Relations: the way an organization interacts with its customers and clientele. p. 300

DISCUSSION QUESTIONS

1. What is the biggest difference between customer relations and public relations?
2. Why is customer relations critical to the long-term success of an organization?
3. What is the difference between customer relations and customer service?
4. What are the primary responsibilities of a customer relations practitioner?
5. What is the connection between employee relations and customer relations?

INDUSTRY CASES AND SPOTLIGHTS

CSR COMPANY SPOTLIGHT: AERIE

Contributed by Isabella Fiorello. Copyright © Kendall Hunt Publishing Company

Aerie, a sub brand of American Eagle Outfitters, officially launched in 2006. The company markets intimate items such as bras, panties, and dorm wear to women aged 15-25. The clothing and intimates brand has 148 stand-alone stores and another 174 stores connected to American Eagle locations. In 2014, the brand launched their "#AerieReal" campaign (Kohan 2020). This campaign is shared through Instagram as a popular hashtag and is a major trademark for the brand. Although the campaign is a huge part of their social media, it is also used to promote Aerie products on its site, commercials, and print ads. Aerie's brand is known for being inclusive and featuring real women of different shapes, sizes, and colors. The #AerieReal campaign aides in promoting these ideas and showcasing its merchandise without misrepresentation or editing of women's bodies in their ads. Over the past several years, Aerie has changed the standards of beauty by inspiring women to be confident and love their bodies (Kohan 2020).

Aerie's Evolution

Aerie is a relatively new brand and has significant amount of competition. Victoria's Secret for example, has been around since 1977 and had become one of the most well-known brands of the 1990s and 2000s. Their fashion shows were iconic, and the brand was at the top of the lingerie market (Hanbury 2020). But in recent years, Aerie made its way to the forefront of the industry, surpassing Victoria's Secret as well as many others. Victoria's Secret is known for showcasing unrealistic body images on its social media and through other marketing strategies (Kohan 2020). In comparison, Aerie uses its social media to promote diversity and inclusion for realistic body types. Aerie is currently on track to top $1 billion in revenues (Ell 2020). Due to the COVID-19 pandemic, stores and businesses were forced to close. But Aerie's Q1 sales were down only 2% because of high demand in its online business which grew 75% from the previous year (Kohan 2020). Victoria's Secret on the other hand, recently announced closure of many of its stores due declining sales (Hanbury 2020). Aerie's sales have continued to rise, as more and more women are looking to shop from a body-positive brand. Aerie's social media accounts allow consumers to see that the brand is inclusive and proud to showcase women of all shapes, sizes, and colors wearing their merchandise.

Vaughan, Ontario, Canada - March 24, 2018—Aerie store front at Vaughan Mills in Toronto.

Research shows social media plays a large role in the fashion industry and has changed the way brands and companies interact with their customers. Social media has given brands a larger voice and in an unprecedented number of ways helped them engage with their target publics. Brands are able to connect and communicate with customers more directly, which results in better feedback. "Businesses who use social media to its full advantage engage with customers by responding to comments on posts, hosting giveaways, and even reposting photos or comments that customers post" (Social Media in the Fashion Industry 2019). Aerie is a great example of a brand that demonstrates these ideas on their social media, as seen with their #AerieReal campaign. Social media can also help an organization improve its customer service. With the use of social media, fashion brands are able to create a concrete image and cohesive messaging. Different platforms can help to project the image, message, and values of an organization. Having a solid image on social media can help improve an organization's brand recognition. Brands no longer have to rely on their website to showcase their products, sales, messages, changes, etc. Social media allows them to post or update at any time on a variety of platforms, which have millions of active potential customers (Social Media in the Fashion Industry 2019).

Aerie currently has 1.4 million Instagram followers, and the company uses this platform to promote their brand and their values. All of its posts include #AerieReal or some of their other popular hashtags. Many of Aerie's posts consist of pictures submitted by real women who buy their merchandise, instead of just professional models (Lopez 2020). This provides a powerful way for the company to connect with its audience. "Making customers feel and be ambassadors for the brand and its mission. Aerie closes the circle, they ask customers what they want, create those items, and then display feedback via social media platforms" (Lopez 2020). Due to its social media, Aerie has become very popular and its interactive campaign has helped boost its sales (Ell 2020). The company's inclusive and interactive campaigns have helped to turn Aerie into one of the biggest stores for women, even competing with and in many ways surpassing the famous Victoria's Secret. Compared to other brands, Aerie utilizes its social media to directly engage and communicate with its audience, create stronger brand recognition, showcase the brand's values and identity, and produce successful and creative campaigns like #AerieReal. Clearly, the company's consistent messaging and social media campaigns have aided in successfully promoting its brand and building its success over the past several years.

REFERENCES

Ell, Kellie. 2020. "WWD: Aerie Aims to Be $3 Billion Brand." *AEO Inc*, 6 March 2020. www.aeo-inc.com/2020/03/06/wwd-aerie-aims-to-be-3-billion-brand/.

Hanbury, Mary. 2020. "The Rise and Fall of Victoria's Secret, America's Biggest Lingerie Retailer." *Business Insider*, 21 May 2020. www.businessinsider.com/victorias-secret-rise-and-fall-history-2019-5.

Kohan, Shelley E. 2020. "AEO's Aerie Brand, Built On Body Positivity And Inclusion, Is Slowly Edging Out Sexy Supermodel Juggernaut Victoria's Secret." *Forbes*, 28 June 2020. www.forbes.com/sites/shelleykohan/2020/06/28/aeos-aerie-brand-built-on-body-positivity-and-inclusion-is-slowly-edging-out-sexy-supermodel-juggernaut-victorias-secret/?sh=a908fe242ba1.

Lopez, Kassandra. 2020. "Social Media Best Practices as Shown by Aerie on Instagram." *Medium*, 12 June 2020. kassandra5511.medium.com/social-media-best-practices-as-shown-by-aerie-on-instagram-fdbc6d04ec75.

"Social Media in the Fashion Industry." 2019. *The Fashion Network*, 16 October 2019. thefashionetwork.com/social-media-in-the-fashion-industry/.

CSR COMPANY SPOTLIGHT: COCA COLA

Contributed by Jacqi Liu. Copyright © Kendall Hunt Publishing Company.

With the continuous growth in business since the dawn of the Industrial Revolution, organizations have been under increasing scrutiny by the public. Due to the accessibility mass communication and the internet provide, consumers are now more aware of a brand's mission, image, and reputation. Most importantly, with Generation Z, individuals born between 1995 and 2015, as the rising generation of the future, the standards organizations are held to are increasing.

Today, corporate social responsibility is one of the most important factors in the growth, and ultimately success, of an organization. Corporate social responsibility is a corporation's social and environmental commitment to its constituencies and greater society. It can make a difference as to whether a consumer purchases a product from brand X or brand Y. Over the long-term, the commitment to and execution of an organization's CSR program plays a critical role in its growth and survival.

On top of the CSR pyramid is Coca-Cola. The company has taken the lead with its latest environmentally sustainable measures and its philanthropic efforts. Coca-Cola has adopted local and international approaches with its CSR programs offering benefits to its constituencies over the short and long term.

The Coca-Cola Company markets, manufactures and sells beverage concentrates, syrups and finished beverages (including sparkling soft drinks; water and sports drinks; juice, dairy, and plant-based drinks; and tea and coffee). (https://www.coca-colacompany.com/company/coca-cola-system).

Coca-cola's target market is everybody. The company's vision is to "craft the brands and choice of drinks that people love." The idea is that any man, woman, child, or senior citizen, can grab a coke "to refresh them in body and spirit." Funny enough, Coca-Cola was first intended to be a medicinal tonic, and it was marketed as a mitigator of headaches.

COCA COLA'S CSR PROGRAM

The focus of Coca-Cola's CSR program is sustainability, which is expressed through the following areas: consumer health, packaging and recycling, water stewardship, employee development, involvement of suppliers, and energy and climate.

Consumer Health: Giving People Options and Choices

Coca-Cola has adapted to the modern world's needs of having healthier eating and drinking options. The company has reduced 10% of the added sugar in its products and, today, 18 out of its 20 top brands have low- or no-sugar option. In addition, the company strives to provide more nutritious and "tasty" drinks by adding vitamins, minerals, electrolytes, and more plant-based beverages. Since 2018, these products have been available in 25 major markets across the world, in such countries as Mexico, Nigeria, Turkey, and Singapore. Coca-Cola has also reduced the size of its products in order for the consumer to easily control portions and added sugar intake while still enjoying their favorite drink.

While reducing packaging and sugar intake might seem insignificant, it helps create healthier eating patterns since diabetes and heart diseases remain the top leading causes of death in the United States. Both of these diseases originate from a bad alimentation and high levels of sugar.

SOURCE: (https://www.coca-colacompany.com/sustainable-business/in-our-products).

Packaging and Recycling: Focusing on a World Without Waste

With plastic as a rising environmental issue, companies have started to transition into biodegradable options to reduce their carbon footprint. Coca-Cola's ultimate goal is to make 100% of its packaging recyclable by 2025 and use at least 50% of recycled material in its packaging by 2030.

Currently, 60% of its packaging is either refilled or collected for recycling, 18 markets offer beverages packaged in 100% recycled pet bottles, and the company offers incentives for constituencies to improve collection. Coca-Cola supports deposit return schemes and packaging recovery partnerships through a "circular solution," a system in which all of the plastic the company produces is designed to be recycled, kept in the economy, and then reused.

SOURCE: (https://www.coca-colacompany.com/sustainable-business/packaging-sustainability).

COCA-COLA'S OTHER CSR INITIATIVES:

- Coca-Cola also provides stakeholders an opportunity to inform perceived violations of workplace rights or any other violations in a secure and anonymous manner.
- Since 2013, Coca-Cola has replenished an estimated 68% of the volume of its finished beverages and returned about 108.5 billion liters of water to communities and nature. This has improved the efficiency of water usage by a total of 8% since 2011.
- Coca-Cola has helped economically empower more than 865,000 women within their 5by20 program in 2014, with a total aim of aiding 5 million women by 2020.

- As part of its attempt to engage in responsible marketing, Coca-Cola does not advertise its product to children younger than 12 years old.

SOURCE: (https://research-methodology.net/coca-cola-corporate-social-responsibility/).

COCA-COLA'S CSR PROGRAM MILESTONES:

According to Coca-Cola's 2019 sustainability report (https://www.coca-colacompany.com/content/dam/journey/us/en/reports/coca-cola-business-and-sustainability-report-2019.pdf):

- To date, Coca-Cola has removed a total of 280,000 tons of added sugar through their product reformulation, which started in 2017 (19).
- The company's new recipe, which began in Mexico, comes with 30% less added sugar and has now expanded to 25 international markets. In addition, 100% of their products provide energy/calorie information in the front of their packages (19).
- Through its sustainability programs, the company has managed to reduce its carbon footprint by 24% since 2010 (22).
- Globally, 88% of Coca-Cola's packaging is now recyclable, a 3% increase from 2017 (27).
- 160% of the water used in the company's beverages has been replenished in nature and communities. Since 2010, at least, 10.6 million people benefitted from Coca-Cola's water and sanitation program with a total of 1.5 trillion liters of water replenished (31).

INDUSTRY CASES AND SPOTLIGHTS

CSR AND COMMUNITY RELATIONS CASE STUDY: DELOITTE

Contributed by Kaitlyn Marcinczyk. Copyright © Kendall Hunt Publishing Company.

Deloitte is a multinational professional services network that provides tax, auditing, consulting, and advisory services to a multitude of brands around the world. Founded in 1845, the company has its headquarters in London, England.

In light of the COVID-19 pandemic, Deloitte altered its crisis management plan to best support its stakeholders. Deloitte's adjusted crisis management plan focuses heavily on its community relations program, focusing on how to support its clients whose businesses are struggling as a result of the pandemic. To communicate this shift, Deloitte issued a press release to inform its publics of the new community relations practices. The press release highlights such initiatives as how Deloitte professionals began 3D-printing medical equipment to send to Spain, due to the country's shortage of PPE. To date, Deloitte has provided over 10,000 masks per day to Warsaw, Poland, and the Ukraine, according to a post on the company's Instagram account.

Deloitte also donated approximately $1.1 million to Civil Protection in Italy to support the purchase of ventilators and other PPE. These actions exemplify the importance of considering multiple stakeholders of an organization in the midst of a crisis, as each is affected in a different way. By considering the hardships of its community and revising its community relations initiatives, Deloitte was able to alleviate the struggles of many countries and individuals (Dutton, 2020).

In an effort to mitigate the risk of COVID-19 in the workplace, Deloitte created a software called DeloitteRESOLVE. This software serves as a business tool to measure employees' risk of being exposed to COVID-19 and assesses response plans. Deloitte's website states that functionality could include tracking the travel, public exposure, personal health monitoring, and mapping interaction with people who are infected. The "DeloitteRESOLVE Solution" supplies relevant and vital information regarding the best way to respond to the outbreak (Deloitte 2020).

Within its crisis management plan revisions, Deloitte also provides resources for its employees to utilize, given the new virtual workplace environment. Deloitte published an article on its website providing tips to employees on how to network virtually. The article explains:

"NETWORKING VIRTUALLY"

1. Identify your networking goals. Think about your approach when networking and consider asking yourself the following questions: Who do you want to connect with? What do you want to gain from making a connection?
2. Be thoughtful when making connections. Whether you're starting your professional career or looking to make a transition into a new industry, your network may be stronger than you realize. Don't forget friends, family, and colleagues you have met along the way of your professional career.
3. Be prepared to communicate your personal brand. Know who you are and how to communicate your own brand. Practice and preparation can pay off when interacting with recruiters.
4. Enhance your virtual profile. Keep your profile of all recruiting platforms up to date. Potential employers might be meeting you for the first time on this site, and first impressions are everything.
5. Schedule a virtual coffee chat. Learn about new industry, careers, companies, etc. Professionals like to share observations about their organization and journey.
6. Attend virtual events. Conferences and forums have gone virtual to offer networking opportunities.
7. Stay in touch. Follow up with new connections and work to build a relationship over time. It's vital for your career to look at each person you connect with as a potential future colleague.

Deloitte publicized its community relations efforts and COVID-19 response on social media and collaborated with employees on how to increase their efforts to assist their publics. The corporation altered its crisis management plan by working to stop the spread in its workplace, and, in turn, created a software program that could provide other companies with the same ability to mitigate the growth of the virus in their workplaces, as well.

REFERENCES

Dutton, S. 2020. "Deloitte outlines global commitments to COVID-19 response and relief efforts: Deloitte Global." 23 April 2020. https://www2.deloitte.com/global/en/pages/about-deloitte/articles/covid-19/deloitte-outlines-global-commitments-to-covid-19-response-and-relief-efforts.html.

Deloitte. 2020. "Networking virtually—Life." 03 September 2020. https://www2.deloitte.com/us/en/pages/careers/articles/careers-blog-networking-virtually.html.

CSR COMPANY SPOTLIGHT: LEGO

Contributed by Lauren Colandro. Copyright © Kendall Hunt Publishing Company.

Founded in 1932, the Lego Group has been one of the most recognizable toy brands in the world, with a corporate history spanning nearly a 100 years. What started out as a Danish carpenter's small toy store transformed into the company's signature plastic bricks and toy sets. Today, Lego's building sets appeal to both children and adults worldwide with themes including popular intellectual properties, iconic architectural feats, and even craft jewelry. In addition to making its toys, the Lego Group has a multi-faceted corporate social responsibility program founded on the principles of and commitment to improving the lives of its customers, workers, and the world.

LEGO'S CORPORATE RESPONSIBILITY PROGRAM

The Lego Group's corporate social responsibility program is divided into three categories: sustainability, children, and diversity. Sustainability is a widespread effort, encompassing all aspects of its production. The company's commitment to the welfare of children cuts across a number of areas ranging from online safety initiatives to educational programs in STEM fields. Lego also prioritizes diversity across all levels of the organization, ranging from the corporate office to the production floor.

SUSTAINABILITY: LEGO'S PACKAGING

Lego's foremost priority in its corporate social responsibility efforts is incorporating sustainability practices into the manufacturing of products and packaging. Lego has made great strides in this area with the majority of its box packaging comprised of 75% recyclable materials. In 2019, Lego phased out plastic bags in its stores, replacing them with recyclable paper bags. The company intends to use paper bags inside of its boxed sets and to eliminate single-use plastic by 2025. Lego also plans to change the way its bricks are produced. In 2018, the

company started making some of its sets out of polyethylene derived from sugarcane. The new material, though non-biodegradable, is ethically sourced and guaranteed the same durability as the original bricks. The company hopes to make all of its sets with these materials by 2030.

PROTECTING CHILDREN

Improving the lives of children is just as important to the Lego Group as its efforts towards sustainability. The company has instituted a donation program to give its used products to children in need. Lego stresses the importance of community service by hosting events to introduce students to STEM programs,

while bringing awareness to real-life issues of sustainability. Though the Lego Foundation, it aims to support children living in areas of conflict and natural disaster zones. As its products are mainly for children, Lego does extensive testing to ensure they meet American and European standards for child safety.

Lego partnered with UNICEF to advocate for the Children's Rights and Business Principles charter, as well as took part in creating the Child Online Safety Assessment. These initiatives aim to protect children's rights on the Internet, as well as define their rights to other companies. The company also has a Child Safeguard Policy, which requires its employees with high child engagement to have background checks. Lego has implemented Child Safeguard Policies and developed a toolkit for other companies to follow to prevent inappropriate behavior toward children online.

DIVERSITY AND INCLUSION

Lego is committed to supporting diversity and inclusion in all areas of the organization—from the toys it creates to the individuals it employs. Every year, Lego employees are given surveys to gauge satisfaction in the workplace and company goals. The company has also created a Diversity and Inclusion Council, working regionally and globally to address issues within the company and the world outside of it. In 2019, Lego launched a new learning program to make the language used within the company, as well as in its advertising, more gender neutral. It also ensures children in its commercials reflect the diversity of society. Lego's corporate social responsibility record demonstrates a deep conscientiousness toward its impact on the world, with efforts that are not only well thought out and far reaching but also tremendously successful.

CSR COMPANY SPOTLIGHT: LEVI STRAUSS & CO.

Contributed by Elyse Whary. Copyright © Kendall Hunt Publishing Company.

Since 1873, Levi Strauss & Co. has been a contributor to the fashion industry since the launch of its first blue jean. Each year Levi's reinvents what it means to wear denim and remains among the most celebrated names in apparel. Today, Levi's is a global leader in denim wear, casual wear, and related accessories for men, women, and children. Sourcing products and materials from 26 countries around the world, Levi's strives for avid sustainability efforts and environmental contribution. Its signature red tab and two horse trademarked logo appear on every garment, becoming so recognized that every pair of Levi's is distinguishable and timelessly well known.

LEVI'S CSR PROGRAM

With its commitment to responsibly and sustainability sourced apparel and the well being of its employees, Levi's sets a great example for other companies to follow. Levi's corporate social responsibility has expanded exponentially throughout the years, from rejecting racial segregation, to ensuring worker protections at every point of the supply chain, to supporting LGBTQ+ rights. Over the years, the company has strived to make things better in the world, while putting science and sustainability first.

Levi Strauss & Co. is committed to recycling, remaking, and reimagining its garments to set the fashion industry standard. The company's plan for using Water<Less renewable resources and incorporating cottonized hemp in its denim is one of its long-term sustainability efforts. Its *WellThread* collection innovates rain-fed cottonized hemp, a natural fiber that leaves less of a footprint on the planet and uses less water to produce. It was developed in a "cottonization process" that softens the hemp fibers to make them look and feel almost indistinguishable to cotton.

Part of Levi's CSR plan also includes its newly established recycling technology, used to develop new denim from old denim, curbing landfill waste and decreasing water and chemical usage in the process. The company partnered with Re:newcell to develop and convert denim fibers into a pulp called Circulose that has helped to close the waste gap in the supply chain of Levi's garments.

The Red Tab Foundation is another one of Levi's initiatives for the financial support of each and every one of its employees. The company believes employees and retirees should have a financial safety net. Levi's is committed to protecting the basic needs and future of its employees who face problems caused by unexpected financial hardship. Over the course of the past year, the company delivered $1.7 million in grants to members of its community, helping to avert of 1,400+ emergencies.

The Levi Strauss Foundation is grounded in advocating for change and changemakers. Its philanthropic and societal work focuses on advancing human rights. From 100+ partnerships in over 40 countries, Levi's takes on issues of social justice, disaster response, worker rights, and HIV/AIDS response. Levi's established a $1 million Rapid Response Fund to support vulnerable communities, immigrants, refugees, the transgender community, and ethnic and religious minorities impacted by the current political environment. Levi's invests $1.3 million annually in Employee Community Engagement initiatives and disaster relief funds globally, it was one of the first corporate funders for HIV/AIDS response since 1983.

PROGRAM MILESTONES AND LEVI'S FURTHER GOALS:

- Founded in 1952
- $10 million-dollar annual budget as of 2020
- $340 million dollars given since inception
- 100 + partnerships in over 40 countries
- Cottonized hemp comes to fruition in the 2020 WellThread Collection
- 100% renewable electricity in Levi's owned and operated facilities by the end of 2025
- 80+% of Levi's jeans and trucker jackets made with Water<Less techniques by the end of 2020

SOURCE: https://www.levi.com/US/en_US/features/our-values

CSR CASE STUDY: MCDONALD'S

Contributed by Mariana Delacqua. Copyright © Kendall Hunt Publishing Company.

As one of the largest fast-food chains in the world, McDonald's has made remarkable strides in the international arena as a restaurant and as a cultural symbol. With its extensive product line, ranging from burgers and salads to all-day breakfast and kid's meals, the company caters to all demographics. According to its website, as of January 2020, McDonald's operates in more than 100 countries, with over 38,000 restaurants globally that serve an estimated 69 million people every day (McDonalds Corporation 2020).

As an international sensation, the company must ensure its campaigns are well received around the world. This is most easily seen through its "McMenu" which features food reflective of the local culture. This strategy is a prime example of glocalization, a concept in public relations based on the idea of combining global and local PR strategies. In addition to buying ingredients from the country in which it is operating, McDonald's adapts its menu items to local tastes, cultural culinary preferences and traditions. For example, in Japan McDonald's serves a pork patty teriyaki burger called the "Seaweed Shaker" and chocolate-drizzled fries; in Germany, it serves a shrimp cocktail; in Italy, its burgers are topped with Parmigiano-Reggiano cheese; in Australia, it offers a guac salsa or bacon cheese sauce as a topping for fries; and in France, customers can order a caramel banana shake (Rosenberg 2020).

SHENZHEN, CHINA - CIRCA NOVEMBER 2018: TOUCH SCREEN to order at McDonald's store.

McDonald's international success has not been accidental; it is part of its strategy is to allocate time and resources to understand the best way to target and communicate with local culture, lifestyle, and traditions. Careful evaluation of these factors allows McDonald's to create a tailored brand message across its markets. As a global brand, McDonald's makes a conscious decision to be culturally sensitive to local tastes, respectful of particular laws and religious traditions (Jankowski 2019). Although understanding culture and being able to adapt accordingly has been beneficial, it is also one of the biggest challenges the company faces. This is due to

11 January 2020; Bangkok Thailand: McDonald's porridge pork bowl is one of the meals choice at McDonald's Weekday Breakfast Specials.

the fact the world is currently changing and with the growth of globalization, no one set mold or strategy is proven to work across all countries. McDonald's is an excellent example of how companies can adapt their global strategies to fit local needs and cultural differences.

REFERENCES

Jankowski, Paul. 2019. "'Glocalization' In The U.S. Heartland: How Global Messaging Can Have A Regional Impact." *Forbes*. https://www.forbes.com/sites/pauljankowski/2019/10/28/glocalization-in-the-us-heartland-why-global-messaging-should-have-a-regional-impact/.

McDonalds Corporation. 2020. "McDonald's Reports Fourth Quarter and Full Year 2019 Results and Quarterly Cash Dividend." *McDonald's Newsroom*. https://mcdonaldscorporation.gcs-web.com/news-releases/news-release-details/mcdonalds-reports-fourth-quarter-and-full-year-2019-results-and#:~:text=The%20Company%20returned%20%242.3%20billion,three%2Dyear%20period%20ended%202019.

Rosenberg, Matt. 2020. "Number of McDonald's Restaurants Worldwide." *Thought.co*, 24 February 2020. https://www.thoughtco.com/number-of-mcdonalds-restaurants-worldwide-1435174#:~:text=According%20to%20the%20McDonald's%20Corporation,69%20million%20people%20every%20day.

CSR COMPANY SPOTLIGHT: STARBUCKS

Contributed by Kennedie McMahon. Copyright © Kendall Hunt Publishing Company.

For 49 years, the universally known green siren continuously lures in millions, with over 30,000 locations worldwide in more than 70 countries. Founded in 1971 by Jerry and Zev Siegl, and Gordon Bowker, the Starbucks Corporation is an American multinational chain of coffeehouses and roastery reserves. The company offers a variety of beverages, hot and cold, from whole-bean coffee, espresso, and micro-ground instant coffee to Teavana tea products, Frappuccinos, and Evolution Fresh juices. A variety of pastries and small snacks are offered as well such as croissants, cookies, chips, and crackers. The company's target market ranges in age between 22 and 60 years old, with a rise in teen customers. To most, Starbucks is seen as simply a coffeehouse that can be a little pricey. However, what they do not realize is this company, is part of something much larger. From its efforts to improve the environment to the opportunities offered to the youth and all the in-between, Starbucks' CSR program makes spending the extra dollar or two on a cup of coffee worth it.

STARBUCKS CSR PROGRAM

The Environment

Starbucks has and continues to work towards helping the environment and making sure its operations around the globe are environmentally responsible. A major shift change by the company is the recent strawless lids for its hot and iced beverages. These new lids are recyclable and contain around 9% less plastic than a regular lid. While still offering straws upon a customer's request, this change eliminates around one billion straws per year globally. The company is working towards switching to reusable packaging and expanding its plant-based/environmentally friendly menu. Looking into the future, the company has established a set of goals to advance its progress in helping the environment. By 2025, the company's goal is to provide 100 million coffee trees to farmers, with 40 million already being distributed since 2015. By 2030, Starbucks plans to have significant reductions of its carbon, water, and waste. It is trying to double the use of reusable cups between 2016 and 2022 and to eliminate single-use straws by 2021. This is just a small fraction of the goals the Starbucks corporation has set to help the environment.

The Workplace

Starbucks is also dedicated to creating a diverse and inclusive environment and is committed to doing its part in ending systemic racism. The company has voiced its support in the Black Lives Matter movement and supplied 250,000 BLM shirts to its partners along with pins employees can wear to support the movement. In an effort to promote equity and create more inclusive communities, the Starbucks foundation committed to $1 million in neighborhood grants. Starbucks has made a Civil Rights assessment, gives anti-bias training, and has partnered with Arizona State University to create the "To Be Welcoming" program which addresses the issues on bias.

The Employees

Imagine your workplace paying for you to attend college and receive your bachelor's degree for a minimum of 20 hours a week. This is exactly what Starbucks has done through its Starbucks College Achievement Plan. Teaming up with Arizona State University (ASU), part- or full-time workers are able to receive 100% tuition coverage for the online program at ASU. Creating and investing in opportunities for people all around the world is just another initiative Starbucks has taken to make the world a better place. In the US, there are 4.6 million individuals between the ages of 16- to 24-year old that are not in school or working. This group is often referred to as Opportunity Youth. Starbucks committed to hiring 10,000 Opportunity Youth by 2018 and by March of 2017 it already met its goal. Because of its success, the company increased its goal to hiring 100,000 Opportunity Youth by 2020. Whether it is through the Starbucks College Achievement Plan or its mentoring program with LinkedIn, the company shows how it is dedicated to helping individuals receive a solid education and providing a jumpstart in the workforce.

In addition to education and training opportunities, Starbucks also has programs to support its employee's mental health. Mental health is a serious issue in today's society and often something that is overlooked. Many insurance policies do not cover mental health and people are not able to get the help needed because of the cost. Beginning in April 2020, Starbucks partnered with Lyra Health to offer employees 20 free sessions with Lyra therapists and coaches for themselves and family members.

ACHIEVEMENTS OF STARBUCKS CSR PROGRAM

Here are some milestones of Starbucks' CSR Program as of 2019:

Environment:

- 99% ethnically sourced coffee and tea
- 40 million trees distributed since 2015
- 160,000+ farmers trained
- 12 major cities recycling Starbucks cups

People:

- 3,200+ diplomas with 14,000+ participants
- 100% pay equity in the US
- 42% women in senior leadership; 17% people of color in senior leadership
- 175,000 employees participating in anti-bias training since 2018

In 2020, the company:

- Donated more than 25 million meals to food banks and mobile pantries
- Converted to strawless lids and is working on a sustainable material straw for 2021
- Distributed 10 million more trees
- Stood up against racial injustice and supplied employees with BLM t-shirts and pins
- Made efforts to break the stigma around mental health and added mental health benefits

SOURCES: www.starbucks.com

CSR CASE STUDY: WARBY PARKER

Contributed by Catherine Moore. Copyright © Kendall Hunt Publishing Company.

Warby Parker is a manufacturer and distributor of eyeglasses. The company makes eyeglasses and sunglasses, distributes contacts, and offers eye exams in its locations across the United States. Warby Parker was founded with the intention of producing and selling designer eyewear for less. Neil Blumenthal, the company's founder, came up with the idea after spending a semester in graduate school without glasses due to the prohibitive cost.

BUY A PAIR, GIVE A PAIR PROGRAM

In 2010, Warby Parker partnered up with VisionSpring to create a program called "Buy a pair, give a pair." Through this program, the company vows for every pair of Warby Parker glasses sold, a pair is donated to someone in need. For every $5 donated, VisionSpring provides one person with eyeglasses that needs them but cannot get them. "Buy a pair, give a pair" also sends professionals to towns and countries to train people to assist in the process of giving eye exams and distributing eyeglasses.

In working with VisionSpring, Warby Parker has "supported their [VisionSpring] social entrepreneurship model internationally, which makes it possible for low-income men and women to acquire and sell radically affordable eyeglasses, earn a living, and care for their families. In addition to providing vocational training, this model makes eyecare significantly more accessible in communities with few or no other options. Over 50% of VisionSpring's customers are getting glasses for the very first time" (**source:** Warby Parker).

VisionSpring is a non-profit, global social enterprise that provides affordable eyeglasses, vision screening and training for non-profits, social entrepreneurs, govt. agencies and corporates clients. Founded in 2001, the organization's mission is to provide affordable, quality glasses to the 2.5 billion people worldwide who need them.

According to data on Warby Parker's website, of the 2.5 billion in need of eyeglasses, over 624 million children and adults cannot effectively work or learn due to the severity of their vision problem.

To date, Warby Parker and Vision Spring have donated over 9 million pairs of eyeglasses to individuals in 50 different countries around the globe.

WARBY PARKER'S PUPILS PROJECT:

In addition to its work with Vision Spring, in 2015, Warby Parker created its Pupils Project. Focused on eliminating barriers to access vision care, Warby Parker teamed up with a number of organizations and local government agencies, such as the Department of Education in New York City and the Department of Health in Baltimore, to offer free vision screenings, eye exams, and glasses to schoolchildren. According to data from the Center for Disease Control and Prevention, vision disability is the single most dominant disabling condition of children in the US. In Mexico, the company supports another program in partnership with the organization Ver Bien to provide glasses to elementary public-school students across the country.

September 2019—Warby Parker retail store in Indianapolis glasses store. For every pair of Warby Parker glasses purchased, a pair of glasses is distributed to someone in need

© Jonathan Weiss/Shutterstock.com

SOURCE: warbyparker.com and visionspring.org

CRISIS MANAGEMENT CASE STUDY: WATER.ORG

Contributed by Kaitlyn Marcinczyk. Copyright © Kendall Hunt Publishing Company.

Water.org is a nonprofit organization founded in 2009 by Gary White and Matt Damon after discovering their shared vision while attending an international summit on poverty. The organization was created with the goal of providing assistance and relief to developing countries without access to safe water and sanitation. Water.org has offices in seven countries throughout the world, and its headquarters is located in Kansas City, MO.

According to the Water.org website, 785 million people globally, or every one in nine people, do not have access to safe water. Additionally, two billion people, or every one in every three people, do not have access to a toilet.

Amid the COVID-19 pandemic, the need to access safe water and sanitation heightened. Water.org saw, firsthand, throughout the pandemic, that safe water is a crucial component in combating the virus. Water.org quickly altered its crisis management plans to meet the changing needs of its publics amid the pandemic. In an effort to continue providing relief to those in need, the non-profit created the COVID-19 Resilience Fund. The fund is closely tied to the organization's goal of providing safe water and sanitation to regions in which they are not available.

Gallons of water recycled attached to tree logs serving as hand washing stations for students to wash their hands at classroom doors in Africa

According to Water.org, The COVID-19 Resilience Fund focuses on assisting in four primary ways:

1. Promote health and support resilience among those living in poverty through hygiene and behavior change messages, as well as advocate for improved public access and investment in water, sanitation, and handwashing facilities.
2. Support an increase in resilience of its partners so it will be able to continue offering critical water and sanitation loans to people in need.

3. Advocate for stronger linkages between WASH (Water, Sanitation, and Hygiene) and health to ensure governments focus resources on these vital, life-saving interventions.
4. Seek new opportunities to drive impact in a COVID-transformed world through continued innovations on the ground to ensure even more people get access to affordable loans.

To publicize its efforts in a time where in-person interaction was not feasible, Water.org used its social media presence to inform followers of the significance of their donations and how safe water is a critical component in fighting the virus. The organization worked to find a balance in posting messages that were appropriate to the crisis. In an article published on *Nonprofit Tech for Good*, Moree Lambeth explained, "The COVID-19 pandemic has fundamentally changed the way organizations execute their social media plans. Posting without a mindfulness of the trending topics and conversations can cause organizations to appear insensitive and tone-deaf. The current social media environment has caused non-profit marketers to re-evaluate their content aware of the acute conversations being had on every channel, at a global level" (Lambeth, 2020). The organization changed its social media plans by incorporating messages on its platforms stating where donations would be going and who these donations would be supporting. For example, they posted on Instagram, "How many times a day do you wash your hands? Now more than ever, handwashing is critical to health, yet millions lack access to the safe water needed to do this powerful act. Celebrate #GlobalHandwashingDay by empowering people in need with access to safe water. Donate through the button in our bio now." Additionally, Water.org continued to encourage donations by utilizing story-telling tactics, as well as providing statistics on the need for safe water and sanitation.

In the past year, Water.org has provided relief to over eight million people, and since its founding in 2009, has collectively provided relief to approximately 31 million people. By adjusting its crisis management plans in accordance with the COVID-19 pandemic, these numbers continue to increase. Water.org strategically measured the needs of its publics and utilized social media to reach audiences throughout the world in an effort to make a difference. In the midst of a crisis, it is crucial for nonprofit organizations to focus on their social media approach, as that is the main form of communication with the media and their stakeholders.

REFERENCE

Lambeth, M. 2020. "How Water.org Adapted Their Content in Response to COVID-19." *Nonprofit Tech for Good*. https://www.nptechforgood.com/2020/07/13/how-water-org-adapted-their-social-media-content-strategy-in-response-to-covid-19/.

REFERENCES

CHAPTER 1

Coombs, W. Timothy. 2014. "Crisis Management and Communications." *The Institute for PR*. 23 September. Accessed June 15, 2020. https://instituteforpr.org/crisis-management-communications/.

Faulkner, Bill. 2017. "Define Consumer Relations." *Bixfluent*. 26 September. Accessed June 15, 2020. https://bizfluent.com/about-6390671-define-consumer-relations.html.

Hawin, Paige. 2016. "Public Affairs vs. Public Relations: What Is the Difference?" *PR Daily*. 19 December. Accessed June 15, 2020. https://www.prdaily.com/public-affairs-vs-public-relations-what-is-the-difference/.

Inc. n.d. "Public Relations." Accessed June 18, 2020. https://www.inc.com/encyclopedia/public-relations.html.

Juneja, Prachi. n.d. "Employee Relations—Importance and Ways of Improving Employee Relations." *Management Study Guide*. Accessed June 18, 2020. https://www.managementstudyguide.com/employee-relations.htm.

NIRI. n.d. Accessed June 18, 2020. https://www.niri.org/about-niri.

PR Council. n.d. "Public Affairs." Accessed June 15, 2020. https://prcouncil.net/inside-pr/public-affairs/.

Sarno, Aaron. 2016. "PR's Vital Role in Human Resources." *Everything-PR*. 23 August. Accessed June 15, 2020. https://everything-pr.com/prs-vital-role-human-resources/.

Verlinden, Neelie. n.d. "All You Need to Know About Employee Relations." *Digital HR Technology*. Accessed June 18, 20. https://www.digitalhrtech.com/employee-relations/.

CHAPTER 2

"1897 American Journalism's Exceptional Year." n.d. *1897 American Journalism's Exceptional Year*. Web. 20 April 2020.

Bates, Don. 2006. "Mini-Me History." Published by Institute for Public relationswww.instituteforpr.org. 2006. Date accessed 17 April 2020.

Bernays, Edward. 1928. *Propaganda*. IG Publishing. New York: Brooklyn.

Bernays, Edward L. 1947. *The Engineering of Consent*, no. 1: 113-20.

Betteke, Van Ruler and Dejan Verčič. 2004. "Public Relations and Communication Management in Europe: A Nation-by-Nation Introduction to Public Relations Theory and Practice." *Walter de Gruyter*: 161.

Brooks, John. 1976. *Telephone: The First Hundred Years.* New York: Harper & Row.
Blanchard, Margaret A. 2013. *History of the Mass Media in the United States: An Encyclopedia.* New York: Routledge, 309.
Clarke, Alan. 1969. "The Life & Times of Sir Basil Clarke—PR Pioneer." *Public Relations* 22, no. 2: 8-13.
Clear, James. 2016. "The 100-Year-Old To-Do List Hack Still Works Like a Charm." 8 August. https://www.fastcompany.com/3062946/this-100-year-old-to-do-list-hack-still-works-like-a-charm.
Cutlip, Scott M. 1966. "The Nation's First Public Relations Firm," *Journalism Quarterly* 43, no. 2: 269-80. Issue published: June 1, 1966.
Cutlip, Scott M. 2013. "The Unseen Power: Public Relations: A History." p. 48.
Evans, Richard. 2013. *From the Frontline: The Extraordinary Life of Sir Basil Clarke.* The History Press.
Greer, Jed and Kavaljit Singh. n.d. "A Brief History of Transnational Corporations." Accessed April 17, 2020. www.globalpolicy.org.
Gunderman, Richard. 2015. "The Manipulation of the American Mind: Edward Bernays and the Birth of Public Relations." https://theconversation.com/the-manipulation-of-the-american-mind-edward-bernays-and-the-birth-of-public-relations-44393.
Hallahan, Kirk. 2002. "Ivy Lee and the Rockefellers' Response to the 1913-1914 Colorado Coal Strike." *Journal of Public Relations Research* 14, no. 4: 265-315.
Heath, Robert S. 2005. *The Encyclopedia of Public Relations.*
Lawrence, A. T., and J. Weber. 2014. *Business and society: Stakeholders, ethics, public policy.* 14th ed. New York, NY: McGraw-Hill, 429.
Litwin, M. Larry. 2009. *The Public Relations Practitioner's Playbooks: A Synergized Approach to Effective Two-way Communication.* Bloomington, IN: AuthorHouse, 9.
Bernays, Edward. 1995. 'Father of Public Relations' and Leader in Opinion Making, Dies at 103." *The New York Times.* Accessed April 19 2020. https://archive.nytimes.com/www.nytimes.com/books/98/08/16/specials/bernays-obit.html.
Hill, Rebkiah. n.d. "Ivy Lee & Edward Bernays: Impact on Public Relations." Accessed April 18, 2020. https://study.com/academy/lesson/ivy-lee-edward-bernays-impact-on-public-relations.html.
Reddi, C. V. N. 2010. *Effective Public Relations and Media Strategy.* New Delhi: PHI Learning Pvt. Ltd., 53.
Seitel, Fraser P. 2006. *The Practice of Public Relations.* 10th ed. Upper Saddle River, NJ: Pearson Publishing.
Vercic, Dejan, Betteke Van Ruler, Gerhard Butschi, and Bertil Flodin. 2001. "On the Definition of Public Relations: a European View." *Public Relations Review* 27: 373-87.
Icco. n.d. Accessed April 18, 2020. www.iccopr.com.
Prsa. n.d. Accessed April 18, 2020. www.prsa.org.
Ipra. n.d. Accessed April 18, 2020. www.ipra.org/history/ipras-story/.

CHAPTER 3

Allport, G. W. (1954). *The nature of prejudice.* Cambridge, MA: Perseus Books.
Amir, Y. (1969). Contact hypothesis in ethnic relations. *Psychological Bulletin, 71*, 319–342.
Capurro, R. (2011). The Dao of the information society in China and the task of intercultural information ethics. In *CEPE 2011: Crossing Boundaries* (pp. 39–45). Milwaukee: University of Wisconsin.

Ganim, S. & Sayers, D. (2014, October 25). UNC report finds 18 years of academic fraud to keep athletes playing. *CNN.* Retrieved from http://www.cnn.com/2014/10/22/us/unc-report-academic-fraud/

Guilherme, M., Keating, C., & Hoppe, D. (2010). Intercultural responsibility: Power and ethics in intercultural dialogue and interaction. In M. Guilherme, C. Keating, & D. Hoppe (Eds.), *The intercultural dynamics of multicultural working* (pp. 77–94). Bristol, UK: Multilingual Matters.

Hesson, T. (2012, December 17). A quarter of deportations are of parents of U.S. citizens. *ABC News.* Retrieved from http://abcnews.go.com/ABC_Univision/News/quarter-deportations-parents-us-citizens/story?id=18000783#.UWyBmrXCaSo

Ishii, S. (2009). Conceptualising Asian communication ethics: A Buddhist perspective. *Journal of Multicultural Discourses, 4*(1), 49–60.

Johannesen, R. L., Valde, K. S., & Whedbee, K. E. (2008). *Ethics in human communication* (6th ed.). Prospect Heights, IL: Waveland Press.

Kane, D. (2014, October 29). UNC spending $782K on PR firm helping with academic scandal. *News & Observer.* Retrieved from http://www.newsobserver.com/2014/10/29/4274697/unc-spending-782k-on-pr-firm-helping.html

Mollov, M., & Schwartz, D. G. (2010). Towards an integrated strategy for intercultural dialog: Computer-mediated communication and face to face. *Journal of Intercultural Communication Research, 39*(3), 207–224.

Moyer, J. (2011, January 7). Ethics and public relations. *Institute for Public Relations.* Retrieved from http://www.instituteforpr.org/ethics-and-public-relations/

Oetzel, J. (2009). *Intercultural communication: A layered approach.* New York: Vango Books.

Quintanilla, K. M., & Wahl, S. T. (2014). *Business and professional communication: Keys for workplace excellence* (2nd ed.). Thousand Oaks, CA: Sage.

Riccio, M. (2011). Democracy as a "universal value" and an intercultural ethics. *Cultura: International Journal of Philosophy of Culture and Axiology, 8*(2), 73–84.

Ting-Toomey, S. (2010). Intercultural communication ethics: Multiple layered issues. In G. Cheney, S. May, & D. Munshi (Eds.), *The ICA handbook of communication ethics* (pp. 335–352). Mahwah, NJ: Lawrence Erlbaum.

Ting-Toomey, S., & Chung, L. C. (2005). *Understanding intercultural communication.* Los Angeles: Roxbury.

Wei, X. (2009). On negative cultural transfer in communication between Chinese and Americans. *Journal of Intercultural Communication, 21.* Retrieved from http://www.immi.se/jicc/index.php/jicc/article/view/48/23

Zhang, X. (2012). Internet rumors and intercultural ethics: A case study of panic-stricken rush for salt in China and iodine pill in America after Japanese earthquake and tsunami. *Studies in Literature & Language, 4*(2), 13–16.

CHAPTER 4

Ball, G. (2014). Sign the petition to end the torture. *NYSenate.gov.* Retrieved fromhttp://www.webcitation.org/6NuWhv25M

Box Office Mojo (2013). *Blackfish (2013)*. Retrieved from http://boxofficemojo.com/movies/?id=blackfish.htm

Coombs, W. T. (2012). *Ongoing crisis communication* (3rd ed.). Thousand Oaks: Sage.

Davis, E. (2014, January 9). BlackFish exposed by former SeaWorld trainers. *MiceChat.com* Retrieved from http://micechat.com/53915-blackfish-exposed/

Duke, A. (2013, December 16). Martina McBride, 38 Special, cancel SeaWorld gig over 'Blackfish' backlash. *CNN*. Retrieved from http://www.cnn.com/2013/12/16/showbiz/seaworld-martina-mcbride-cancels/

Durrant, R., Wakefield, M., McLeoud, K., Clegg-Smith, K., & Chapman, S. (2003). Tobacco in the news: An analysis of newspaper coverage of tobacco issues in Australia, 2001. *Tobacco Control, 12*, 75-81.

Entman, R. M. (1993). Framing: Toward clarification of a fractured paradigm. *Journal of Communication, 43*, 51-58.

Garcia, J. (2014, January 21). Dawn Brancheau family Blackfish statement. *Orlando Sentinel*. Retrieved from http://articles.orlandosentinel.com/2014-01-21/business/os-dawn-brancheau-blackfish-statement-20140121_1_killer-whales-blackfish-orca-tilikum

Goffman, E. (1974). *Frame analysis: An essay on the organization of experience*. New York: Harper & Row.

Gordts, E. (2014, August 20). Here's what newspapers around the world are saying about the Ferguson shooting. *The Huffington Post*. Retrieved from http://www.huffingtonpost.com/2014/08/20/ferguson-world-views_n_5693062.html

Grunig, J. E. (1992). *Excellence in public relations and communication management*. Hillsdale, NJ: Lawrence Erlbaum Associates.

Grunig, J.E., Grunig, L.A., & Dozier, D.M. (2006). The excellence theory. In C. H. Botan & V. Hazleton (Eds.), *Public relations theory II* (pp. 21-62). New York: Routledge.

Hallahan, K. (2005). Framing theory. In R. L. Heath (ed.). *The encyclopedia of public relations* (pp. 340-343). Thousand Oaks: Sage.

Hearit, J. M. (2006). *Crisis management by apology: Corporate response to allegations of wrongdoing*. New York: Routledge.

Kazoleas, D., & Teigen, L. G. (2009). The technology-image expectancy gap: A new theory of public relations. In C. H. Botan & V. Hazleton (Eds.). *Public relations theory II* (pp. 415-433). New York: Routledge.

Martinez, M. (2014, March 7). California bill would ban orca shows at SeaWorld. *CNN*. Retrieved from http://www.cnn.com/2014/03/07/us/california-bill-orca-killer-whale-seaworld/

Rovell, D., & Keneally, M. (2014, September 19). NFL commissioner Roger Goodell admits he 'got it wrong' regarding Ray Rice domestic violence incident. *ABC News*. Retrieved from http://abcnews.go.com/Sports/nfl-commissioner-roger-goodell-addresses-domestic-violence-issue/story?id=25610774

Stock, K. (2013, August 29). SeaWorld's slump raises a question: Is Shamu too sad, or too expensive? *Bloomberg Businessweek*. Retrieved from http://www.businessweek.com/articles/2013-08-29/seaworld-slump-raises-a-question-is-shamu-too-sad-or-too-expensive

Stout, D. (2014, August 1). So long, Shamu: Southwest, SeaWorld end ties. *Time*. Retrieved from http://time.com/3069051/so-long-shamu-southwest-seaworld-end-ties/

USA Today Sports (2014, October 8). Timeline: NFL's month of woe. *USA Today*. Retrieved from http://www.usatoday.com/story/sports/nfl/2014/10/08/timeline-nfls-month-of-woe/16889819/

Vercic, D., Grunig, L. A., & Grunig, J. E. (1996). Global and specific principles of public relations: Evidence from Slovenia. In H. M. Culbertson & N. Chen (Eds.). *International public relations: A comparative analysis* (pp. 31-65). Mahwah, NJ: Lawrence Erlbaum Associates.

Volin, B. (2014, September 14). NFL commissioner Roger Goodell under fire for handling of Ray Rice situation. *The Boston Globe*. Retrieved from http://www.bostonglobe.com/sports/2014/09/13/nfl-commissioner-roger-goodell-under-fire-for-handling-ray-rice-situation/yZCnuCQhxzcjQ9GrDaHLMK/story.html

CHAPTER 5

Becker, R. (2010). Writing for public relations: The importance of planning. *Words. Concepts. Strategies.* Retrieved from http://www.richardrbecker.com/2010/03/writing-for-public-relations-importance.html

Black, L. M. (2011, March 8). 5 smart social PR campaigns to learn from. *Mashable*. Retrieved from http://mashable.com/2011/03/08/social-pr-campaigns/

Bobbit, R. & Sullivan, R. (2013). *Developing the public relations campaign* (3rd ed.). Boston: Pearson.

Bosker, B. (2011, December 10). Qwikster is dead: Netflix kills DVD-only service weeks after unveiling it. *HuffPost Tech*. Retrieved from http://www.huffingtonpost.com/2011/10/10/qwikster-dead-netflix-kills_n_1003098.html

Coombs, W. T. (2007). *Ongoing crisis communication: Planning, managing, and responding* (2nd ed.). Los Angeles: Sage.

Coombs, W. T. (2012). *Ongoing crisis communication: Planning, managing, and responding* (3rd ed.). Los Angeles: Sage.

Gonring, M. P. (2004). Making public relations indispensable to the CEO. *Public Relations Strategist*, 12-15.

Harshbarger, R., & Schram, J. (2014, April 22). NYPD's Twitter fail: Trolls hijack campaign with 'police brutality' pics. *New York Post*. Retrieved from http://nypost.com/2014/04/22/nypds-twitter-outreach-completely-backfired/

Hendricks, D. (2014, July 9). Spohn CEO defends Memorial plan. *Corpus Christi Caller-Times*. Retrieved from http://www.caller.com/news/local-news/spohn-ceo-defends-memorial-plan_43184892

Maresh-Fuehrer, M. M. (2013). *Creating organizational crisis plans*. Dubuque, IA: Kendall Hunt Publishing.

Ulmer, R. R., Sellnow, T. L., & Seeger, M. W. (2011). *Effective crisis communication: Moving from crisis to opportunity* (2nd ed.). Thousand Oaks: Sage.

Wagstaff, K. (2011, October 24). Netflix loses 800,000 subscribers after price hike, Qwikster debacle. *TIME Tech*. Retrieved from http://techland.time.com/2011/10/24/netflix-loses-800000-subscribers-after-price-hike-qwikster-debacle/

CHAPTER 6

Begos, K. (2014, January 6). Water pollution from drilling confirmed in at least 4 states, casting doubt on safety of boom. *HuffPost Green*. Retrieved from http://www.huffingtonpost.com/2014/01/06/water-pollution-drilling_n_4548561.html

Born, M., & Hamill, S. D. (2014a, February 12). Greene County shale well continues burning. *Pittsburgh Post-Gazette.* Retrieved from http://www.post-gazette.com/local/south/2014/02/11/Gas-well-explodes-in-southeastern-Greene-County/stories/201402110126

Born, M., & Hamill, S. D. (2014b, February 19). Remains found at drilling site in Greene County: Worker has been missing since blast. *Pittsburgh Post-Gazette.* Retrieved from http://www.post-gazette.com/local/marcellusshale/2014/02/19/State-police-hope-to-search-gas-well-pad-for-missing-worker-today/stories/201402190136

Colaneri, K. (2014, March 25). Chevron pizza 'scandal' leaves small town divided. *NPR.* Retrieved from http://www.npr.org/2014/03/25/293875192/chevron-pizza-scandal-leaves-small-town-divided

Hardway, A., & Belanger, M. (2014, February 13). One fire out, second still burning at Chevron natural gas well blast in Greene County: Cameron International worker still identified by officials as missing. *WTAE Pittsburgh.* Retrieved from http://www.wtae.com/news/local/explosion-reported-at-gas-well-in-greene-county/24407710#!bgdr5k

Iunescu, M. (2012, September 13). Social media engagement: How to put a ring on it [Web log]. Retrieved from http://lightspandigital.com/blog/social-media-engagement-definition-practice/#axzz38VJsS8FF

Kaushik, A. (2011). Best social media metrics: Conversation, amplification, applause, economic value [Web log]. Retrieved from http://www.kaushik.net/avinash/best-social-media-metrics conversation-amplification-applause economic-value/

Rahorn, R. (2006). *Defense Information School broadcast writing style guide.* Fort George G. Meade, MD: Defense Information School Broadcasting Department. Retrieved from http://www.impact-information.com/impactinfo/BROADCAST_WRITING.pdf

Saint Louis Zoo (2013). Edward K. Love Conservation Foundation Cypress Swamp: New exhibit in 1904 Flight Cage commemorates World's Fair centennial [Backgrounder]. Retrieved from http://www.stlzoo.org/files/1513/7528/3973/CypressSwamp_mediakit2013.pdf

The Public Relations Society of America (2014). Fact sheet [Fact Sheet]. Retrieved from http://media.prsa.org/about+prsa/fact+sheet/

CHAPTER 7

"Barcelona Principles 2.0" *PR News.* Accessed 24 April 2020. www.prnewswireonline.com.

Batchelor, B. 1938. *Profitable Public Relations.* New York: Harper & Brothers.

Cavey, Raleigh. "Measuring PR Correctly: Four Tips on Getting the Most from PR Analytics." 25 June 2019. https://www.prweek.com/article/1588877/measuring-pr-correctly. Accessed 20 April 2020.

Butler, John M., and Scott M. Cutlip. 1994. *The Unseen Power: Public Relations, a History.* Hillsdale, NJ: Lawrence Erlbaum Associates, 1994. 807 pp. *American Journalism* 11, no. 4: 370-371.

Davis, Jenn Deering. "The 5 Easy Steps to Measure Your Social Media Campaigns." 24 April 2012. https://neilpatel.com/blog/social-media-measurement/.

Griese, N. L. 2001. *Arthur W. Page: Publisher, Public Relations Pioneer, Patriot.* Atlanta: Anvil Publishers.

Hill, L. 1937. "Advertising local government in England." *Public Opinion Quarterly* 1, no. 2: 62-72.

"How to Effectively Measure PR." Faith PR. 23 August 2018. www.faith-pr.co.uk.

Kucharski, Matt, and Heidi Wright. "For Best PR Results Follow, the 3 Os of Metrics: Outputs, Outtakes & Outcomes." *PR News Online*. 27 August 2012.

Lee, M. 2006. "Empirical Experiments in Public Reporting: Reconstructing the Results of Survey Research, 1941–42." *Public Administration Review*. March/April. 252-262.

Margee, Kate. "First global standard of proving value of PR created at European Summit on Measurement." *PR Week*. 18 June 2010.

Ochieng, Neil. "Understanding PR outputs, outtakes, outcomes and impacts." *AXIA Public Relations*. 5 June 2018.

"Setting SMART Objectives Checklist 231." "Chartered Management Institute (CMI)." 11 March 2011. https://www.managers.org.uk/~/media/Files/Campus%20CMI/Checklists%20PDP/Setting%20SMART%20objectives.ashx.

Watson, T. 2001. "Integrating Planning and Evaluation: Evaluating the Public Relations Practice and Public Relations Programs." In *Handbook of Public Relations*, edited by R.L. Heath, 259-268. Thousand Oaks, CA: Sage Publications, Inc.

Wilson, Laurie J, Joseph D. Ogden, and Christopher E. Wilson. 2019. *Strategic Communications PR for Social Media and Marketing*. Dubuque, IA: Kendall Hunt.

CHAPTER 8

Grossman, Andrew. "The PR Pro's Guide to Effective Media Relations," *AdWeek*. 14 September 2015. Accessed 16 June 2020. https://www.adweek.com/digital/the-pr-pros-guide-to-effective-media-relations.

Linton, Ian. n.d. "How to Make A Media Pitch," *Chron*. Accessed 15 June 2020. smallbusiness.chron.com/make-media-pitch-54785.html.

Roolf, Anna Julow. "Public Relations vs Media Relations: Do You Know the Difference?" 6 September 2017. *Powderkeg*. Accessed 12 June 2020. https://powderkeg.com/public-relations-vs-media-relations-do-you-know-the-difference/

"The Role of Content in the Consumer Decision Making Process," Nielsen/inPOwered MediaLab Study, December 2013-January 2014.

Sheares, Adirenne. "4 Media Tips to Live By." 14 April 2015. *Cision*. Accessed 15 June 2020. https://www.cision.com/us/2015/04/4-media-relations-tips-to-live-by/

Universal Accreditation Board. n.d. "Accreditation Study Session: Media Relations." Accessed 15 June 2020. https://www.praccreditation.org/resources/documents/APRSG-Media-Relations.pdf.

CHAPTER 9

Amadeo, Kimberly. 2019. "Sarbanes-Oxley Summary: Four Ways Sarbanes-Oxley Stops Corporate Fraud." 10 October. *The Balance*. Accessed 10 May 2020. www.thebalance.com.

Beatty, David R. 2017. "How Activist Investors Are Transforming the Role of Public-Company Boards." *McKinsey Special Collection: Activist Investors*. 2017. Accessed 10 May 2020.

Blackburn, Virginia. "Top Accounting Scandals 2018." 20 March 2019. Accoutancy Age. Accessed 10 August 2020. www.accountancyage.com.

Corporate Finance Institute. n.d. Accessed 2 May 2020. https://corporatefinanceinstitute.com/resources/careers/jobs/role-of-investor-relations-ir/.

"Effective IR: Becoming a Trusted Proxy for Management." October 21, 2014. Deloitte module of CFO Journal, *CFO Program, Deloitte LLP*.

"Effective IR: Building Trust with Clarity, *Candor* and Consistency." July 9, 2014. Deloitte module of CFO Journal, *CFO Program, Deloitte LLP*.

"Effective IR: Know Your Audience and 'Tell It Like It Is.'" September 23, 2014. Deloitte module of CFO Journal, *CFO Program, Deloitte LLP*.

"Effective IR: Maintaining a Responsive *Dialogue* with the Street." September 2, 2014. Deloitte module of CFO Journal, *CFO Program, Deloitte LLP*.

"Effective Investor Relations (IR): Lessons from the Trenches." n.d. Deloitte module of CFO Journal, CFO Program, Deloitte LLP. Accessed 10 May 2020.

Gackowski, Tomasz. 2017. "The idea of investor relations in the modern economy: a communication approach." *Economic Research-Ekonomska Istraživanja*, vol. 30, no. 1, pp. 1-13. doi: 10.1080/1331677X.2016.1265894.

Hanna, Julia. "The Costs and Benefits of Sarbanes-Oxley." 10 March 2014. Forbes. Accessed 10 May 2020. www.forbes.com.

Jolly, Jasper. "Ted Baker Balance Sheet Error Worse Than Fear as Woes Deepen." *The Guardian*. 22 Jan 2020. Accessed 10 August 2020. www.theguardian.com.

Lemke, Time. 2020. "What an Activist Investor Means for Your Investments." 06 February. Accessed 10 May 2020. www.thebalance.com.

National Whistleblowers Center. n.d. Accessed 10 May 2020. www.whistleblowers.org.

NIRI. n.d. Accessed 2 May 2020. www.niri.org.

Phelan, Paula. 2014. "Why Investor Relations and Public Relations Should Work in Harmony." *Entrepreneur*. 6 June. Accessed 11 May 2020. https://www.entrepreneur.com/article/234546.

Salvo, Leigh. 2018. "The Relationship Between PR and IR." The Gilmartin Group. 9 March. Accessed 11 May 2020. www.gilmartinir.com/the-relationship-between-ir-and-pr/.

CHAPTER 10

Blanding, Michael. "Businesses Need a 'Catalyst' to Make CSR Practices Stick," *Harvard Business Review*, 2020.

Diversity Best Practices. "Community Relations and Philanthropy." *Diversity Primer*, pgs. 200–212. 9 September 2009. https://www.diversitybestpractices.com/publications/diversity-primer#page-2.

Googins, Bradley. "Why Community Relations is a Strategic Imperative," *Strategy+Business*. Third quarter, no. 8. 1 July 1997. Accessed 28 May 2020. https://www.strategy-business.com/article/17964?gko=27dcc.

Inc. n.d. "Community Relations." Accessed 1 June 2020. https://www.inc.com/encyclopedia/community-relations.html.

JPMorgan Chase. n.d. https://institute.jpmorganchase.com/impact. Accessed 4 June 2020.

Kaplan, Robert, George Serafeim, and Eduardo Tugendhat, "Inclusive Growth: Profitable Strategies for Tackling Poverty and Inequality," *Harvard Business Review.* Jan/Feb 2018. Accessed 9 June 2020. https://hbr.org/2018/01/inclusive-growth-profitable-strategies-for-tackling-poverty-and-inequality.

Kane, Gerald C., Robert G. Fichman, John Gallaugher and John Glaser. "Community Relations 2.0," *Harvard Business Review.*

Loscocco, Pete. "Community Relations Programs 101 (part 2)." *Freeman Communications.* 27 October 2016. Accessed 5 June 2020. https://freemancommunications.com/community-relations-programs-101-part-2/.

Patagonia. n.d. Accessed 9 June 2020. www.patagonia.com.

PR Council."Taylor Case Study: P&G's #NFLDraftRedCarpet." n.d, n.a. Accessed 10 August 2020. www.prcouncil.net

SCORE. "SCORE's Top Marketing & Public Relations Tips," *Entrepreneur.* 6 December 2005. Accessed 8 June 2020. https://www.entrepreneur.com/article/81286.

Warrillow, John. "The One Quote Every Entrepreneur Must Read," *Inc.* 9 March 2015. Accessed 8 June 2020. https://www.inc.com/john-warrillow/the-one-quote-every-entrepreneur-must-read.html

CHAPTER 11

Cone Communications. 2015. "2015 Cone Communications/Ebiquity Global CSR Study." https://www.conecomm.com/2015-cone-communications-ebiquity-global-csr-study-pdf.

Cone Communications. 2017. "2017 Cone Communications CSR Study." Accessed 8 July 2020. https://www.conecomm.com/2017-cone-communications-csr-study-pdf

"Triple Bottom Line." *The Economist.* 17 November 2009. Accessed 18 May 2020. https://www.economist.com/news/2009/11/17/triple-bottom-line.

Elkington, John. "Twenty-Five Years Ago, I Coined the Phrase Triple Bottom Line. Here's Why I Am Giving Up On It.". *Harvard Business Review.* 25 June 2018. Accessed 18 May 2020. https://hbr.org/2018/06/25-years-ago-i-coined-the-phrase-triple-bottom-line-heres-why-im-giving-up-on-it.

Glavas, Ante. "Corporate Social Responsibility and Employee Engagement: Enabling Employees to Employ More of Their Whole Selves at Work." *Frontiers in Psychology.* 31 May 2016.

ICMR. "Coca-Cola India's Corporate Social Responsibility Strategy" n.d. Accessed 10 August 2020.www.icmrindia.org

HP. n.d. Accessed 25 May 2020. https://www8.hp.com/us/en/hp-information/social-innovation/hp-foundation.html.

Kanter, Rosabeth Moss. 1999. "From Spare Change to Real Change: The Social Sector as Beta Site for Business Innovation," *Harvard Business Review.* May-June.

Kotler, Philip. *Corporate Social Responsibility: Doing the Most Good for Your Company and Your Cause.* 13 December 2004. Hoboken, NJ: Wiley.

Kraaijenbrink, Jeroen. "What the 3Ps of the Triple Bottom Line Really Mean," *Forbes.* 10 December 2019. Accessed 18 May 2020. https://www.forbes.com/sites/jeroenkraaijenbrink/2019/12/10/what-the-3ps-of-the-triple-bottom-line-really-mean/#76e6f6215143.

Lanphear, Kimberly. "Three Reasons Why CSR is Important for Your Business," *US Chamber of Commerce Foundation.* 8 April 2019. https://www.uschamberfoundation.org/blog/post/three-reasons-why-csr-important-your-business.

Nielsen. "The Sustainability Imperative." 12 October. 2015 Accessed May 28, 2020. https://www.nielsen.com/us/en/insights/report/2015/the-sustainability-imperative-2/.

Newsweek. n.d. Accessed 25 May 2020. https://www.newsweek.com/americas-most-responsible-companies-2020.

Porter, Michael E., and Mark R. Kramer. "Strategy & Society: The Link Between Competitive Advantage and Corporate Social Responsibility." *Harvard Business Review.* December 2006.

Rangan, V. Kasturi, Lisa Chase, and Sohel Karim. "The Truth About CSR." *Harvard Business Review.* January/February 2015.

Tharp, J., and Chadbury, P. D. "Corporate Social Responsibility: What It Means for the Project Manager." January 2008. Paper presented at PMI® Global Congress 2008—North America, Denver, CO. Newtown Square, PA: Project Management Institute.

UNIDO. n.d. Accessed 18 May 2020. https://www.unido.org/our-focus/advancing-economic-competitiveness/competitive-trade-capacities-and-corporate-responsibility/corporate-social-responsibility-market-integration/what-csr.

CHAPTER 12

Arpan, L. M., and D. R. Roskos-Ewoldesn. 2005. "Stealing Thunder: An Analysis of the Effects of Proactive Disclosure of Crisis Information." *Public Relations Review*, 31: 425–433.

Carney, A., and Amy Jordan. 1993. "Prepare for Business-Related Crises." *Public Relations Journal*, 49: 34-35.

Coombs, W. Timothy. 2004. "Impact of Past Crises on Current Crisis Communications: Insights from Situational Crisis Communication Theory." *Journal of Business Communication*, 41: 265-289.

Coombs, W. Timothy. 2007a. "Protecting Organization Reputations During a Crisis: The Development and Application of Situational Crisis Communication Theory." *Corporation Reputation Review*, 10, no. 3: 163-176.

Coombs, W. Timothy. 2007b. *Ongoing Crisis Communication: Planning, Managing and Responding.* Los Angeles: Sage.

Coombs, W., and S. J. Holladay. 1996. "Communications and Attributions in a Crisis: An Experimental Study of Crisis Communication." *Journal of Public Relations Research*, 8: 279-295.

Coombs, W., and S. J. Holladay. 2001. "An Extended Examination of the Crisis Situation: A Fusion of Relational Management and Symbiotic Approaches." *Journal of Public Relations Research*, no. 13: 321-340.

Coombs, W., and S. J. Holladay. 2006. "Halo or Reputational Capital: Reputation and Crisis Management." *Journal of Communication Management*, no. 8: 123-137.

Dean, Dwane Hall. 2004. "Consumer Reaction to Negative Publicity: Effects of Corporate Reputation, Response, and Responsibility for a Crisis Event." *Journal of Business Communication*, 41, no. 2: 192-211.

Doane, Beth. 2018. "What To Do When Crisis Strikes: Five Tips On Crisis Management." *Forbes*. https://www.forbes.com/sites/theyec/2018/10/17/what-to-do-when-crisis-strikes-five-tips-on-crisis-management/?sh=1b37c8fd7709

Fombrun, C. J., and C. B. M. van Riel. 2004. *Fame & Fortune: How Successful Companies Build Winning Reputations*. New York: Prentice-Hall Financial Times.

Institute for Public Relations. 2007. "Crisis Management and Communications." 30 October 2007. https://instituteforpr.org/crisis-management-and-communications/

Sturges, David. 1994. "Communicating Through Crisis: A Strategy for Organizational Survival." *Management Communication Quarterly*, 7, no. 3: 297-316.

Taylor, M., and M. L. Kent. 2007. "Taxonomy of Mediated Crisis Responses." *Public Relations Review*, no. 33: 140-146.

Ulmer, R. R., T. L. Sellnow, and M. W. Seeger. 2006. *Effective Crisis Communication: Moving from Crisis to Opportunity*. Thousand Oaks: Sage.

CHAPTER 13

Blumenthal, Danielle. 2015. "The Difference Between Public Affairs and Public Relations." *Government Executive*, 17 September 2015. https://www.govexec.com/management/2015/09/difference-between-public-affairs-and-public-relations/121238/

Drutman, Lee. 2015a. "How Corporate Lobbyists Conquered American Democracy." *The Atlantic*, 20 April 2015. https://www.theatlantic.com/business/archive/2015/04/how-corporate-lobbyists-conquered-american-democracy/390822.

Drutman, Lee. 2015b. *The Business of America is Lobbying: How Corporations Became Politicized and Politics Became More Corporate*. Oxford University Press.

Hayley-Jones, Lisa. 2017. "Public Affairs Management." *PR Week*, 4 January 2017. https://www.prweek.com/article/1461024/job-description-public-affairs-manager.

Morley, M. 2002. Public Affairs. In *How to Manage Your Global Reputation* (p. 126). London: Palgrave Macmillan.

Morley, M. 2019. "Public Affairs Versus Public Relations." *Public Strategies Impact*.

Musters, Reinier, Ellora-Julie Parekh, and Surya Ramkumar. 2013. "Organizing the Government-Affairs Function for Impact." *McKinsey Quarterly*. https://www.mckinsey.com/business-functions/strategy-and-corporate-finance/our-insights/organizing-the-government-affairs-function-for-impact#.

Post, James E., Robert B. Dickie, Edwin A. Murray, Jr., and John F. Mahon. 1983. "Managing Public Affairs: The Public Affairs Function." *California Management Review*, XXVI, no. I: 135-150.

Public Affairs Council. n.d. https://pac.org/

Public Affairs Networking. n.d. "What is Public Affairs." https://www.publicaffairsnetworking.com/what-is-public-affairs.php

See, Andy. 2020. "Creating Successful Public Affairs Campaigns: The 5 Step Approach." *PRGN*, 23 May 2020. https://prgn.com/tips-trends/creating-successful-public-affairs-campaigns-the-5-step-approach/.

Sitton, Jennifer. 2018. "Differentiating Between Public Affairs and Public Relations." *Hubbell Communications*, 22 August 2018. www.thinkhubbell.com/differentiating-public-affairs-public-relations/.

US Chamber of Commerce. 2020. "Public Relations vs. Public Affairs: What's the Difference?" 27 April 2020. www.uschamber.com/co/grow/marketing/public-relations-vs-public-affairs.

CHAPTER 14

Accenture. 2020. "Care to do Better: Building trust to enhance employee potential and leave your people and your business: Net Better Off". https://www.accenture.com/us-en/insights/future-workforce/employee-potential-talent-management-strategy

Bolden-Barrett, Valerie. 2018. "Workers Unhappy with Managers 4x More Likely to Job Hunt." *HR Dive*. https://www.hrdive.com/news/workers-unhappy-with-managers-4x-more-likely-to-job-hunt/542515/

Cheremond, R. J. 2019. "3 Ways to Increase Employee Satisfaction and Drive Business Results." *Gartner Group*. https://www.gartner.com/smarterwithgartner/3-ways-to-increase-employee-satisfaction-and-drive-business-results/

Childress, John. 2019. "The Evolution of Corporate Culture & Culture 4.0." *Medium*. https://medium.com/@jrchildress1348/the-evolution-of-corporate-culture-culture-4-0-12ebfc509dc9.

Craig, William. 2018. "The Importance of Having a Mission-Driven Company." *Forbes*. https://www.forbes.com/sites/williamcraig/2018/05/15/the-importance-of-having-a-mission-driven-company/?sh=5b5f5b6e3a9c

Deloitte. 2019. "Leading the Social Enterprise: Reinvent with a Human Focus." https://www2.deloitte.com/content/dam/Deloitte/cz/Documents/human-capital/cz-hc-trends-reinvent-with-human-focus.pdf

Duran, Annemaria. 2020. "7 Strategies to Improve Employee Relations." *HR Magazine*. https://www3.swipeclock.com/blog/7-strategies-to-improve-employee-relations-for-a-phenomenal-workplace/

Great Place to Work. 2019. "2019 Fortune 100 Best Trends Report: Employee Experience at the Best Workplaces in America." *Fortune*. https://www.greatplacetowork.com/resources/reports/2019-fortune-100-best-trends-report?zd_source=hrt&zd_campaign=5188&zd_term=chiradeepbasumallick

Lee, Sophia. n.d. "What Is Employee Experience?" *Culture Amp*. https://www.cultureamp.com/blog/what-is-employee-experience/

O.C. Tanner. 2020. "5 New Workplace Culture Insights You Must Know." https://www.octanner.com/insights/white-papers/5-things-you-might-have-missed-about-workplace-culture.html

Purdue Global. n.d. "Generational Differences in the Workplace." https://www.purdueglobal.edu/education-partnerships/generational-workforce-differences-infographic/

Ross, Marie-Claire. 2015. "5 Reasons Why Mission-Driven Leaders Are the Most Successful." http://corporateculturecreator.com/tag/mission-driven-leadership/

Sams, Caroline. 2020. "Top 5 Strategies to Improve Employee Relations." *HubWorks*. https://hubworks.com/blog/top-5-strategies-to-improve-employee-relations.html

Solow, Marc. n.d. "Culture and Engagement: The Naked Organization." *Deloitte*. https://www2.deloitte.com/us/en/insights/focus/human-capital-trends/2015/employee-engagement-culture-human-capital-trends-2015.html

Starner, Tom. 19 June 2019. "How Employee Experiences Impacts Your Talent Pipeline." *HR Executive*. https://hrexecutive.com/how-an-enhanced-employee-experience-improves-the-talent-pipeline/

Watkins, Patricia. 2018. "2018 Millennials At Work Research Report." *Udemy*. https://about.udemy.com/ideas-and-opinions/2018-millennials-at-work-research-report/

CHAPTER 15

Bernazzani, Sophia. 2020. "What Is Customer Satisfaction?" *HubSpot*. https://blog.hubspot.com/service/what-is-customer-satisfaction

Fontanella, Clint. 2020. "What Is Customer Relations? Everything You Need to Know." *HubSpot*. https://blog.hubspot.com/service/customer-relations

LaMarco, Nicky. 2019. "What Is Customer Relations." *Small Business Chronicle*. https://smallbusiness.chron.com/customer-relations-43230.html

Microsoft. 2019. "State of Global Customer Service Report." https://info.microsoft.com/rs/157-GQE-382/images/2018StateofGlobalCustomerServiceReport.pdf

Smith, Anthony. 2018. "How To Build Lasting Customer Relationships." *Forbes*. https://www.forbes.com/sites/anthonysmith/2018/08/01/how-to-build-lasting-customer-relationships/?sh=3e159a0d447a

The Economist. 2019. "How to Keep Your Customers Happy." https://www.economist.com/business/2019/08/22/how-to-keep-your-customers-happy